HEY DAD, REMEMBER ME?

July 8th

To Kendrick

Remember that the father's could challenges
issues or become the you are
not conquer the shoulders
the son must overcome.
or your father's
I will do more
amazing

Hey Dad, Remember Me?

CREATING THE RELATIONSHIP WE ALWAYS WANTED

James Andrew Beck

SerfBliss Press
Irvine, CA
First Edition

To my dad, thank you for owning your mistakes and changing for the better, when few men ever do.

To my mom, thank you for keeping me happy when I was miserable.

To my sister, thank you for making me feel handsome when I only felt ugly.

ACKNOWLEDGMENTS:

IF YOU ARE MY FRIEND and received a B or better in English classes, then thank you for your wisdom and guidance because I used it. There are so many people who helped me with this book that I've lost count. However, there are five people without whom I could not have written this book:

Annmarie Morais—my writing mentor—taught me to be committed to the truth, especially when it is ugly. Thank you for teaching me how to turn a scene.

Malia Probst—my former roommate—taught me to be open to new things, even when uncomfortable. Thank you for teaching to 'go with it'.

Roya Vakili—my sister from another family—taught me that you can't load punctuation into a shotgun and blast it on the page. Thank you for teaching me to rewrite and rewrite and rewrite…

Christina Beck—my love—taught me that you can't just write what you think and place it wherever you wish. Thank you for teaching me that everything has a place and a home. I'm glad my home is with you.

Jim Beck—my father—taught me that you always can and must change for the better, without saying a word. Thank you for the countless interviews that dug through your painful past. The story of your change has inspired lives, so rest assured it was worth it.

THE HOUSE BY THE SIDE OF THE ROAD

Let me live in my house
by the side of the road
Where the race of men go by—

They are good, they are bad,
they are weak, they are strong,
Wise, foolish—so am I.

Then why should I sit
in the scorner's seat
Or hurl the cynic's ban?

Let me live in my house
by the side of the road
And be a friend to man.

Sam Walter Foss

TABLE OF CONTENTS

PREFACE

AT ELEVEN YEARS OLD, I know I won't amount to anything beyond the stupid shithead with his head up his ass that Dad tells me I am.

The cold barrel slides into my mouth. It doesn't seem real, like I am in a movie. Teeth clench cold steel. My tongue presses the curved metal, tasting the oil. The pistol's sight rests against the roof of my mouth. Lungs draw in the summer's air dusted with gunpowder residue.

No one wants me here. I don't want to be here. Just pull the trigger and solve everyone's problem.

I sit, waiting for something to happen. Heart pounding, chest heaving, I wait.

Great, I'll probably screw this up and shoot my cheek off. I've got to add another bullet, just to be sure.

Another round quickly slips into a neighboring chamber. It is easy; my father taught me how to use a gun. The weapon slides back between my teeth. I cock the hammer and rest my thumb on the trigger.

I am ready.

WELCOME TO OUR STORY

In 1999, my father and I were asked to speak at a Father's Day church service at Life Center in Tacoma, Washington. Until that point, the journey of our relationship had been kept a secret. Religious circles knew him to be a pillar of strength and I was the dutiful son, following in his footsteps. From the outside, our lives looked picture perfect. As we prepared our message, it felt disingenuous to keep up the facade. My father and I agreed that the openness, transparency, and honesty which enabled us to save our relationship, needed to continue throughout every aspect of our lives.

Over a thousand people listened as we spoke our truth for the first time, sharing our family's dark secrets. After we finished, a line of familiar faces waited to speak with us. In front, a beautiful middle-aged woman approached me. She was church royalty and had everything a person could want: the perfect waterfront home, powerful political friends, a good-looking husband and kids, plenty of money, beloved in the community, exotic vacations, beautiful clothes, and expensive accessories. She is the type of person that makes you look to the heavens and question the fairness of God. When she walked through the foyer, her strut defined jealousy. This day, however, mascara streamed down her face and stained her ivory-colored Chanel jacket.

She gripped my arm and pleaded, "My kids hate me, and my husband wants to leave. They say I'm just like my mother and they are right, but I don't know what to do. How did you and your father change everything?"

I was shocked. She believed in my lies, as I believed in hers.

"I—I don't know how to summarize it. My dad and I worked on our relationship for over a decade and only recently fixed it. Things that worked for us might not work for you."

Tears flowed faster and faster. "You have nothing to give me, no advice or specifics?"

I felt impotent.

Finally, I said, "Well, there are many things I could tell you. Some of the stuff worked and some didn't. I could fill books with everything we did. I don't even know what you need."

The mascara stain inched down her pristine jacket. She pulled me in close and whispered sharply, "Write it down. Promise me that you will write it down. Put it in a book. Let me decide what I need."

"Okay, I promise."

This book fulfills that promise. To my church royalty friend, this is for you.

INTRODUCTION

HEY DAD, REMEMBER ME? REVEALS how a child can believe suicide is the answer. It is the true story of a boy evolving into an abusive, rage-filled, religious zealot; it's a story about my dad. This narrative nonfiction book begins from the perspective of a suicidal eleven-year-old son (me). To gain understanding, the book shifts to the perspective of my father, recounting how his past justifies the man he became. It then returns to the son's perspective as he grows up, revealing the cycle of generational dysfunction that was created through abuse. By walking in the footsteps of both father and son, we learn how good people destroy their children.

After the father realizes that he is continuing the same abusive cycle that he endured as a child, he commits to spending the rest of his life turning the relationship around. He builds a relational framework that ultimately transforms destructive patterns into healthy ones.

Writing was and still is my greatest insecurity. I've spent the last sixteen years learning how to write and rewrite this story. All the pages in this book are written to the best of my memory and ability. Some names have been changed and some haven't. This is the best I have to offer. My commitment is to the truth of what happened, how it was experienced, and uncovering rare gems of learning that tend to get lost in the dark parts of our lives.

A REQUEST

This is the author's father—the real James Beck. My perspective is in bold throughout the book and that was my son's decision, not mine.

For years, my actions destroyed my boy's emotional well-being and ruined his childhood. I've always been willing to die for my kids, but I didn't know how to live with them. The biggest problem: I actually thought I was doing a good job as a father. I had no idea the damage I was causing my son or my family. The pages of this book contain the most shameful moments of my life. I am not proud. In fact, I cringe knowing what the world will learn of me.

The redemptive aspects of my life are how my son, Bubba, and I have been able to repair and rebuild our relationship. It is the only thing in life that I am actually proud of. I agreed to share my past in hopes that the lessons I learned might help you. My request is that you read beyond the first chapter, otherwise, please put this book down. The resolution of our relationship is the only thing that makes this story worth reading. Plus, if you don't, I'll just end up looking like an asshole.

Also, when my son asked my permission to write this book, I kept thinking of all the bad grades he received in English. His request seemed like he was asking if he could fly to the moon.

Yeah, kid, write whatever you want.

Call when you land.

RING, RING. It's too late to change my mind now.

Jimmy and Bubba floating down the Kettle River

OUR SECRET...

CHAPTER 1

THE GOOD BOY

KEY CENTER, WASHINGTON, 1986
(SON, ELEVEN YEARS OLD)

The summer sun beats down on my shirtless back. Afternoon sweat beads cling to my skin as I push the mower back and forth, across the three-acre lawn. A quarter-mile gravel road splits two rolling alfalfa fields down the center, separating our mint-green farmhouse from a distant country highway. Living near the Puget Sound means that we can usually count on a cool breeze blowing, but not today. It is hot. The only break from the heat is when I cut grass in the shadows cast from towering evergreens. Five horses along with a lonely cow watch from behind a barbed-wire fence. The farmhouse my family rents stands sentinel and empty.

Bubba at eleven years old

Suddenly, the vibrating mower gasps and convulses in my grip. I watch, motionless. The machine ends its choking garble with a dull hum and a *POP!*

Running out of gas is the only acceptable excuse for not finishing the lawn. Either the grass needs to be completely manicured or I need to be seen cutting it upon my father's return. Anything less than these two options validates that I am a lazy piece of shit—and my dad doesn't need more confirmation. To my father, my being worthless is a scientific fact the same as the earth being round and water being wet. This "lazy piece of shit" title is given to anyone that takes longer breaks than he thinks are necessary. Under his watch, minutes are like hours and hours are like days. My dad is a poor judge of time, but makes up for it with quick eyes. Nothing escapes his notice. Even trips to the bathroom are accounted for.

Every summer, my father and I work out in the forest, gathering firewood for the upcoming winter. At some point nature forces the question, "Dad, can I go up to the house to go to the bathroom?" It's assumed that country boys piss on the ground when women aren't around, so this means I have to go number two.

"Make it quick," he'd reply.

I would take off like a jackrabbit, running as fast as I could while clenching my butt cheeks together. Once back at the house, I'd poop, wash up, and sprint back as fast as possible. No matter how quick, Dad always asks the same question: "Why did it take you so long?"

"I had to wipe," I'd reply, careful not to make eye contact.

"You were trying to get out of work again, lazy piece of shit." Dad then moves off into the woods, chainsaw in hand, grumbling about me.

If Dad follows me into the house, I trumpet wiping efforts from the porcelain throne. I have to. It calms him and lets everyone know that my workload isn't being intentionally neglected. Taking a sip of iced-tea or soda is acceptable, but if I stop for longer than a minute, there had better be a damn good reason. A one-minute break can slide by if I have dirt in my eye. He'll help, kind of. After spreading my eyelids open, pursing his lips, he'll blow, violating my eye socket. The tears push the muck toward the edges. He gives me an extra minute or two to work the eyelids in a circular motion to get tears flowing again so that I can blink normally. Removing a splinter takes anywhere from one to three minutes, depending on how deep it is and what tools are available. However, if I am working at pulling out a sliver with my teeth, then the time clock stops. After all, I am still working.

Today is different. I am by myself—free from my father and free of everyone else who calls this place home. I don't remember ever being totally alone. There are always a few foster kids around, doing chores or just hanging out. Now everyone is gone. My biological sister, Rachel, went to Emily Baker's house for a whole week. My mom is chauffeuring the rest of my foster sisters around town to friends' homes or court-approved family members. Dad is at Grandma's house, fixing a broken wall and won't be home for at least two hours. The farm animals are fed, chicken coop is clean, garden is weeded, firewood is brought in, garbage cans are empty, and my room is spotless. The only thing left to do is mow the lawn and I am out of gas. Loophole.

Every kid in the home receives five dollars twice a month for allowance. This is enough to keep a waistline chubby with Snickers candy bar residue, but not enough to fill up the gas cans. Sure, my father expects me to volunteer to walk twenty minutes to the gas station and carry full cans back to the house, but he does not expect me to pay for it. That is his job. I already told him of the gas shortage a few days ago, but the reminder was ignored. Technically my obligation was fulfilled, but somehow the problem will become my fault.

If placing blame was a sport, my father could compete at the Olympic level. He is a natural. There is always something I should have done. With a dead lawnmower sitting in front of me, I now realize how inadequate my reminder was.

I should have left a note.

"Aw, fuck!"

My head whips around, looking to see if anyone is listening. Christian boys aren't supposed to use words like *fuck*, *shit*, and *cocksucker*. It's against God and Jesus wouldn't like it. My heart sinks into my belly. Anger is of the Devil and I just committed a sin, a bad one. My heart pounds. Anxiety tears through my chest. Eyes darting around the sides of the house, I scan the front porch and the surrounding woods. Luckily, I am still alone.

Because my father is a part-time minister, there are no restrictions on his vocabulary. He and God have some sort of understanding. However, since I'm a kid, my mouth isn't exempt. Any disagreeable words not held tight or whispered under hushed breath demand a combination of soap, screaming, or a backhand. Proverbs 13:24 "He that spares his rod hates his son: but he that loves him chastens him." Dad loves me, in the Christian way. Kids need to be purged of

5

unrighteousness. It is just a natural part of being religious. These feelings are my fault, my sins. My family has the right answers; Jesus is the answer. Shame pushes against my chest, making it difficult to breathe.

Head hanging low, looking into the grass, I pray, "I'm sorry God. It was an accident. Please forgive me. I didn't mean to swear."

One positive result comes from assuming all household problems are your fault. When you start from the bottom rung of the ladder, you can't fall very far. It's like being the worst kid in dodge ball: everyone expects you to lose the game or let the team down. On the off chance my father recognizes that I have nothing to do with a problem, I find myself pleasantly surprised, even encouraged.

The best is when the foster kids living with us get into serious trouble. Their problems become my relief. The greater the challenge, the easier it is to blend into the surrounding chaos. When a runaway returns home, I am off my father's radar for three days. If a foster sister gets raped or beaten by her pimp, nobody thinks of me for a week. When my foster brother Pat stole my dad's truck and went joyriding, I didn't get yelled at for more than two weeks. Whenever any of the girls try to commit suicide, there is at least a month of peace.

Peace is all I want.

No matter what happens around the house, Dad's frustrations eventually refocus on me. His screaming voice never leaves my mind, like the ringing in your ears after a gunshot. I am grateful; this helps me avoid problems. Walking toward our front steps, I hear his voice again.

"Look at all the grass on your pants. Are you gonna just drag it all over the floor right after your mom vacuumed? Pull your head out of your ass and think!"

Steps come to a halt. I look down. Grass clippings cover my jeans and tennis shoes. My feet stomp against the cement walkway, wads of mashed-up green fall from once-white sneakers. I whip my pant legs back and forth. More stray grass falls to the ground.

"Hey, stupid, do you think that is clean? Take off your damn pants!"

Pants, shoes, and socks are wadded up next to the door. I stroll inside wearing only tighty-whities, clean and grass free. Threads from the mustard-brown shag carpet slip between my toes as I pad across the room. Removing evidence of my whereabouts keeps me safe. I can never tell what will piss off Dad.

Will he be mad that I am walking around the house? He will probably think I should be looking for more work to do, but there isn't any.

My parents started taking in "Last Chancers" when I was three. A "Last Chancer" means our house is the last place these foster kids can live before they are stuck out on the street, a last chance at a normal life. Mom wanted a big family, but after three miscarriages and other health complications, doctors said that my older sister and I are all the children she can birth. She is content. Dad is the opposite. He wants to help as many kids as our house can fit. There are seven "Last Chancers" staying with us now; sometimes it can be up to nine. They live with us from three months to nine years.

On any given day, a random kid shows up on our doorstep. Within minutes, they are as much a part of the family as I am. We've had local parents kick their kids out of their car and onto our lawn. Driving off, they'd yell, "You take care of them." We do. On other days, the kids run away. Sometimes they'll be gone for a week, a month, maybe forever. We never know unless they come back, if they come back. The lesson "nothing ever lasts" is taught week after week, like a skipping record.

The home's number one rule: Foster kids can run away as many times as they like, but only move out once. Teens roll like tumbleweeds into our home; they are here for a few holidays and then blow away. I wish I could blow away, go somewhere peaceful.

With all the random kids coming in and out of our house, it is difficult to tell them apart. Names get mixed up, some duplicated. Qualifiers like "the girl that ran away, had a pimp, and was raped" don't help at all. Everyone who moves in has been raped, beaten, and runs away at some point. Half of them have had a pimp. A three-month stretch in Juvenile Hall or "The Juvie" is a rite of passage, just one more stop on the way to adulthood. Most have at least one abortion under their belt. To be remembered, my siblings have to either live at our house for a long time or do something significant.

Pat stole Dad's truck.

Willie got in a fistfight with the school principal.

The Eskimo-looking boy smells like stale rice.

Kristen is a mentally slow fifteen-year-old. Mom says it's because her father, grandfather, and brothers raped her. They all brought friends over to have sex with her since she was an infant.

Kristen often says funny things like, "I like hookin' 'cause I get paid; most people just take my pussy for free."

The best was when we were all around the dinner table and she told Dad, "I know the difference between a good dad and a bad dad. You're a good dad."

My father responded, "Well, thanks, Kristen. What makes you say that?"

Without missing a beat, she answered, "Because you don't make me give head."

Mom asked, "What's 'head'?"

"Oh, you know." Kristen stuck her fist by one cheek and pressed her other cheek out with her tongue, miming a blowjob.

Brenda is a fourteen-year-old who tells lies even when the truth sounds better. If Mom asks about her homework and it was completed hours ago, she will say, "I haven't done it yet." Return trips from the country grocery store are filled with bogus stories about receiving backstage passes to upcoming Van Halen concerts or meeting local celebrities who are going to whisk her away. My parents are only uneasy when she *isn't* pregnant.

The only truthful information Brenda gives involves teaching the other girls the streets in Tacoma that turn a blind eye to prostitution, the way to pick out a good pimp, and how to slit your wrists if you really wanted to die—down the road, not across the street. Luckily, Brenda makes the cry-for-help cut only every other month. You know, the horizontal one.

The prettiest is Angie. Rumor has it that she started hookin' when she was nine, even though Mom and Dad won't confirm it. She has multiple personalities; we've counted six so far. In the blink of an eye, she changes. Walking into her room, it is a roll of the dice as to which you are going to get.

The more you've endured, the more respect you get. One of my sisters had burns on her arms where her real dad extinguished his cigarettes as a punishment. A brother of mine was beaten with a crowbar and had twisted skin from where his mom threw a pot of boiling water on him when he was five. Honor comes from these scars. Scars mean you are tough. I don't have any scars.

Our farmhouse is silent except for a breeze and house sparrows chirping in nearby trees. Walking toward the refrigerator, I pass a deep indentation in the malachite countertop. The genesis of this particular imperfection is easy to remember.

A few months ago, Mom told Dad, "You're being too hard on Bubba."

He warned, "Back off."

Mom wouldn't let up.

Red faced with anger, he yelled, "Get the hell outta my face!"

She stood her ground.

Enraged, my father grabbed a Martinelli's cider bottle by the neck and hit it against the countertop. He kept hitting, trying to break it. After a few good whacks, she backed down. The bottle remained intact, but the broken counter still serves as a warning to those who wish to confront my father.

A hollowness settles in my gut when Mom covers for me. Whenever I do anything, no matter how hard I try, I screw everything up and create problems for her. Dad says that boys need to be toughened up, that he is teaching me how to be a man. Mom tries to buffer any tension and takes the bulk of his anger. More often than not, it makes matters worse because "A man is supposed to take care of his own problems." That's what I'm learning: how to be a man. Eventually, everyone in the house learns to stay away when Dad is yelling at me. It is like calming a beehive; distance and time are the only things that work. That's why I hide from him.

Oversized windows look across rolling alfalfa fields. It feels freeing to walk around the house in my underwear. The long gravel driveway gives early warnings of cars coming up the drive. Until gravel grumbles under moving tires, I am free. I have at least two hours to do whatever I want. Rummaging through the fridge for leftovers, I remembered what Nick, a Little League buddy, told me: "Bubba, every man has porn under his bed. I bet that even your dad has a stash."

I am confident that my dad does not have a stash. Everyone in my family follows the Bible and Jesus doesn't like porn. Just few months ago, after Dad made captain at the Fire Department, he pissed off all the other firefighters by purging the station of all images degrading to women. Averting my eyes happens every day. If there is a PG movie with a boob flash, my family leaves the theater. TV shows with cussing get turned off. Even the lingerie section of the Sears catalog is thrown in the trash.

Does Dad have a secret stack of dirty magazines under his bed? I wonder if he likes Hustler *or* Playboy? *What if there are a couple of videotapes or sex toys? Finding that kind of stuff will sure knock him off his high horse. He won't be so fucking...er, I mean frickin'...high and mighty. That'll put him on the hot seat for a change. There's only one way to find out.*

My parents' waterbed lies motionless. The folds of the blankets rest at perfect military angles. Snooping around their bedroom is the second biggest crime in our home. Nothing to fear, the long gravel driveway will inform me of my parents' return. I'll have plenty of time to cover my tracks. My heart thumps so hard I can hear it beating, trumpeting the opportunity of a lifetime.

If there are naked girls hiding in this room, I will find you. Come out, come out, wherever you are.

My grip tightens around a cold brass handle. The balance of power shifts as wood scrapes against wood. The first drawer slides open. It holds an old neck brace, several knee and ankle wraps, and a sixty-foot telephone cord. I pull the drawer all the way out and examine the secret hiding space underneath—dusty carpet.

Damn it. Two left.

The second drawer is full of spiritual books and do-it-yourself craftsman manuals.

Come on, God, really?

The final drawer slides open, revealing a couple of *Better Home and Garden* magazines, scattered receipts, and a white plastic Safeway grocery bag. I flick the bag aside. Underneath hides a classic Winchester revolver with an oak handle, sheathed in an oiled leather holster. It is one of many guns in Dad's collection, here to protect the family. The wood handle feels smooth. I pull it from the holster. Loaded. Dad keeps this gun "ready" in case something bad happens. Handling a weapon without his permission is direct disobedience, the greatest crime. I've never touched his guns without permission, until now.

Are these hollow-point bullets?

Releasing the cylinder, the tip of my index finger presses against a round, keeping it in its chamber. Tilting the gun back, the remaining bullets fall to the carpet. Flicking my wrist, the cylinder rotates back into place. A lonely bullet rests four clicks away. I aim the barrel at a picture of my father and pull the trigger.

CLICK.

CLICK.

CLICK.

One more squeeze and the gun fires. Power. Each breath is shorter than the last. Through the window, rays from the sun warm my skin. Sweat rolls down my back and soaks the elastic of my underwear. House sparrows chirp outside. The wind is absent. Cold sweat leaks from every pour. The bullet is patient. The barrel aims at my face as I stare deep into the revolver.

Why does Dad say I'm stupid? I always try. Maybe he is right. Maybe I am worthless.

The weapon wobbles. Gripping the handle, it stops shaking. Control.

Everyone thinks he's the greatest guy in the world. I wish he would die. People would hate him if they were his son. I wish the world knew who my father really is.

My thumb releases the safety.

I'm always wrong, screwing everything up. No one wants me around. Everyone would be better off if I were gone.

The gun slides between my teeth. The sight scrapes against the roof of my mouth as I insert the barrel. My lungs draw in gunpowder residue with each breath. Teeth clench cold steel as I tongue the curved metal against my cheek. Gun oil coats each taste bud, cutting the taste of gunpowder.

No one wants me here. I don't want to be here. Just pull the trigger and everything will be over.

I sit quietly, waiting. Heart pounding, chest heaving, my hand twitches.

Great, I'll probably screw this up, too, and shoot my cheek off.

Another bullet quickly inserts into the neighboring chamber, just in case. Fast. After all, my dad taught me how to use a gun. The weapon slides back in between my teeth. Arm shaking, my thumb cocks the hammer.

All I have to do is pull the trigger and everyone's problems will be solved. They will be better off when I'm dead.

Silence.

Trigger finger motionless. I half expect to become demon possessed and jolt forward, but the room remains still and peaceful. I can't tell if each passing moment contains more or less courage.

Will my ears ring?

Will I even hear the gunshot?

How long will it take me to die?

Am I supposed to aim at the roof of my mouth or the base of my spine?

Is this is why they don't teach you about suicide, so you don't know?

The handle adjustment aims the gun toward the roof of my mouth, because that makes the most sense. The site scrapes more skin from my palate. Maneuvering the weapon, I find a comfortable position.

Do it! Just do it!

Pull the trigger and it will all be over.

CRUNCH. Gravel grumbles under moving tires. A baby-blue station wagon cruises up our driveway. My thumb jumps from the trigger.

Oh, shit! I'm not supposed to be here.

In seconds, the weapon is reloaded and back in its holster. The white plastic Safeway grocery bag slides back in place.

I look down.

I'm still in my underwear.

In a flash, I'm up in my bedroom, pulling on a fresh shirt and jeans. The car rolls to a stop. The new arrival is Mabel, one of my mom's church friends. Mom said that she might stop by.

Control breath.

Smile.

You have to smile. Mabel can't think anything is wrong. No one can.

Keeping a Christian smile on your face is a well-developed skill, practiced every Sunday on our way to church. Dad screams on the ride there and then we go off to Sunday school keeping up the illusion that our family is perfect. Walking outside, I paste on a grin.

Mabel asks, "Hey, Bubba, is your mother home?"

"No, but she should be back in a couple hours."

"Oh, okay. She said I could pick some squash from her garden, but I don't want to do it while she is gone."

"It's fine. She told me you might come by. Dad planted a couple packages of seeds so we have plenty."

Mabel scrunches up her face, thinking. "Squash is a hardy plant. They grow anywhere. You don't have to plant that many seeds to have a decent crop."

I reply, "That's why we have plenty. Would you like some help?"

"Yes, could you be a good boy and fetch a wheelbarrow?"

"Of course," I reply with a smile.

Mabel walks beside me as I navigate our wheelbarrow down a dirt path. She asks, "How are things with the family?"

"Great," I reply and load up vegetables for my mom's friend. After all, that's what a good boy is supposed to do.

THE PAST...

CHAPTER 2

WHISKEY COULD

ST. LOUIS, MISSOURI, 1943 (FATHER)

Newspapers tell everyone that the Great Depression's grip on the throat of America is loosening. The tide of World War II favors the Allies. Hope is on the horizon. The country's female labor force is in full swing, filling factories.

Standing in the aisle of a bus, on her way to a manufacturing job at an airplane factory, nineteen-year-old Sarah Francis looked for a seat. She passed by an elderly couple and a young mother trying to quiet a screaming infant. On her way down the aisle, a few passengers shot unwelcoming grimaces, wanting to keep the whole bench. Eventually she reached a crossroad: a scruffy boy with a mischievous grin sat on her left, and a smart-looking businessman sat on her right. Both made room for her and motioned an invitation.

For the next thirty years, Momma told anyone who would listen that sitting next to that scruffy boy was the worst mistake of her life. That boy was my father, James Beck.

LOUISIANA, MISSOURI, 1945

On January 13, Sarah Francis Beck obtained her first legitimate excuse to leave work early: her water broke. Over the past two years, it had been her job to get the local men to play her husband's carnival game: the Ball Toss.

Show a little leg and bat the eyelashes. That was the life of a female carnie. She loved playing the tease, traveling from town to town, seeing the world as a carnival worker. In her prime, she was a pro at seducing money out of the local men's battered wallets. Even at nine months pregnant, she wrangled in plenty of Pike County boys. Today, the young chaps waiting eagerly in front of her shuttered stand didn't get the flirt show they typically enjoyed.

The carnival "big boss" assured the disappointed men, "Don't worry. Sarah will be back the day after tomorrow, in full strength, and slimmer than ever."

The "big boss" had given an unprecedented treat for Sarah and Jimmy Beck: two days off with pay. For Sarah, it meant she could labor away in the hospital and push out their firstborn. For James, it meant he could escape to a tavern, drain a couple racks of beer, and both get paid for it. It was a golden opportunity for both of them. Daddy tossed back longnecks as Momma gave birth to me.

It was after 3:00 a.m., the following day, when Dad finally stumbled back to our run-down singlewide trailer. Momma had fallen asleep on the couch while keeping vigil for her "son of a bitch" husband. I cooed nearby in a dresser drawer.

The coast was clear. My father shushed his giggling barfly companion. Together, they slipped through the front door, past the couch, and into the back bedroom.

CREAK. The hallway announced footsteps. Instantly alert and aware, Momma snatched me up and thrust me toward Dad.

He recoiled. She started screaming.

"You goddamned motherfucker! You don't even come to the hospital to see your son be born. You worthless piece of shit!"

"Shut up, bitch. You should be happy I put a roof over your head!"

He pushed her down the hall and locked the door. Mom pounded and screamed for a while, but it was too late. Dad's head was elsewhere.

My first day isn't something that I remember firsthand. That would be impossible. But listening to all the screaming matches my parents had over the years, it isn't a difficult story to piece together.

Hungry Horse, Montana, 1948 (Three years old)

"Learn your manners! A spoon isn't a goddamn shovel! How many times do I have to show you how to eat your peas? Hold it like this!"

Momma made balancing a mound of peas on a spoon look easy. Her pinky extended and a folded napkin remained on her lap. For the moment, she looked almost dainty. Her deliberate pinky movement was the only refinement in our singlewide trailer.

I grabbed the silverware exactly like she did. The spoon slowly dipped into the bowl. My fingers adjusted and I raised the mound of peas to my lips.

SMACK. Her backhand flew without warning. The high chair toppled and crashed to the floor. I spilled out onto the linoleum. Within seconds she jerked me up off the ground and threw me back into the chair.

Momma yelled, "If you don't do it right this time, ya little shit, I swear to God, I'll kill you." She shoved the spoon back in my hand and screamed, "All the other kids in the neighborhood hold their spoon right. I guess I've just got a stupid shit for a son."

After Momma taught me how to hold a spoon, she wanted me to stay inside. That way, no one could see my face. I tried my best to hold the spoon the right way, but my hands were too small. When she left the room, I ran away, but didn't get very far. When Dad caught me running down the street, he asked how I got all the cuts and bruises because Momma said I fell down.

Dad brought me home and locked me up in the bathroom. A few minutes later, Momma came in and smacked me around for running away.

I fell down a lot back then.

Grand Coulee Dam, Washington, 1950 (Five years old)

Rumors floated around that World War II might be ending soon. Soldiers would be returning home, jobs would be scarce, and money would become even tighter. Hearing that the carnival work would dry up, Dad abandoned the Ball Toss booth and returned to his true calling: high angle welding. Because Dad's education never went beyond the eighth grade, he made all his money by taking the high-risk positions that no one else wanted. It didn't matter whether he was walking across an I-beam fifty feet above a packed highway or five hundred fifty feet over a rushing river; he loved it all just the same. Armed with a flask of Jack Daniels, he would throw on a mask, strike an arc, and work at the top of the Diablo Dam in the Skagit River, or wobble one hundred fifty feet in the air on missile silos in Arkansas. Right now he's spot welding the Grand Coulee Dam.

Did he ever get fired for drinking on the job?

Yes and often, but the Ironworkers Union was hard-pressed to find someone else who would monkey climb and free-weld five hundred feet in the air without a safety harness. Dad's lack of fear was his job security.

James and Sarah Francis Beck

Momma never had any education or marketable skills, and never worked another job. She raised seven children, but to call her a "stay-at-home mom" would be an insult to mothers. Technically, she did stay at home, and she did birth offspring, but Sarah Francis was an angry, frustrated woman, with little maternal love to spare for the children of the cheating, lying drunk she'd married. In short, my mother is the meanest person I've ever known.

HOPE, IDAHO, 1951 (SIX YEARS OLD)

It was a Saturday. We lived in a tiny shack out in the country with cattle fields that surrounded our yard. A long gravel driveway cut through trees, bisecting cow pastures and ended up at our front porch. Behind our home was a forest so heavily wooded that I was the only kid brave enough to scout it out.

My family never stayed in a town long enough for me to make real friends. So I filled the woods behind my house with make-believe friends: a band of cowboys and Indians, Robin Hood and his Merry Men, even a wild black stallion. All of my imaginary friends wanted me to lead because they thought I was really smart and strong. I was the only one brave enough to venture into the dark cave and fight the bad guys. I proved my courage by being the only one who would dare ride the dangerous black stallion.

On this particular day, we kids were told to stay in the house so we could "be together as a family." I sat on the couch with my two little sisters, Mary and Gracie. We watched Dad drink beer after beer while Mom screamed at him. Occasionally, he would chuck an empty beer can at her, just to make her jump.

Momma yelled, "You worthless bastard. What the hell am I supposed to cook, the damn cans?"

"I'm the one that works for a livin'. You just sit around here on yer fat ass. Go fishin'. Catch somethin' from the river."

"You don't work for a livin'. You work for gawdamn beer."

"Listen, heifer, no one's gonna tell me how to spend my paycheck. Especially not you, ya worthless bitch."

This was family time. We Beck kids learned to sit still when our parents were fighting. Pretty soon the punches would come; better they beat each other up than hit us kids.

Whenever Mom and Dad had a blowout fight, they would make up for it by doing something really nice like have a marshmallow roast, take a trip to the local store for candy, or go for a ride in the country. I knew this was going to be one of those times. On the drives, Dad would have me open the barbed wire gate that connected our driveway to the outside world. After the fight ended, they cleaned themselves up: Dad in the bathroom and Mom in the kitchen. His knuckles were bloody and her nose still bled. Today, I was going to be the hero and surprise my dad—I'd show him how smart I was. While he washed his hands, I slipped out the front door, bravely mounted my imaginary black stallion, and galloped as fast as I could toward the barbed wire gate. I was sure I would get an extra piece of candy for such a carefully planned good deed.

A smile stretched from ear to ear. I ran a quarter mile. I was so far that I couldn't hear what my dad was yelling.

"You better turn around right now, ya little pecker head or I'm gonna beat the shit outta ya."

I kept running.

CLICK. The gate unlocked.

I stood against the wire. Dad was going to be proud of me and tell me that I'm a good boy. Mom will clap. I will be the hero.

The station wagon revved—*RRRRHHHUUUNNNN.* It was my papa. I turned toward the house, still grinning.

The car barreled down the driveway, coming closer and closer.

It was going really fast.

Something was wrong. The car closed in, the brakes locked, and the car skidded, sending gravel and dust flying. I was frozen with shock. CRASH.

The station wagon bashed me against the barbed wire, pinning me. The fence popped free from the cedar posts. Each strained breath forced metal barbs further into my back.

The station wagon backed up.

I fell to the ground, aching, crying, and confused. The car door opened. Heavy boots crushed the gravel a few feet from my head.

Dad yelled, "Get in the fuckin' car."

I couldn't move. It had to be a mistake.

I looked up through tears and dirt.

"Did you hear me?" A scuffed black leather boot sailed toward my face.

WHAM. It landed right between my eyes. I held my face. He kicked me in the stomach. I curled up in a ball. Dad kicked through any opening I gave him.

WHAM. My head split open. He kicked and he kicked.

WHAM. My ribs broke.

CRACK. A gunshot.

Dad's arms rose into the air. Momma held a .30-30 Winchester in the distance.

This was my chance. With adrenaline pumping, I took off. I ran like the wind, like the Devil himself was after me. No one could catch me. I sprinted to my safe place, into the woods where my friends could help me: the cowboys and Indians and Robin Hood and his Merry Men. There was no way I was going to get caught because my parents didn't have a wild black stallion to help them.

In no time, I slipped into my secret cave—a vacated badger den under a tree, just big enough for me to fit. It was dank and dark. My face was puffy and warm. It became harder and harder for me to open my eyes. The skin on my face was tight. My body shivered. I could taste blood, dirt, and tears. Whenever I wiped tears away, more dirt would get into my eyes.

Hours passed.

Occasionally, I would hear my parents' footsteps and voices around me. It was cold, but I was safe. Alone, I was peaceful and that's all I wanted. Curling into a ball, I relaxed and talked to myself.

I'm going to leave these crazy assholes the first chance I get. When I have kids, I'm going to be good to them. I'll never treat them like this.

Eventually, I fell asleep.

The chill of nightfall woke me. It felt like fifty bees stung my face; my eyes were swollen shut, zero visibility. Everything throbbed or shivered. A cool breeze carried the distant pleas of my parents, searching for me. "Come back, Jimmy. We're sorry. We miss you."

My swollen face made their words difficult to believe. I had no intention of coming out from under the tree, but where else could I go? Despite a firm resolve to remain underground, my cramping legs and empty stomach won the battle and convinced me that it was time to leave my cave.

I called out, "Here I am! Here I am!"

A stampede of footsteps—within seconds, a weathered hand reached inside the cave and pulled me out. Dirt covered my entire body.

Jimmy at six years old.

Dad hugged me. I cringed and hugged him back; the barbed wire cuts still stung. Mom and Dad started kissing my swollen face, as if their lips were going to make me feel better. It hurt. I wanted to yell, "Stop fucking touching my face," but I didn't because they were finally being nice.

A few hours later, I was on the couch and moved an ice chip around my cheek like Dad showed me. He sat down beside me and asked, "How ya doin'?"

"Fine."

Dad scooted close to me and put his hand on my knee. "Yer gonna have to stay inside for a couple weeks, till you heal up. Those damn neighbors get nosy. You gotta listen to me when I say something. You got that?"

I nodded, got it.

"If anybody asks, tell 'em you fell down the stairs."

I nodded again in agreement.

"Good boy."

Dad pulled something out of his pocket, slapped it into my hand, and said, "This is for after you get well."

I strained. My eyes opened a crack. Four nickels rested in my palm: candy money.

ABERDEEN, WASHINGTON, 1956 (ELEVEN YEARS OLD)

Life wasn't all bad. I've always been proud of how I had to hustle to survive. I started picking up coal alongside the railroad tracks when I was five. People would easily pay me twenty-five cents a bag and that was a lot of money back then. Sometimes I'd swipe free yardsticks from Sherwin-Williams paint supplies and sell them house to house.

KNOCK, KNOCK. I'd wait for the next sucker to answer the door.

"Hi, my name is James Beck. I'm selling these swell yardsticks for a nickel apiece to support our next Boy Scout Father-Son Banquet. Would you like to buy one? They are only a nickel."

Everyone bought at least one. Occasionally, I'd get caught repeating the same line.

"Hey, weren't you selling these last month for the same event?"

"Yes, sir, but we didn't raise enough money last month, so it was postponed. Would you like to buy another yardstick?"

Worked every time.

By the end of elementary school, I had several moneymaking and charity scams down pat. The local baker set aside fresh breads and treats for me every week, and the Christian grocer had a special "Jimmy Jr. Bag" filled with fruits and vegetables for me to take home. Sometimes, I'd take the goods home and other times I would trade it for other things my family needed.

NEWHALEM, WASHINGTON, 1957 (TWELVE YEARS OLD)

The prospect of hanging out with my father always lit me up with excitement. Classmates bragged about the cool stuff they did with their dads. I knew it was a matter of time before it was my turn. Soon, he would teach me how to play football or take me on a fishing trip. Meanwhile, I didn't mind tagging along on his "business trips" to the tavern. I liked being around him. The car rides were the only time we spent together. He was always happiest when en route to a bar. His good mood put me on top of the world.

However, once he slipped inside a tavern, the fun was over.

I'd sit out in the car, doors locked, windows cracked. There are only so many things you can do in a car, waiting. After what seemed like an eternity, Dad would swagger out with a soda and a grin. After sitting alone in the car for a couple hours, it was exciting to see him again.

He'd stumble over to the car, hand me the soda and some potato chips. He'd ask, "You havin' fun, Jimmy?"

"Yeah, Dad. Are we going to go do something fun now?"

"Not yet. Got a bit more business to take care of. Just drink your soda and be a good boy."

Sons are supposed to listen to their fathers, so I did. He would slip back in the tavern and I would wait.

A couple hours later, he would come out with another soda pop and a bag of potato chips. A few hours later, he'd come with another. Each question came with the same reply.

"Hey, Dad, are you ready to go now?"

"Not yet. Just a bit more business."

Moments later, the tavern door would shut.

I never knew how those nights would end up. Sometimes, I would find him in a back alley, puking his brains out. Other times, I'd walk home, if I knew how to get there. On good nights, we slept in the car. On great nights, I woke up in my own bed. Usually, the evening ended with me roaming the streets, looking for my drunken father. Sometimes, he would be passed out on someone's front lawn. The homeowners would watch as I carried him off their grass. If it were one of my classmates' homes, I heard about it the next day at school.

CONCRETE, WASHINGTON, 1957 (TWELVE YEARS OLD)

By the time we moved to Concrete, Washington, I'd had enough. I was excited to get another fresh start. No one, ever again, would know that the drunk passed out on their lawn was my dad.

This new place was a clean slate and I made good friends: John and Joanne. She was a bit of a tomboy and could out-fish anyone I'd ever met. John was big and gangly for his age. His dad was a drunk, just like mine. The difference was, his dad owned a liquor cabinet. Even though we were best buddies, neither of them saw my house nor met my family.

A few times a week, John and I met in an old tree fort about twenty-five feet up a giant oak. John would pass me the booze that he stole from his father's stash. We'd take pulls. It didn't matter what it was—gin, vodka, peppermint schnapps, whiskey, tequila—we drank it all. We never got caught and stashed the extra liquor in the tree house for later. We thought we were hot shit and stayed drunk all summer.

In this new town, no one knew whose son I was and I was determined to keep it that way. In Newhalem, I learned that there was never going to be baseball lessons or fishing trips with my father. Unless I turned into a bottle of booze, my dad didn't want me.

The next time Dad asked, "You wanna go into town with me?"

I replied, "No, thanks. I got something else I have to do."

That afternoon, he drove to his favorite bar to drink alone and I walked across town, to the tree house, to drink with my buddy.

We never spent another afternoon together.

BELLINGHAM, WASHINGTON, 1958 (THIRTEEN YEARS OLD)

I'd steal cartons of cigarettes and boxes of condoms and sell them to classmates. Boys would gather around me at the playground.

"Hey, Jimbo, I only got a quarter. Can I get a rubber and a cigarette?" a classmate would ask.

"Nope, prices are a nickel a smoke and twenty-five cents for a rubber. I've gotta cover my costs. But if your buddy buys a second rubber, I'll throw in a smoke for free."

I'd sell a couple boxes of Trojans every day to forth- and fifth-grade pals. We'd put them in our wallets and thought the ring looked cool as it pressed through our blue jeans. It signified "Hey, babe, I'm with it. I have sex."

Each time I returned home from school, Momma held out her hand and I'd fill her cigarette-stained palm with nickels, dimes, and quarters. This change and occasional bills filled up a money jar, the contents of which bought anything for the household I could not get with a grin, a sob story, or quick fingers. Because Momma stayed at home with my siblings and Dad drank away his paycheck, the responsibility to put food on the table was mine. I did it for years. There was never a "Thank you" or "Good job" for my efforts. This contribution was expected because I was the oldest, the man of the house. It was the only way our family was going to eat.

The money jar was my family's financial safety net. Only Momma knew where it was hidden and guarded its location from everyone. If Dad found it, the money would disappear into the nearest bar and we'd go hungry. No person, holiday, or special occasion could keep my father from his beer. However, sometimes whiskey could. When times were tight, which was always, the hidden money jar was the Holy Grail and Dad relentlessly pursued it. He would shake down us kids, upend the house, and beat it out of anyone he thought knew of its location. At some point, each of us kids had prized possessions pawned off for beer money because we didn't give in.

Momma would yell, "Gawdamn it. We don't have another stash."

"Yer lyin' to me, bitch. Give it up."

"There ain't no more money."

Dad went through our rooms to see if there were any toys he could trade the bartender. Once Dad found the money jar, he was gone. With cash in hand, he would head down to the nearest bar and drink. And drink. And then drink some more. When that watering hole shut down, he would find another place with booze: a barfly's apartment, neighboring towns with later last calls, or even jump a boxcar and toss a few back with hobos as he crossed the country. It didn't matter if rent was due, Christmas was tomorrow, or there were over a half-dozen hungry mouths waiting at home. Whenever he got his hands on a paycheck, borrowed cash, our valuable possessions, or raided the money jar, he would spend every last dime the family had on booze. When Dad went on a bender, we would not hear from him for weeks, months, even years.

My father had many weaknesses, but he was a master at one thing: the art of starting a new life. He'd begin the process by creating a facade of stability in a new town, whether it was in the next county or hundreds of miles away. Then he'd contact the local union and find some welding work. With the legitimacy of a new job, he would sucker unsuspecting townsfolk into extending credit lines, acquire a car, and a low-rent house.

After tiring of one-night stands with the local barflies, getting sick of meals served in greasy diners, and being lonely in his run-down shack, he'd start calling Momma. He'd demand that she bring all of us kids to wherever he was living. Despite Dad's constant promises that "things will be different this time," she would ignore him.

My father was not a man to give up, though. He knew that every time he split town, Sarah Francis would head down to the state welfare office and sign up for food stamps and other government assistance programs. Then, with taxpayers' help, she would feed all of us kids. All Dad had to do was contact that welfare office, give them a sob story about how he wanted to support his family, but his stubborn wife wouldn't let him. After he sent a little money, the deal was set.

There was no way the state was going to financially assist a family who had a "willing husband and father" to provide for them. Once Dad's cash arrived, the spigot of state assistance would turn off and the family would be forced to move to wherever Dad was living.

Momma's lack of education and nonexistent diplomacy skills gave her zero leverage with the welfare officials. She would go down to the office and scream, "That no-good son of a bitch does this every couple months! He steals all the fuckin' money, spends it on booze, and then convinces you pricks to make us follow him. You assholes can't make us move back there. I just won't do it!"

Mom's demands were ignored.

The only "assistance" the local welfare office would give us consisted of pointing a finger toward the transportation Dad had to pay for. I'm sure they were glad to dump the "Beck problem" on another town. We would have just enough time to grab a couple changes of clothes before we hopped in the army-green station wagon that carried us to the bus or train station. If you didn't carry it, "it" didn't make it. Nothing ever lasted.

This cycle repeated about every six to nine months, causing our family to move back and forth across America, landing in towns like Ketchikan, Alaska; Searcy, Arkansas; Butte, Montana; Memphis, Tennessee; Beach, North Dakota; and Port Orchard, Washington.

The one good thing about moving all the time was that each new town was a clean slate that could be hustled. As soon as we settled in, I would start working the old angles and get free stuff from local stores. Things would start off great and stay that way for a while. Before long, bounced checks would pile up, taverns would stop offering tabs, the car would get repossessed, and Dad would skip town in another drunken stupor. The day after, all of us kids would follow Momma down to the welfare office where she filed for state assistance.

The welfare office was the worst place in the world: sticking your hand out and moving at a snail's pace. Everyone looked pathetic. It was another reminder that our family was at the low end of society, the sludge that accumulated at the bottom of the barrel. We were the people who didn't have cars, live in nice houses, or pay bills. Everyone who stood in line were either angry or in tears. Momma was one of the angry ones.

In small towns, standing in a welfare line spelled trouble. If somebody from school spotted you, you were fucked. When in line, you kept your head down, mouth shut, back turned, and hat pulled tight. Every car that drove by could have someone in it who would gladly destroy you. The only safe people were those standing with you. It was an unspoken "don't ask, don't tell" policy if you recognized a classmate in line. A kid in junior high armed with that type of information would execute a social death sentence. Everyone was potential threat, so I hid my face and blended into the crowd. I spent enough time being the poor kid who everyone teased: rocks thrown at you, spit on, kids telling joke after joke at your expense until you walked away and spent the summer alone.

CHAPTER 3

BLOOD WINGS

BELLINGHAM, WASHINGTON, 1958
(FATHER, THIRTEEN YEARS OLD)

Most of the local jobs were gone. Employers were going out of business. Even Pacific American Fisheries, one of the largest canneries in the world, was going belly up. There was little work to be found. Times were tough. Dad got fired from his welding job and went off drinking.

The next morning, Momma dragged us kids down to the welfare office. She lied to the officials, saying that Dad had been gone for several weeks. I shielded my face like always. The controlling officer took one look at my family and gave us food stamps on the spot. I'm still not sure how Mom figured out that Dad was on another bender, but she was right. After being gone only one night, she knew. It might have been instinct, experience, or maybe she just didn't want to take a chance of being wrong.

Sarah Francis Beck—Jimmy's momma

Burned-yellow wallpaper bubbled up and peeled at its edges. The kitchen in our current house was a rush job two decades after its prime: busted linoleum, a leaky sink that only had cold water, and an uneven floor. It held all the stuff that Dad needed to fix. Dishes were stacked up in the sink, spilling out onto the counter, cemented with week-old food. Sacks of new groceries and cigarettes sat next to dirty plates: food stamp items. Momma only stuck with three priorities: smokes, food, and rent. Smokes were the only nonnegotiable. We didn't own a broom, vacuum, or cleaning supplies because nobody would have used them. The rotary telephone hanging on the wall was our only decoration. The phone company turned it off months ago.

I boiled a pot of water on the stove and filled the sink. Plates needed to be washed now that we finally had groceries. Momma's face sagged as she lit up a Winston cigarette. She took a long pull, held, and then blew smoke around the room. Hard years pressed into deep wrinkles on her face. It looked like she had a permanent frown.

Dad had been gone for months. The phone bill never got paid because Momma thought that he wouldn't be able to find us if we didn't have a working telephone. She was wrong. Dad persuaded the welfare office to personally deliver his "come live with me" message to our address. The guy who showed up from the state office looked like a linebacker, which made him impossible for Momma to ignore.

Momma screamed, "You need to get the hell off my property. I got rights."

The man from the welfare office pulled out an envelope. "Calm down, Mrs. Beck. I'm here about your husband."

"I know what yer here for and I won't go. Ya can't make me," Momma replied.

"I'm not trying to make you do anything. I just wanted to show you your husband's—"

Momma cut him off. "Don't wanna see nothin' from that son of a bitch. He hadn't done nothin' fer me or fer these damn kids ever, except take. Take, take, take. He's been gone for four months."

"Well, he wants to give back now. The reason you haven't heard from him is because he has been out to sea on a commercial fishing boat. He's doing well up in Alaska and wants you to come live with him. Here is his pay stub."

Momma snatched the paper out of the man's hand. Her eyes widened. "This is what he's makin'?" she asked.

The man nodded.

Her jaw dropped. "This is more money than he made all last year, holy shit fuckers."

It seemed something had changed.

The man continued, "Your husband has been clean and sober for three months. He's been faithfully attending Alcoholics Anonymous meetings. He also accepted Jesus Christ as his personal Lord and Savior."

Momma went into a fit of laughter. "Ha, ha, ha, James Beck found Jesus. You gotta be shittin' me. Did you actually see him at church?"

"No, but I did talk to his pastor. He assured me that James has turned over a new leaf. More than that, a reformed Baptist Church in Bellingham and Ketchikan pooled their tithes together and bought these plane tickets so that your family could be together."

Momma grabbed the envelope from the man's hand and looked inside. Sure enough, several plane tickets were there.

"My Jimmy, the Christian, this I gotta see." She tucked the plane tickets into her bra and took another pull from her Winston cigarette.

"I'll leave this last document with you. It is a map to the waterfront home your husband's going to rent, as soon as you arrive."

Momma snatched the papers out of his hands and flipped through them. "All right, we'll go. You can leave now." The man left.

Midchuckle, Momma asked, "Whatdaya think, little Jimmy? You think yer daddy got saved?"

"I don't know. He sure is making lots of money."

This stumped Momma, valid proof at least one thing was different.

I scrubbed the dishes.

"Do you think James Beck really found God?" she asked.

"Maybe." I shrugged my shoulders, hoping he did.

Christians were nice people. They were the type that lived in the same town, had clean clothes, and got visits from Santa Claus. The grocery store owners who helped me out were all Christians. They might be easy marks, but they seemed like good people. They drove nice cars and lived in nice homes. With paychecks like the one Dad was getting now, we could become Christians in no time.

Momma hollered, "Religion ain't shit. Christians are liars and fakes. Fuckin' lunatics."

"He might be better now," I followed.

Momma yanked the plate I was scrubbing out of my hand and tossed it in the sink. She slapped my face. "Your father ain't no better. He does the same shit over and over. He leaves us for drinking and takes all our money. How good is that? Just 'cause someone rubs a couple words together for a few weeks don't mean they've changed."

I tucked my head away and kept washing.

"Use your shit brains: people don't change. And you're just like him. You're gonna leave me, too. You got the same fuckin' grin he got. Worst mistake of my life was sittin' next to the son of a bitch on that gawdamn bus."

I kept scrubbing dishes, hiding my grin. She was right. I was leaving the first chance I got. Momma was wrong, too. I would never be like my dad.

Flying twenty thousand feet in the air, I knew that I could fall to my death at any moment. No matter how many times the pretty flight attendant assured me everything was fine, my fingers dug into the armrest. I could only handle looking out of the airplane window for a few seconds. Houses, cars, and streets were too small to make out. Mountains looked like anthills. Nothing was recognizable. Every once in a while, the plane would drop and my stomach would stick to my throat. I didn't know how far Ketchikan was, which direction we were flying, or how long it would take to get there, but landing couldn't come fast enough. The rest of the passengers were eating and drinking as if everything was fine and dandy. They obviously didn't know that we could die at any second.

The flight attendant asked, "Would you like a soda?"

"No, thank you."

She was sweet, but still made me feel poor.

"Well, would you like something to eat? We have turkey sandwiches."

"No, thanks." I was hungry and thirsty, but the church people didn't give us any lunch money and I was certain that airlines didn't take food stamps.

The flight attendant leaned in and whispered, "It's free."

"Are the sodas free, too?" I asked.

"Yes." She smiled.

"How many can I have?"

She leaned down and whispered softly, "As many as you can carry."

For the rest of the flight, I ate and drank until my belly was ready to burst. Right before we started our descent, the flight attendant loaded me up on roasted peanuts, half dozen soda pops, and a couple more sandwiches for the road.

The mountains and trees surrounding our new community were breathtaking. Beautiful homes dotted the coastline. All of us kids were farmed out to different church families in the area until Dad scratched enough money together to rent our waterfront mansion. The Christian family that hosted me were tops. They cooked three warm meals every day, had super-clean sheets, and even bought me a brand-new winter coat. Having a house on the water seemed uppity. This new town had a great school and I could finally stay in one place and learn. Reading and writing was tough; I was so far behind in my education I didn't think I'd ever catch up with people in my grade. At this point, the past didn't matter. Things were finally going to be different.

KETCHIKAN, ALASKA, 1959 (FOURTEEN YEARS OLD)

It took two weeks for Dad to exchange Jesus for whiskey. He got drunk while working on the fishing boat and was fired. The local preacher stopped by—the one who raised all that money for our plane tickets—and wanted to encourage my father in the faith. Dad was still sauced. He chased him off with a pistol.

Things were back to normal. Life sucked.

The promised waterfront mansion turned out to be a rickety dump, just like every other place we lived in. It was the worst house on our street: a two-bedroom shack, on stilts, that hovered over the ocean. When we first drove up, I thought it was a joke. From the looks of things, one good shove would send it crashing into the water. The place didn't even have real plumbing. The toilet was a hole that emptied straight into the saltwater. Used toilet paper and other nasty things floated below until the outgoing tide washed our crap out to sea. The walls were insulated, but there were so many holes in the floor that it didn't matter. Walking around, you could see the seawater below. Parts of the flooring were rotten. I nailed down scraps of plywood over the really bad spots, so my little brother and sisters wouldn't fall through.

The only good part about this waterfront house was being able to live in the attic. My parents took one bedroom and my five siblings shared the other. Every day, I would climb the ladder and no one would notice I was gone. I had a sleeping bag, candles, and a wad of clothes. I was free of everyone. It was awesome being alone, except all the warmth was insulated away from me. Living in the attic was better than being downstairs with my family. It would have been a great room if it weren't Alaska. Being cold was a small price to pay.

WHAM, WHAM. Jolts ripped me from dreamland. I gripped the attic floor. It was the middle of the night. The whole house shook. Rhythmic thuds vibrated throughout the shack. Lightning flashed and thunder clouds roared. Storm winds whistled through the holes in the floor. Waves crashed hard, tossing mist up through the floorboards. It felt like the whole place was falling apart. Bracing myself, I tried to understand why my room was shaking.

This house is going to fall into the water. I've gotta get outta here!

WHAM, WHAM. Tears and terrified cries from my younger brothers and sisters magnified as I pushed down the folded attic stairs and jumped down the steps. My little brother Dennis clutched my sisters Gracie and

Mary. Linda, with her pigtails and tattered dress, attempted to rock baby Marguerite back to sleep. Dad hadn't drunk up all the remaining money, so he and Momma were still down out at a local tavern "taking care of business."

WHAM, WHAM. Logs slammed against the pilings, shaking the house.

Dennis pleaded, "Jimmy, what are we gonna do? The sea is gonna kill us."

I peeled a large piece of plywood off the floor, the one that covered the biggest hole, and told Dennis to turn off the lights. The moonlight revealed six enormous logs—each about two feet in diameter and twenty feet long—that had lodged themselves under the house's bracings. The waves were tossing the logs against the shack's foundation.

Within a minute, my clothes were off and I was down to my skivvies. You don't realize how cold snow is until you have to walk barefoot in it. Pink skin, shivering limbs, and numb toes were pricked with the winter cold as I stepped down the access ladder. Our waterfront dump seemed luxurious compared to the Alaskan ocean. The saltwater felt like a million icy-cold needles stinging every inch of my skin. Breath was strained and constant, panting in the cold night. Puffs of frozen air hovered around my lips as I waded toward the first log. With each step cautiously placed, I was careful not to let barnacles cut into my feet.

The moonlight reflected off the water, giving warnings of large waves to come. Bobbing up and down with the stormy current, I waded toward the pilings. At the lowest point, the water level was right at my nipples; there were other places where I couldn't reach the bottom. When a large wave came, there was no touching the ground. It lifted me up toward the bottom of the house and then dropped me just as fast. Treading water, I navigated between tar-plastered pillars covered with kelp, crabs, and barnacles. Saltwater crashed everywhere as rogue timber slammed against the foundation.

My siblings shouted down from the holes in the floorboards overhead, "Be careful, Jimmy. Don't let the logs smash you!"

WHAM. A rogue log hit a bracing just a few inches away from my head. This was the moment I realized that my plan to push the logs out from under the house was a bad one. The waves tossed me around like an anchorless buoy. Vibrations from the logs slamming against the bracing rippled against my skin. Numb hands gripped the middle of a log and I kicked with all my might, guiding it away from the family home. A huge wave dragged me under and across the barnacles, cutting into my back and arms.

Pushing my head above water, the first few seconds were the scariest. I quickly cleared saltwater from my eyes and got my bearings, hoping another log wasn't aimed in my direction. Working my way toward the backside of the house, I grabbed a log that blocked several others. Pushing the butt end, I kicked with all my might. The log and I set out for the open ocean. I swam back. The passing current carried the log away and I fought to retrieve the next one. Each log took about twenty minutes to push out to sea. After a couple hours, all the timber floated in the channel. The logs were headed for the foundations of other people's homes, but I didn't care. They weren't my problem, not anymore.

My sister draped a hot washrag across my forehead as I sank in the tin tub. Washing saltwater off never felt so good. My brother brought the kettle to a boil and poured water into my bath, bringing it to a warm temperature. All my siblings sat around, recounting my "log wrestling" adventure. I saved the day. They treated me like a hero. It felt great. Even the cold draft whistling through the floorboards didn't bother me.

Alaska just became a state, but that didn't make life in Ketchikan any more interesting. I had only one good friend: my eighteen-year-old buddy, Tommy Stack. He was the size of a truck, with sausage fingers. Tommy and I hung out all the time, drinking and shooting the shit. I looked up to him; I guess he was kind of a father figure. All Tommy talked about was getting out of town and seeing the world. He'd pick me up after junior high school and give me a ride home. I'd give a greaser strut out to his beat-up '49 Ford coupe. It was cool having a buddy who could drive.

One day, as we drove off, he leaned over and said, "Jimbo, today is the day. I'm signing up for the National Guard. It's my time. I'm finally going to see the world."

His words socked me in the gut. I didn't have any other friends. My throat choked up. "But I'll miss ya."

"I'll miss you, too. But I gotta leave. A man's gotta do what a man's gotta do."

If Tommy left Ketchikan, then there wouldn't be any reason for me to stay. I asked, "Why don't I sign up for the National Guard, too?"

"Gotta be eighteen. You're not even close. You don't even have facial hair."

Tommy wasn't trying to be cruel. At five foot three and a hundred twenty pounds, I didn't even look fourteen. Ever since Dad traded in Jesus for whiskey, I looked for a way to escape. I wanted to leave and never look back. No one wanted me around and I didn't want to be around either. I was just another mouth to feed. My brothers and sisters would understand one day that a man's gotta do what a man's gotta do.

Looking up at Tommy, I grinned and said, "Betcha I can find an old drunk that'll sign a piece of paper saying I'm eighteen."

That afternoon, Tommy and I stood by a bar and waited for an easy mark to enter. Within a few minutes, a grizzled barfly moseyed toward us.

"Excuse me, miss."

She looked up, without a word.

"I need your help. Commie bastards killed my mom and dad in the war. I grew up in an orphanage and all my paperwork was burned when it caught fire. I have no proof of age or birth certificate. I feel it is my duty to defend my country and join the National Guard."

She looked me over. "You want me to say I'm your mom so you can get in?"

"Well, yeah." Tommy and I rehearsed a lot more details, but now they didn't seem necessary.

"Two shots of whiskey. That's what it will cost you."

Tommy said, "Done."

A few minutes later, we entered the recruiting office.

That old drunk was a better liar than I was. The recruiter didn't even question my age. She told an award-winning tale. Within five minutes, we all signed on the dotted line and were out the door. Tommy slid our girl some money. The old barfly licked her lips, gave us a toothless grin, and slipped into the tavern. I never saw her again.

For the next two weeks, I walked around the house with a "shit eatin' grin" on my face. Getting shipped off was the light at the end of the tunnel, the secret that kept me going. Nothing bothered me, not even Momma's scratchy voice. Time flew by.

Momma asked me a couple times, "What the hell are you so happy about?"

I answered, "Nothing, I'm just happy."

One morning, no different from any other, I climbed down the attic staircase. Momma was in the kitchen, sucking on a Winston, the brand that tastes so good like a cigarette should. She glanced at me, but didn't say anything when I passed. The rest of the family was still in bed. I walked out the front door, grinning. The station to catch a seaplane out of town was only a few blocks away. It was the main way off the island. Each step felt like walking on a cloud. I waited for someone to call out my name or at least try and stop me. Nothing. The only sound came from my sneakers squeaking against the asphalt. I never looked back.

The next day I arrived at Fort Ord, California, for boot camp. It was a big jump: playing war in the cold Alaskan woods with stick guns and rocks one week to shooting rocket launchers and machine guns in the warm California sunshine the next. Monterey Bay was just a few miles away. It contained the nicest beaches and swankiest restaurants I'd ever heard of. Some of the guys said that a highfalutin golf course was built a few miles outside the base: Shores Course at Pebble Beach.

I never saw it. Golf was stupid.

I loved California. Heck, anything was better than freezing my ass off in Alaska. Every day, I had three hots and a cot (three meals and a place to sleep) and pocket money. Sometimes the mess hall cooked *steaks* for dinner! I could eat my fill. At breakfast, the cooks dished out eggs, bacon, and taters. I could have all the orange juice and milk I wanted. Some of the guys in my platoon would wiggle the bacon and complain that it wasn't "fresh" enough. It was ridiculous. To me, the military was heaven.

Drill instructors would yell inches from my face. Bits of spit would hit my cheek. Some guys would cry when it happened to them. I thought it was funny and had to fight back a laugh. One day, my sergeant screamed at me, "What the fuck you smiling at, pussy lips? My fifteen-year-old son looks older than you."

Your fifteen-year-old son is older than me and my momma can out-curse you.

"Just happy to be here, sir." I knew better than to speak my mind, so I kept still and fell in line.

The six-month National Guard training tour flew by. Before I knew it, I was discharged and back in Ketchikan. Surprisingly, the shack was still standing. The neighbors told me that my family moved to Memphis. Tommy got a job working for the seaplane company. I had no family, no friends, no way to make money, no place to live, and nowhere to go.

I was stuck.

Memphis seemed like fun, so I used the rest of my cash to buy a one-way plane ticket. I landed at Memphis International Airport the next night and then hitchhiked to Grandma Beck's house. Walking through the door, I was excited to share my National Guard experience with my family; nobody had heard from me since I left. Going back to school seemed like the best option after my military experience. However, I didn't know how I was going to negotiate finishing the eighth grade with my National Guard commitment to be a weekend warrior and protect my country.

Grandma was sitting in the kitchen, drinking a cup of coffee when I entered. She gave me a hug. "Well, hi, Jimmy. When did you get here?"

"Just now. Where's my dad?"

Grandma relaxed back in her chair. The smile faded from her face. "He's in town, taking care of some business."

"Where's my mom?"

"In the back bedroom. I know she'd like to see you."

I skipped through the hallway and opened the bedroom door. Momma relaxed on a bed with an ice pack pressed against her face. She pulled the ice away, revealing a shiner.

"What are you smiling about?" she asked.

"I'm home," I said.

"You shouldn't have left, worthless kid," she replied.

"Don't you want to know what I've been up to?"

"Did you make any money?" she asked.

"I spent it all to fly back."

"Lot of fuckin' good that does me. Why don't you make yourself useful and fetch me some ice."

I got her some ice.

Dad never came home.

The next morning, I walked into town. Just as I passed an army recruiter's office I remembered some of the guys in boot camp saying that the only easy way out of a National Guard commitment was to become active duty. I turned around. If the army didn't work, I'd try the navy. Upon entry, the recruiter looked me up and down. Before he questioned my age, I handed him my DD214 (papers verifying age and employment with the National Guard). The recruiter glanced over my paperwork and said, "Looks like everything is in order. When do you want to get shipped off?"

"As soon as possible," I replied.

"You've already been through basic training, so you don't have to waste time there. Ever think about becoming a combat engineer?"

"No, sir, but I am now," I said.

"I can get you on a bus this afternoon. You barely have enough time to go home and pack."

"No need to pack. Just point me toward the bus station."

A few hours later, I was on a bus headed to Fort Leonard Wood, Missouri-combat engineer school. It was about seventy miles northeast of Springfield, smack dab in the middle of nowhere. After that, I went off to jump school at Fort Campbell, Kentucky—sixty miles northwest of Nashville.

All the sergeants gave me shit for looking young, but they gave everyone shit. There were tons of recruits who were slow to develop. Somebody in the group has to be the youngest and smallest. I was that guy. Everyone assumed I was a late bloomer and let my appearance slide. However, one paratrooper didn't: Ron Howard. He was a fair-skinned, athletic prick who had a stupid expression permanently etched on his face.

In "jump school," paratroopers were gods and trainees were called "leg" because we hadn't earned our "wings" yet.

Leg = shit.

As soon as Ron saw me in the chow hall, he made it his personal mission to make my life miserable. This guy would seek me out and fuck with me every chance he got. I'd walk by and he'd toss food on the floor and say, "Pick it up, leg."

Then I picked up his food. I had to.

One day in the chow hall, I wasn't paying attention and I sat down right across from Ron. I wanted to run, but Airborne Steel doesn't run from anything. I pretended that I sat there on purpose.

Ron got in my face. "Hey, leg, when you gonna fuckin' grow up and be a man?"

I ignored him and started eating.

He yelled, "Did you hear me, runt?"

The food on my plate held my gaze. Focused. I hoped Ron would get bored with my lack of response and leave me alone.

He had his wings and wasn't going anywhere.

"Where are you from, leg?"

Being from so many places, I grabbed the first town that came to mind. "Bellingham, Washington."

Ron brightened up like a peacock and got real friendly. "What? I'm from Bellingham. That's awesome. What school did you go to?"

"Whatcom Junior High."

He rolled his eyes. "What high school, dumb ass?"

Oh no, I'm fucked.

My mind reeled for a bit. "Bellingham High."

"I went to Bellingham High."

Awesome. What are the odds?

I didn't know what to do. My archenemy was finally being buddy-buddy with me. I didn't want this to change, but continuing this conversation could only land me in Shitsville.

Ron asked, "Do you know Lisa Headmen?"

"I know Katie Headmen." It slipped out before I gave it thought.

"That's her little sister. She was in junior high."

The gears in Ron's mind started turning. I could feel him put the pieces together.

"My little brother dated her," I mumbled, which came off well enough to sound believable. He went through a long list of possible friends. I nodded my head, pretended to know them, and laughed at his stories. I only knew the people on his list through their younger siblings.

I wolfed down my chow and told him, "Gotta go, man. It's so great that we are from the same place."

Ron said, "I don't ever remember seeing you around."

I laughed. "I'm small, easy to miss." My exit was quick and friendly.

Bellingham High isn't big enough to hide in and neither is the army. With only two weeks left of jump school, I had to become a ninja and disappear. Ron had to be avoided at all costs. As fate would have it, Ron looked for me. We became fast buddies. He made sure we talked every meal. Trying to avoid him felt rude. It was nice to have someone that shared roots, which was new for me. It also felt dirty to keep the lie going, but a man's gotta do what a man's gotta do. There was only one way to survive: do your work, answer questions when asked, be quiet when possible, deflect when necessary, and lie if you have to. I had to stay off everyone's radar.

On graduation day, our commanding officer gave us a choice: we could have our Jump Wings gently placed on our uniform like a pussy or he would remove the metal backing and punch his fist against the paratrooper pin. Having metal sink into your flesh gives you Blood Wings.

I'm no pussy.

WHAM. The instant those pins sunk into my pecs I was a member of the 101st Airborne, an elite fighting force. Legs were the other worthless rats running around. Within seconds, bullies turned into buddies. Officers gave me respect. For the first time in my life, I belonged.

After getting Blood Wings, the platoon dispersed. Ron followed me back to the barracks.

When we were alone, Ron pulled me aside. "Jimbo, let me ask you a question."

"What do you want to know?"

"How old are you really?" he asked.

My stomach tied in knots. I could lie to anyone, but I couldn't lie to another man in the 101st Screaming Eagles. Crossing my fingers, I hoped my new friend wouldn't turn me in. "According to my enlistment papers, I'm twenty-one."

He looked me over. "And?"

"I just turned sixteen."

Ron doubled over in laughter and kept on laughing. I couldn't tell if it was a good or bad thing. It was too late; the beans were spilled.

He said, "You made it through jump school and you're only sixteen?"

"Please don't tell anyone."

"Come on, Beck. That is the coolest thing I've ever heard. I ain't gonna tell a soul."

I became a member of the 101st Airborne Paratroopers—"The Screaming Eagles"—a member in the 326 Engineers Battalion and still had not passed the eighth grade. The army was the best thing that had ever happened to me. It showed me adventure and revealed another world. I would have stayed in forever if our division hadn't been dropped into a group of trees, busting me up. I broke my arm and leg. When I was in the hospital, they went through my medical records and figured out my real age.

A couple officers chewed me out, but quickly dropped the issue. What could they do? I was just a kid.

In the end, they gave me an honorable discharge for fraudulent enlistment and sent me packing. The two-hundred-mile bus trip to Memphis was one of the most depressing rides of my life. A few weeks prior, my commanding officer gave me Blood Wings. The bruise on my chest still throbbed as the bus rolled through Middle America. I leaned back in my seat, rested my head against the window, and whispered a favorite cadence under my breath:

I made my living as an Airborne Ranger
Blood, guts, and a whole lot of danger

If I die on a Chinese hill
Take my watch or the commies will

If I die in the Korean mud
Bury me with a case of Bud

Put my wings upon my chest
And tell my mom I did my best

They could have taken the "tell my mom" part out, but it worked with the song. Even though I lied about my age, I earned those wings fair and square. No one could ever take them from me. It was hard to believe that the one place I was going back to was the only place I didn't want to be. I was headed home, wherever that was.

SEARCY, ARKANSAS, 1961 (SIXTEEN YEARS OLD)

Two years had passed since I stepped foot in junior high. Leaving Alaska felt like someone else's life. The principal, a tiny leprechaun man, escorted me through the empty hallways. Everyone was already in class as we toured the building. He knocked on a door, interrupting the English teacher's lecture. She welcomed me into class, said my name at the front. I took a seat in the back.

The teacher lifted a short story off her desk and began teaching about *The Life of an Airborne Ranger*.

Is this a setup, some sort of elaborate joke?

Looking around, everyone in the room was a country bumpkin to the core. There was no way they could know.

The teacher continued, "Just think about how exciting it would be to be a paratrooper and jump out of a plane." She rambled on and on, giving a lame explanation of what the army was like. Descriptions of training exercises and night jumps were way off. She also had no idea how someone qualified.

I wanted to correct her.

Airborne training is completely different. You have to perform five satisfactory jumps: two with combat equipment. Your knees and feet stay together. You don't squat land!

It felt like an episode of the *Twilight Zone*. My whole body itched to speak, to yell. I had to remain quiet. If I ran my mouth, I'd be the crazy new kid with a ridiculous imagination. It didn't matter that I had discharge papers and army photos. Even with solid proof, it would seem like I was trying too hard to fit in. I would be a suck-up, kiss ass, or show-off—take your pick. If I told anyone about the last couple years of my life, people would think I was a liar because the military doesn't let eighth graders enlist.

Lying is easy. My whole life I've been able to get people to believe lies. I'm a natural. Telling the truth is a different story. Truth has to be kept a secret. Truth gets you kicked out or made fun of. Truth holds you back. People don't like the truth; they like lies and I give people what they like.

As the teacher lectured on the life of an Airborne Ranger, the class listened in amazement. I tuned out all the bullshit and doodled on my desk.

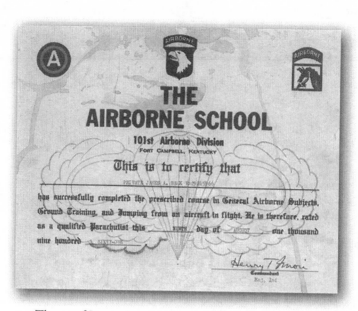

The proof Jimmy kept hidden—the Airborne certificate

CHAPTER 4

EXCESS BAGGAGE

BUTTE, MONTANA, 1963 (FATHER, EIGHTEEN YEARS OLD)

The sun was shining. A cool breeze blew wheatgrass sideways as our thoroughbreds grazed nearby. It was my only day off that week. I spent it with my girlfriend, Mary-Jo Silver. She was a cute, freckled-faced brunette. After an afternoon of horseback riding, Mary-Jo and I sprawled out on a picnic blanket. We alternated sips of wine, bits of cheese, and kisses. I acted a little more intoxicated than I was, checking to see how far my girl would go-third base.

Yeah, baby!

After Mary-Jo put on the brakes, we gathered our picnic basket and headed down the mountain, back to her parents' home. We put the horses away before nightfall, just like Mr. Silver wanted. He made this rule because he said "he knew my type."

Mr. Silver was a roughneck miner, one of those good-natured men who masked eagle eyes with a disarming smile. The guy was sweet as pie to anyone who wasn't dating his daughter. I was cautious. That guy would kill me if he found out I had sex with his baby girl and made sure I knew it.

Luckily, I had a bit of a death wish.

Mary-Jo and I brushed down the horses. Once finished, I gave her a peck on the cheek as her father watched through the window. I smiled and waved, a nice touch. I hopped on my 1960 Allstate motorcycle and kick-started the beast. The custom baby-blue and chrome gas tank rumbled between my legs. After I was off the Silver property, I opened up the throttle on the open country road. Parched grassy hills and abandoned mining rigs passed by as the wind whipped my hair back. Squinting, I saw pavement pass beneath me. I hollered at the top of my lungs. The engine thundered between my thighs. Wind pushed moisture from my eyes, forcing salty water to roll across my cheeks.

I was wide open.

I was free.

When I wasn't chasing tail, I was backfilling a pipeline trench for a local concentrator mining company. I busted my hump six days a week, eight hours a day, time and a half on Saturday, for $2.80 an hour. It didn't matter what the weather was like, we worked. Blizzards, hailstorms, we did it all. Someone had to take care of my brothers and sisters. I wanted to finish high school, but there was rent to pay, food to put on the table, and a motorcycle to keep up.

As far as Dad was concerned, I still owed him $450 on the 1956 Ford Crown Victoria I bought off him. Two days after I gave him a $150 down payment, he split town with my car and the cash. I heard the fucker got a bridge job in Medora, North Dakota. Good riddance. I was glad the prick was gone.

I pulled into our driveway. A few dirt-stained toys were scattered about the lawn—a raggedy doll, a plastic tea set, and a rusty tricycle—but no one was home. Mom had left the clotheslines up, but there was nothing hanging out to dry.

This was unusual.

When I tried to open the back door, it was locked.

Strange, we never lock our doors. We don't have anything worth stealing.

I shimmied through the window and crawled inside. Cigarette butts, soda cans, and empty beer bottles were strewn about the floor. The place looked abandoned. Our imitation Tiffany lamp was missing. In a flash, I knew what happened: Momma followed the money. She took the family to go live with Dad.

She told me countless times that if all the bills were paid she'd never move again. Lies. All lies. Every week I handed her my paycheck and paid her bills. This obviously wasn't enough; nothing ever is.

The few outfits I owned still hung in my closet. I wadded them up and stuffed them under my arm. Rummaging around, I picked up the tea set and doll. I searched for other things my family might appreciate: a teddy bear, a paddleball, and clothes. I brushed the dirt off and shoved everything in my motorcycle saddlebags. No one will expect to see any of these toys again. My siblings will be happy. We Becks learned not to get attached to toys, homes, or friends. Nothing ever lasts.

The engine rumbled between my legs. The five-hundred-mile motorcycle ride to Beach, North Dakota, was an empty drive. My entire life fit into one small leather sack. I didn't know why I was going back home. They obviously didn't want me around. I paid all the bills and I'm still excess baggage.

They didn't even leave me a fucking note.

BEACH, NORTH DAKOTA

I cut the engine. My butt was numb and asleep, stuck to the motorcycle. My legs stretched as I peeled myself off the bike. I tugged a crumpled piece of paper from my leather jacket and double-checked the address, a formality. The Crown Victoria Dad stole from me was parked cockeyed on the overgrown lawn. It was in one piece, so I had no complaints. The new shack had a wooden porch and some old rocking chairs. Grayish paint peeled off the walls, revealing an off-white undercoat. My family wasn't squatting, so that was good.

I pulled off my helmet.

Momma's smoke-strained voice echoed across the lawn. "Ya cocksucker, you can't have 'em! We need to go down to the damn store and get some gawdamn food."

Sounds like home.

I grabbed all the stuff from my saddlebags and headed inside. When I entered, Momma slapped Dennis across the back of the head for her own private reason. He staggered out of the way. She lit another cigarette and saw me in the doorway.

With a grimace, she barked, "Oh, great. Show up after we already finished unpacking, fucking lazy kid."

Dad shot me a sober grin and gave the room a tight look.

He asked, "Hey, Jimmy, how do ya like the new place?"

I gave him a nod of approval. At least the place had hot water.

Dad spun around and faced Momma. "Listen, heifer, gimme them keys!"

Momma shoved the keys into my palm. "Jimmy, he wants to take your car."

I clenched them tight. Dad whipped his head back and forth between us. "You trying to gang up on me, bitch?"

Momma backed away.

Dad took a couple friendly steps in my direction and said, "Jimmy knows what's good for him."

Looking me square in the eye, as if my response was obvious, he commanded, "Gimme them keys. I gotta take care of some business."

We all knew what "business" meant.

I shot a glance over to the couch. Linda and Gracie were sitting quietly, watching. They looked hungry, and were careful not to get involved.

Time to be a man and face my problem head-on. Airborne Steel doesn't run from anything.

"Not with my car, you're not."

In an instant, his rage flared. "Oh, big man, huh? You think that *you* can tell me what to do in my own goddamn house? Give me them keys if you know what's good for you."

"No. It's my car."

Time to test my Airborne training.

The room spun out of focus. Gracie and Linda ran into the back bedroom. Mom backed against the wall. Only my father and I existed. Fire was in his eyes. One of us was going down, we both knew it. He looked at me, then down at the keys. I stood between him and his beer.

I wasn't budging.

"I'm gonna knock your teeth out of yer head and make you pick 'em up off the floor if you don't give me them damn keys!"

Dad was giving me an out.

This was my last chance. It was now or never, fold or stand tall.

I looked him in the eye and said, "Take them from me, if you think you can."

In a flash, he swung. His weather-beaten fist sailed toward my face.

Before, whenever Dad was angry, I froze up and he landed his punches with ease. But today I was ready. He didn't realize that every army exercise and fight I had gotten into, it was his face that I was punching. I had been looking forward to this moment my whole life. Six months backfilling a pipeline, bar brawls, and Airborne training were on my side. My reflexes and strength kicked in as I dodged his punch, clenched my hand, and with every ounce of my being, sank my fist into his gut. I hit him with all the rage I possessed.

My father crumpled like a lifeless puppet.

I stood over his unconscious body, the victor. It didn't feel like a victory. I'd never hit anyone that hard. One punch dropped the son of a bitch. That was all it took. I wasn't sure I had it in me. I wished I had done it sooner. I just stared at my father as he lay motionless on the floor.

He didn't move.

I thought he was dead.

Mom lunged at me, screaming and scratching. "You killed Daddy, you son of a bitch!"

My hands held Momma's wrists, containing her flailing blows as her fingernails reached for my eyes. She kept fighting, but I held on tight. There was no way I'd hit my mom. Men aren't supposed to hit women.

Eventually, Dad lurched, coughing and sucking in breath. The old fucker was okay. Mom rushed to his side as I tucked the keys inside my pocket.

Grabbing the sacks full of abandoned toys, I went into the back bedroom. My siblings were all there, sprawled out on an old saggy mattress, happy to ignore another bout of yelling. Dennis, the charmer of the bunch, was playing Go-Fish with Mary as Linda and Gracie watched. Marguerite lay fast asleep.

Dennis smiled as I entered. "It's good to have you home, Jimmy."

"Thanks, buddy. It's good to be home."

BEACH, NORTH DAKOTA, 1964 (NINETEEN YEARS OLD)

A bloodcurdling plea called out from the living room, "Help me. Somebody help me!" It was Momma's voice. It reminded me of all the times I cried out when she was giving me a good thrashing. She probably deserved the beating, so I stayed in my room and let Dad give it to her.

When we kids were smaller, Momma would only stop when she got tired. She beat us kids more often than Dad ever did. Of course, he was rarely home. Nothing was off limits to her: belts, punches, kicks, sticks, garden hose, and hair pulls. Her grabby hands were the reason I still kept a high-and-tight military haircut.

BAM, BAM. Rhythmic thuds and loud crashes reverberated against the thin walls of our house. Momma screamed out again, "Somebody help me!" She had obviously pushed Dad too far.

Each thud was her getting what she had coming. None of us kids raised an eyebrow. This happened all the time. Dad did work around the house and she would hover over him, nagging. Then finally, he'd snap and go after her.

BAM, BAM. Mom gasped for breath and screamed bloody murder. "Please, somebody help me! This asshole is gonna kill me! Help—"

Usually everything calmed down after she started begging. Her voice would end in a scratchy, high-pitched drone. These last words, however, were drowned out into a choking garble.

It was time to check out the situation. Rancid garbage slime covered the kitchen floor. It smelled bad. Dad had finally taken out about a dozen bags of trash that had piled up for a few months. The residue made my nose hairs curl.

I rounded the corner. In the living room, Dad pinned Momma's arms against the floor with his knees, sitting on her stomach. His hands clamped down on her windpipe, choking away her scratchy voice. Momma writhed underneath, trying to bite his wrists and break free. She was fighting for her life and losing.

After our first fight, my dad avoided me when he got angry. He was bigger and stronger, but I was a better fighter. We both knew it. Once Mom realized he wouldn't tangle with me, she began taunting him, intentionally pissing him off, and then hiding behind me. I was her human shield. She relentlessly humiliated him, and it wore my patience thin.

This time, though, he went too far.

WHAM, WHAM. Momma's flabby limbs flailed with less vigor as her consciousness faded. Dad was in a trance, choking and slamming her head against the floor.

WHAM, WHAM. He wouldn't let up. It looked like he was going to finally kill the bitch.

No matter how much I hated Momma, I couldn't let Dad take her life. Charging up from behind, I blindsided him with a kick to the head. He launched sideways and smashed against the far wall. Whipping around, his eyes met mine.

I jumped on top of him. Elbows, knees, and fists began flying. Nothing was off limits. We were alone in our own violent world. Time didn't exist. The fight carried us from the living room, into the kitchen, and out to the parched front lawn. Our faces and knuckles were bloodied and mangled. I couldn't feel cuts or bruises. Adrenaline was the only thing I knew. We were animals, fighting in a cage of hate.

I lunged at him and slammed him to the ground. He was stunned. Capitalizing on the moment, I mounted his chest and pinned his arms to the grass with my knees, just like he did to Momma.

Choking is for pussies.

WHAM, WHAM. Face shots landed at will. Blood streamed from his nose and mouth. I remembered opening the gate when I was a little boy.

WHAM, WHAM. My fists kept connecting.

WHAM, WHAM. Meaty hands dug into my shoulder, then threw me to the ground.

The cage broke.

I spun around more beast than human, ready to destroy the person who touched me. Scrambling to gain footing, I sized up my new opponent: a mountain of a man, each arm was bigger than my torso. He had no neck to speak of and was in police uniform. His shiny badge brought me to my senses. There was only one cop in our town and he was standing in front of me, ready to tangle.

I raised my hands in submission.

I'm getting hauled off to jail. Great. This is what you get for helping family.

Momma stopped the officer. "No, that's my son. He's just protectin' me. Take my husband. He's the son of a bitch I called about."

The police officer faced off against my bloodied father, who was rolling around in the dirt, moaning. Dad wasn't a threat anymore. He looked like a dirty rag.

The officer relaxed.

Adrenaline slowed.

Tension left as an empty feeling took over. I never wanted to hurt my dad, but he never gives me a choice. It was the only way he would stop, the only way he'd learn.

Cuffed and secured, the officer supported my father as he hobbled over to the police car. Sharp glares fired in my direction as he yelled, "Fuckin' cunts, I swear to Christ I'm gonna kill…" The cop pushed Dad's head down and he ducked inside the patrol car.

The door slammed shut.

He kept hollering as the cop hauled him away.

The next morning, in eleventh-grade biology, I sat in the back of the class wearing sunglasses, pretending that the bruises on my face didn't exist. My knuckles still throbbed. If I played my wounds right, I'd become the tough new kid who nobody fucked with. That helps with making buddies and hooking up with chicks. I remained silent throughout the lecture, trying not to draw attention.

In small towns, once somebody knows your family had a run-in with the law, everybody knows. Life goes downhill fast. We pulled up to this town only a few weeks ago. It was another clean slate about to be tarnished. With any luck, nobody would learn about yesterday's domestic disturbance. It might even take a few more months to establish my family as the "drunken lowlifes who ruin the neighborhood."

KNOCK, KNOCK. The door opened. A cop entered, a familiar face. Everyone stared at the mountain of a man in police uniform like he was a celebrity. He walked over to our teacher. I tucked my chin into my chest, hiding behind my book. There was no reason he should look for me here. It had to be a coincidence.

The officer made small talk with the teacher. Classmates looked around with curious fascination. Many shifting glances took greater notice of my fresh bruises. This was the type of thing that gets talked about for lifetimes. Good or bad, it was too early to tell.

The officer pointed back at me. My teacher nodded.

The cop approached my desk.

Expressionless, my movements betrayed no information. In a bouncy Minnesota accent, the oversized officer said, "Grab yer books and come with me ya."

Following the cop out of the classroom, I gave a strut that would sow seeds of respect and mystery. Chicks dig bad boys. In the hallway, the principal stood nearby as if the cop needed him as backup. The police officer whipped out an envelope and handed it to me.

"Open it," he commanded.

I did.

A pink piece of paper was folded inside: a collection notice from the phone company.

"Is that your name and address?"

I pulled out the note. It read: "James Beck, 421 S. Central Ave, Beach, North Dakota 58621."

Do cops in this town do collections for the phone company?

"Yeah, it's my name and address. So what?"

"Do you know it's a criminal offense to litter?"

"What are you talking about?" I was puzzled.

"Don't ya lie to me ya," he said in his thick accent.

"I have no reason to lie to you. I have never seen that piece of paper in my life. It wasn't even opened."

All of a sudden, pieces started coming together: the garbage bags, Dad taking out the trash. Images of him driving my car down a deserted country road, tossing out trash bags, and leaving them for someone else to pick up came to mind.

"There's a whole lot of trash down on Black Diamond Road and it has your name on it."

"My dad is the one you want, not me. We just have the same name. He's the one that littered. He's down at city hall; you locked him up yesterday. Make him pick it up. He's not doing anything."

The principal shrugged.

The cop thought for a second and then slapped the envelope into my palm. "Share the name, share the responsibility. Yer doing it. You got a car?"

"I don't know where my car is. My dad took it and I don't know where he parked."

"I'll give ya a ride."

While my classmates sat around lunch tables, speculating why the older kid in junior biology got yanked from school by a cop, I walked down the Black Diamond Road, picking up rancid trash. The cop sat in his car, watching. All twelve bags were strewn about the asphalt. Animals had torn into most of them, eating garbage and leaving collection notices strewn about the landscape.

The sun was hot. Beads of sweat clung to my forehead. Golden-brown hills rolled across the distant horizon. Parched and dehydrated land stretched forever. I bent down and picked up a sea of rotting trash with my name on it. I flashed the police officer a grin and filled another garbage bag.

The courthouse was an old brick building in the center of town, about four blocks from our house. Security was minimal. There were no fences or barbed wire. A person could walk right up to place. The top of Dad's holding cell was underground. If he stood up, his head was right about ankle level. Bars covered the busted-out windows. Fresh air and evening light was unavoidable.

I sat against the backside of the building and whistled.

Dad came to the window. He waited for me to speak.

"How do ya like prison?" I asked.

"Ya asked that question last night," Dad responded.

"You didn't answer."

"'Cause it's a stupid fucking question," he said.

"You must like it a little or you wouldn't come back so often." This was my trailer-trash logic.

Dad thought for a bit; I had a point. "The food is good. Betcha I ate better tonight than you did. Yer momma can't cook worth shit."

He was right. The last time I ate a good meal was in the school cafeteria.

Dad barked, "You ain't gonna bring up the trash bullshit again, are ya? Them pricks should have made garbage men pick it up. Their fault, not mine."

"Dad, where's my car?"

"Sold it," he said, matter of fact.

"Why did you sell it? The car was mine. I bought it from you."

"The family needed to eat. You don't want your family to starve, do you?"

This seemed like a foolproof argument. However, there were no groceries in the house and his latest blowup was fueled by a healthy supply of Jack Daniels.

"Whatever," I responded.

"It's kinda stupid to keep your title in your dresser, under your T-shirts," Dad said, as if it were my fault for tempting him.

I asked, "You gonna pay me back?"

"Of course I will," he responded.

"When?"

"When I get outta here."

I knew he was lying, but it was a nice lie. Sometimes lies are nice to hear.

That week, we had some great conversations. Every night, we would talk for hours. He told me about growing up, what his childhood was like, his days as a merchant marine, and the welding jobs he did around the country. We created good memories through those bars. It was the best time I ever spent with my dad.

At the end of the week, I called into his cell.

Silence.

I peeked through the broken glass. It was empty. My father was gone.

CHAPTER 5

RINGS AND KINGS

BEACH, NORTH DAKOTA, 1965
(FATHER, TWENTY YEARS OLD)

Once Dad was released from jail, it took six months for him to resurface. He called again and gave Momma the same old story: "I love you and miss you. I want you to come live with me. I've changed, quit drinking, and have a great job. I'm in Port Orchard, Washington. There is so much work here. Little Jimmy could easily find a good job. Everything's going to be different this time."

My younger brothers and sisters still believed. Momma and I knew better, but we didn't have much of a choice. After Daddy called the welfare office, the only money they would give was for transportation out of town. With below-zero temperatures and no way to pay the heating bill, we wouldn't last long. The state gave us two days to pack up. I had a decision: stay in Beach and keep working on the Medora Bridge, a job Daddy helped me get before he got fired, or take a chance at a better life in Port Orchard.

I never got my high school diploma and wasn't qualified for a good job. Working in the freezing cold sucked. Moving was worth the risk. Taking a chance on Dad, seeing if he was right about all those jobs in the northwest seemed like the best call. There was also a small part of me that wanted to go because I was still hoping to connect with my family. It was all I had. Having only two days to sell my motorcycle forced me to accept half what it was worth. All of my possessions again fit in a duffel bag. All of us Becks crammed into an army-green social services station wagon and then got on a train. We headed out west.

Port Orchard, Washington (Three months later)

I held a telephone. An abandoned cigarette smoldered in an ashtray next to me, in the kitchen. It added to the gray haze. Several mashed butts lay among ash. Momma was in the living room, lighting up another. There were traces of the shiner Dad gave her a couple weeks ago.

The receiver slipped from my grasp and landed on the cradle, ending the call. This was the first time I had talked with my dad since he got released from his last stint in jail. I didn't visit him. There were always plenty of opportunities and this jail wasn't within walking distance.

When the authorities set Dad free, he moved into an apartment in Tacoma, about thirty miles away. Momma was healing up good. Her face wasn't swollen anymore. It was breakfast time. Dad was already drunk. He wanted me to check out his new apartment. Because the restraining order was still in effect, he couldn't pick me up. At least, that was his excuse. Even if he was sober, none of us owned a car.

There weren't any jobs like Dad promised. I'd spent the last few weeks trying to scrounge up some work and earn some cash, but came up empty-handed. I didn't have anything planned that day, so I went out to the highway and stuck out my thumb. It was cold and windy. Fingers quickly turned pink from the winter chill. Cupped hands kept in the warm air as I blew air to warm my knuckles. I walked backward along the highway, trying to look nonthreatening. Whenever a car approached, I stuck my thumb out.

It took five minutes to score a ride. The driver had rosy-red cheeks and a happy disposition. He reminded me of a TV version of Santa Claus, minus the beard. He was a jolly man heading to eastern Washington to be with his wife and kids. The car was warm and conversation was lively. Time flew by. Before I knew it, we were at the Tacoma city limits. There was more enjoyment in that thirty-minute car ride, with a complete stranger, than I'd had with my entire family for years.

The man was headed to Pasco, a couple hundred miles east of Tacoma. The jolly driver asked, "What exit should I take?"

"Uh, I'm not sure."

Directions came to mind, but I held my tongue. Thoughts of hanging out with my drunken father, hearing him bitch, and having to pick up all his beer cans made me nauseous. I'd already wasted too much of my life cleaning up his mess.

I reached into my pocket and pulled out all my money: fifty-seven cents and pocket lint. The next off-ramp was Pacific Avenue, my exit.

I told the driver, "Just head on out to Pasco, if you don't mind. I'm not staying here."

"Then where are you headed?" he asked.

My mind raced.

I had a standing invitation to live with Grandma Beck.

How long will it take me to get to Tennessee?

"I'm going to Memphis," I replied.

"Aren't you supposed to visit your dad?" he asked.

"I was going to, but...change of plans."

"Won't your father be upset?"

"Nope," I said. It was considerate of this stranger to be concerned. This was not something I was accustomed to.

He continued, "Shouldn't you call him or at least let your family know where you are going? I'm sure they will be worried sick."

I pictured my dad passed out on his apartment floor and chuckled. "Nah, they won't even notice that I'm gone."

When we arrived in Pasco, my ride dropped me off at a cousin's house; he happened to live nearby. He'd gotten fat since I'd seen him last, gained about forty pounds. We drank a few beers, talked about our crazy family, and then I crashed on his couch.

The next morning I got up early and started hitchhiking east.

A free-loving hippie picked me up. The guy was cool, had long dreads, wore a thin strand of beads, and remained shirtless despite the freezing weather. We smoked weed and cruised along a little slower than the rest of the traffic. I was high, so I wasn't sure how much progress we made. As long as I was headed east, I didn't care how far north or south we went.

Late that night, we rested in the back of his van, on the side of the road. It was the dead of the night and we were in the middle of nowhere.

A roaming hand brushed my side.

I moved away.

The hand followed.

In an instant, I doubled up my fist and I popped the hippie in the jaw. He squealed like a little bitch. I jumped out of the van and took off walking. I would have been a little more diplomatic had I known the weather forecast. Rain poured down on me. I spent all night walking along Happy Jack Road, soaking wet, moseying through a torrential downpour. The closest town was Cheyenne, Wyoming. I hoped my steps carried me in the right direction.

The next morning, the road was empty. Aspen and willow trees shielded me from the wind. The rain blew sideways. My flannel shirt and jeans were soaked; every inch was wet to the bone. Socks sloshed around inside my shoes. I pulled my flannel in tight to keep in some warmth.

Shivering in the cold, I kept walking.

Out of the corner of my eye, a police car rolled up. A couple oversized good ol' boys were behind the wheel. Mixing police and my family never yielded positive results. Instincts told me to run, but I was too tired and wet.

I kept walking, pretending to not notice. The patrol car inched up alongside me. They cracked the window. The officer called out, "Why don't you come with us?"

I kept walking, hoping they would just go away.

He said, "Hop in back. This is the last time we'll ask."

Too exhausted to resist, I jumped in the backseat without question. The car was warm, better than being outside, exposed to the elements. My crime was a mystery, but I didn't care. If warmth was part of the punishment, I didn't mind facing anything else they had in store. Going to jail didn't seem like a bad option. A small part of me began to understand my father.

When we arrived at the station, the officers issued me prison clothes. The jail was toasty, a hell of a lot better than walking down Happy Jack Road. The guys left me in my cell.

After a few hours, I checked the cell door. It was unlocked.

CLICKETY-CLACK. I heard footsteps down the hallway and jumped back on my bunk, pretending to be asleep.

I could bust out of here at any time. Those stupid guards forgot to lock the cell.

CLICKETY-CLACK. Footsteps marched across the tiled floor. I lay motionless.

An officer appeared in the doorway. "Hey, man, would you like a turkey sandwich or ham?"

"Uh, ham, please."

I was ill at ease. These cops were setting me up for something. They were uncommonly large and uncomfortably nice. I would make my escape after I examined the ham sandwich.

Are they trying to poison me?

A few minutes later, the officer brought a ham sandwich along with my old clothes, dried and folded. It was then that I realized I wasn't arrested. They were helping me out.

I left my cell and they invited me to join their poker game. We played for a few hours. I hustled a few bucks off them and then went to bed.

The next morning, a lanky officer with thick sideburns dropped me off at a truck stop at the edge of town. He even hitched me a ride with a truck driver into Salt Lake City, Utah.

Life on the road got old real quick: living out of thrift stores, eating scraps of meals, and having to scrounge shelter every night. Having a safe place to lay your head every evening is a luxury most people take for granted. The faster I got to Memphis, the faster I could begin a new life. Staying on the road meant progress. I made sure to shower often enough not to stink. The difference between traveler and homeless is decided by your body odor. It also decreases the distance people are willing to drive you.

As it turns out, my "just head east" mind-set wasn't a good game plan. I went way too far north and south, zigzagging across the United States. There was a lot of time wasted. When I landed in Albuquerque, New Mexico, I was fed up. After one solid day of washing windows at a gas station and panhandling, I spent every dollar I scraped together on a bus ticket to Jonesboro, Arkansas. I couldn't afford the ticket to Memphis. Jonesboro was as close as I could get and that was close enough.

When the bus pulled out of the station, a beefy black man sat next to his pregnant Negro wife, right across from me. I pushed my rucksack against the window and used it as a pillow. My belongings were secure. Momma always told us kids that "ya can't trust dem niggers." I figured she was right.

The idling bus rumbled. I woke.

Passengers left their seats and lined up to enter a greasy spoon for breakfast. I stayed on the bus, pretending to be asleep. There was no point in getting off; I had no money. The less I moved, the less I felt hungry. It had been three days since I had eaten. Memories of the police officer's ham sandwich filled my mind. When everyone was inside, focused on breakfast, I scrounged the seats for loose change. I found only a dime.

Everyone came back. The Negro couple took their seats across the aisle. He glanced at me.

I didn't like it.

I glared back.

His arm had ink. The tattoo read, "Army Ranger."

I asked, "Hey, are you Airborne?"

He grinned. "Yeah, 101st."

"Me, too." I lit up like a birthday cake. We shook hands as brothers.

"I'm Quincy. This is my wife, Rita," he said in a thick southern drawl.

Quincy and I chatted for the next eight hours. He was visiting his wife's family before being deployed to Vietnam and was leaving in a month. They had a three-year-old daughter, Sarah. The kid was staying with Rita's sister because she was hospitalized with some sort of sickness that sounded like a foreign language. Their next baby was due in less than three months and Rita couldn't fly.

"I hate leaving my little girl, but at least she is with family. It's what had to be done. A man's gotta do what a man's gotta do."

I nodded in agreement.

Quincy took in a giant breath and then sighed. Rita kissed him on the cheek.

He continued, "If we waited any longer, Rita wouldn't make the trip due to her pregnancy. Rita's sister is going to bring our daughter out to Atlanta after she gets healthier. The doctor said it should take about a month or two."

The bus rolled to a stop: Fayetteville, Arkansas. It was another roadside diner. The air filled with the aroma of burgers and greasy fries. Everyone stood up and filed off the bus.

Quincy hit me on the shoulder. "Come inside. Eat with us."

"Nah. I'm not hungry. I'd rather relax on the bus."

"Then keep me company. There's no harm in that."

The three of us went inside and sat around the table. Conversation continued right where it left off. Rita talked about her little girl while Quincy listened.

Quincy ordered, "We'll have three number 2 specials and three cokes, please."

Hearing his food order, I panicked. I had only a dime to my name. I tapped Quincy repeatedly under the table, before the waitress left. He ignored me.

I called out to the waitress, "Excuse me, miss—"

Quincy looked over and cut me short. "Don't worry, man, I got you covered."

The waitress turned around. Quincy repeated, "It's fine. Just put the order in." Then he leaned in close and whispered, "I know how it is. I know where you are at. I've been there."

"I don't have any money." For the first time, I felt embarrassed.

"It's okay. I don't want your money."

"But I can't pay you back," I said. It was odd, having someone offer you exactly what you needed without pulling a con or taking an angle. Quincy and his wife obviously didn't have much.

He smiled. "When you see someone in a tough spot, help them out. Pay it forward. Pay me back that way."

"I will, I promise."

This was the first time in my life that someone better than me didn't make me feel poor. Quincy shot me wink and we started talking about the army again. When the food came, I dug in. It was the best meal I'd ever tasted, with the nicest man I'd ever met.

The next morning, the bus dropped me off in Jonesboro, Arkansas, where my aunt Izzy and uncle John lived. I had never met them before and didn't even know their last name. Grandma Beck talked about them the last time I was in Memphis. She said they lived on a street named Word.

Once I found Word Street, I started going door to door asking if anyone knew a woman named Izzy who had a husband named John. Within a half hour, I was sitting at my aunt and uncle's table, wolfing down a half pound of bacon, a dozen eggs, and fried taters.

After I finished eating, I slumped over in my chair, and did a face plant in the ketchup. *PLUNK.* My aunt and uncle cleaned me off and carried me over to the couch. I slept for twenty-four hours.

When I woke up, my clothes were laundered, folded on the chair next to me, and breakfast was cooking again. Grandpa Beck entered as I was cleaning my plate. He looked just like my dad, except older, less worn, and had more muscle.

Grandpa didn't say much on the drive. When we reached the Memphis city limits, he said, "You're gonna have to pay your own way if you're gonna live under my roof."

"Yes, sir." This wasn't a problem. Most of the money I made was either taken by Momma or stolen by my dad. Only having to pay for myself seemed easy. I didn't take it personally. I'm sure Grandpa got suckered by my dad more times than he could count. Grandpa Beck was a hard worker who had zero patience for mooching or laziness. I was worried about my brothers and sisters, wondering how they were going to survive. I abandoned them, but every man has got to make his own way. One day, they'd understand.

Crossing the Memphis city limits, I reached in my pocket and felt something hard. I pulled it out: a shiny dime glistened between my fingers. I had made it and still had money left over.

MEMPHIS, TENNESSEE, 1966 (TWENTY-ONE YEARS OLD)

Two weeks after landing in Memphis, I had more work than I could handle. In the evening, I bagged groceries at Piggly Wiggly on Cooper Street. At night, I'd drive over to 899 Madison Avenue and work as an orderly at Baptist Memorial Hospital, graveyard shift. One of the doctors gave me a sweet deal on a 1965 Oldsmobile Rocket with a 454 big block engine. It took only a month to get on my feet and move into my own apartment.

The following week, I enrolled in Memphis Technical High School. Before I started, the principal pulled me into his office. Mr. W. A. Bourne was a shrewd, protective man. I told him my sob story and appealed to his good graces: I was an adult without a formal education because I lacked childhood opportunities.

Mr. Bourne paced around my chair, stopping dramatically in front of his chair. He placed both hands on his desk and leaned toward me. His button-up shirt collar was a size too small, forcing his pudgy neck to spill over the creased white fabric. His beady hawk eyes surveyed me from behind horn-rimmed glasses.

"Mr. Beck," Bourne said in a quick, cutting tone. "This is an unusual situation, very unusual. However, I think I have a solution. I will allow you to attend my school if you promise me one thing."

I listened.

No matter what came out of his mouth, I'd agree.

Bourne gave me another dramatic pause. I hated dramatic pauses.

"You can finish out your education at Memphis Tech as long as you never date any girl that is under eighteen."

"Agreed, sir." I stood up and extended my hand.

It was a fair request that could easily be observed. After all, I didn't want to go back to jail.

We shook on it.

"The faculty and staff are well informed of your age and background. They have each promised to keep a close eye on you. If you violate this agreement, I promise that I will find out, kick you out, and prosecute you to the fullest extent of the law. Is that understood?"

"Yes, sir."

"Welcome back to high school."

"Thanks, sir. It's good to be back." I couldn't help but grin.

On the first day of school, I felt like a rock star. The gigantic three-story brick building was my castle. The whole school knew who I was and literally stood in line to be my friend. The principal gave me the best advertisement a guy could receive: an adult with a new car, his own apartment, money, cool clothes, who could legally buy beer for any party, was attending high school. After all those years of feeling like a worthless piece of shit, I finally felt like a king.

Not dating chicks under eighteen was the easiest stipulation the principal could have made. I had no intention of dating younger women. This school was filled with hot-blooded teachers, primed for action. I already scouted out my social sciences teacher, Miss Reynolds. She had blond hair, a shapely waist, perky tits, and legs for days. The principal gave every staff member leeway when it came to my education, to protect the young female students. He laid the groundwork; all I had to do was collect. Each teacher was more than accommodating, excited to help me out. Some viewed me as a "down-on-his-luck military man," while others saw a bit more. I played every angle.

RING. The bell rang. Makeshift art projects hung around the room. Classmates put finishing touches on clay sculptures while others cleaned the pottery wheel. I had been making eyes at Miss Penderson, the petite art teacher, all hour. She liked it. While the kids grabbed their book bags and file out into the hallway, I lingered.

Miss Penderson told the other holdouts, "Just leave the wheel. I'll clean it."

Strolling past her, I cocked a grin and said in a sultry tone, "Good-bye, Miss Penderson."

The pocket-size teacher grabbed my hand and asked, "Can you help me clean the wheel?"

"Sure, but I might be late for class."

"I'll write you a note."

While washing off the pottery wheel, our hands glided across each other. "Were you really in the 101st Airborne?"

"Yes."

"Where have you been?" she asked.

"I've been all over the country, seen all sorts of things. A better question is, 'Where haven't I been?'"

For the next thirty minutes, we talked about life. I shared some adventures and exaggerated the details. Afterward, she scribbled on a notepad and handed me a slip of paper.

"Here is your late pass for math," Miss Penderson said and followed it up with a long kiss on my cheek. Then she whispered, "There's more where that came from."

Joining the army was the best decision I ever made, until I decided to go back to high school. I'd been drinking beer, jumping out of planes, and shooting machine guns for years. If I got in trouble in the service, I got court-martialed. In high school, I got detention. Not chewing gum or running in the halls seemed a little bit juvenile. That's not my style. I never ran and I always looked forward to "punishment." Sometimes I'd walk up to Miss Reynolds's desk and whisper in her ear, "I need you to send me to detention. I'm thinking about doing something really bad. There is nothing you can do to stop me. You should get involved."

Miss Reynolds would whisper back, "Come back after sixth period and lock the door behind you."

There were a couple days when my art teacher called in sick. We met at my apartment and took off for the day on my motorcycle. We'd finish things off at her place. I'd get late phone calls from married teachers to perform "extra credit" assignments while their husbands were off at war and got straight As doing it.

My dad taught me one lesson: "Get it while you're young."

I did.

After graduation, girls got a lot more conservative. Legs tightened. Marriage talks were the only thing that would loosen them up. Engagement rings got them wet. Chicks now needed to set a wedding date before they gave up the cookie.

It was an easy problem to overcome. After a couple of dates, when the time was right, I'd pull out a "go-to" engagement ring I always kept in my pocket and propose. We'd speak softly about love and our future. Once the ring was on her finger, it was easy to get some nookie. It was practically a fiancée's obligation.

The rushed wedding plans would inevitably freak out my bride-to-be and she would back out. Some of the engagements lasted only a few days, while others dragged on for months. Tears would be conjured when it fit the situation. It was all part of the dance. Because they rejected me, I'd get my engagement ring back. Within the hour, I would be playing the field, calling up the next chick in line. There were always a few girls prepped. As soon as the diamond ring was in my pocket, I'd get it resized and slide it on someone else's finger. They were all special, in a Beck sort of way. One of my rings was recycled seventeen times.

Memphis women were the only things that made life in Tennessee exciting. I was going to a trade school, learning how to fix typewriters. The brochure said that it was a promising career that guaranteed a permanent future in an ever-growing job market. During school one day, Louie Nelson, a drinking buddy, came over to my workstation. He was a "life of the party" type of guy. Today, he was quiet. It got my attention.

Louie leaned in and asked, "How would you like to do something special?"

He never acted gay, so I said, "Sure, man, I'm in."

"Meet me at the Memphian Theater at eleven o'clock. I'll explain later."

The Memphian was a run-of-the-mill neighborhood theater that ran alongside a strip mall. It was on Cooper Street, just north of Union Avenue, close to the hospital. There were always a couple flicks playing. I had taken a few dates there; it wasn't anything special. However, when I showed up at the Memphian, there were hundreds of people surrounding the building.

What the hell is going on?

The closer I got, the more difficult it became to navigate through the crush of people. Jumping up, I attempted to locate Louie; he was nowhere to be found. Eventually, I worked my way to the front and tried to get inside. A monstrous hand jutted out and gripped my shoulder, stopping me instantly. A beefy security guard, with oversize biceps straining a cotton T-shirt, blocked my path.

Louie called out to the security guard, "It's okay. This is Jimbo. He's with me."

After seeing Louie, the security guard was all smiles and guided us inside.

Despite the throngs of people outside, the Memphian was nearly empty. Standing next to Louie felt safe, so I remained a little closer than I normally would. Several men huddled around the concession stand, helping themselves to candy, popcorn, and sodas. Strangely enough, they didn't buy anything and nobody seemed to mind that they were stealing. It was like a friendly stickup in an alternate universe. The theater staff handed them whatever they wanted.

Weird.

The group of guys finished their sugar quest and walked our way. A smooth face led the pack. The leader was "The King" himself—Elvis Presley. Instantly, it all made sense. Louie gave me an unnecessary warning look. I knew better than to spoil this. The unspoken rule was: if you bug The King, you don't come back.

If the best way to appreciate my host is to ignore him, I'll be happy to oblige.

Elvis looked at Louie and me. We gave him slight smiles, following up with a nod.

He returned the nod.

After that, I was in. Whenever Elvis wasn't shooting a movie, he would rent out local attractions so that he could hang out with his hometown friends. It didn't take long to get in good with the bodyguards. All the guys working the place were people Elvis knew since high school. A few strategic conversations secured me standing invitations to every party: the Memphian, the bowling alley, the fairgrounds, wherever. Most of the time, Louie and I wouldn't even bring dates. The crowd outside held hotter women than we could ever pull on our own. We would show up, point to the hottest chick we found, and then point to our arm. I'd tell them the two rules: "Don't ask for autographs or take pictures. Just be cool." No girl refused.

People started recognizing Louie and me as the guys with the inside track. We were the cool cats, the select few. To say I was a friend of Elvis would be a stretch. He called me by name. That might count for something. The King would often send Louie and me over to The Three Pigs to grab a hundred pulled-pork sandwiches for everyone and paid for it. Carrying bags of Memphis BBQ was the least I could do.

One thing most people don't know about Elvis is that he loved to serve his guests, probably because he never got to. Everyone was too busy kissing his ass.

By my fifth Elvis party, my friendship with The King graduated from nods to backslap and small talk. We were back at the Memphian. Louie didn't want to see *Planet of the Apes,* so I flew solo. I showed up thirty minutes early to get a lay of the land. There were the usual groupies, thousands huddled close together, pushing to get in. I spotted a smoking-hot brunette with a sexy look of desperation.

"What's your name?" I asked.

"Becky. Becky Wright." Upon closer inspection, Becky was drop-dead gorgeous: curves in all the right places and beautiful lips. Becky Beck would be a funny name, but I wasn't planning on marrying her.

We walked in and took our seats.

Becky squeezed my arm, hard.

I looked up.

Elvis was walking up the aisle toward us.

The King saw me, gave me a nod, and slapped my shoulder. I returned the nod, as if it happened every day. The truth was, this was the first time Elvis ever formally recognized just me in front of another person.

Becky had a "deer-in-the-headlights" look, mouth gaping open, devoid of sound.

Elvis and I exchanged knowing glances.

Becky remained speechless, gripping my arm as hard as humanly possible, hyperventilating.

Elvis sat a few rows back and Becky started to quiver. Her grip remained firm. The opening credits rolled. Finally, she blurted in my ear, "Oh my gawd, Elvis just looked at me."

The lights dimmed.

That night, Becky did everything I wanted. It was a luscious lips marathon. Being able to hang around The King was an aphrodisiac that provided unparalleled benefits. Come to think of it, I never even had to give that girl one of my engagement rings.

CHAPTER 6

SET ME FREE

MEMPHIS, TENNESSEE, 1968 (FATHER,
TWENTY-THREE YEARS OLD)

A shot rang out in the Memphis sky. Martin Luther King Jr. was gunned down at the Lorraine Motel, 450 Mulberry Street. Overnight, Memphis went up in flames. The weekly civil rights protests and antiwar demonstrations sprung up all over the city, several times day. The streets were no longer safe. Life in Memphis wasn't fun anymore.

I went to school at 6:00 a.m. and afterward, I'd work down at the hospital for eight hours. On my drive home, I'd have to predict where the local uprisings would occur in order to avoid traffic jams. After a quick shower, I would pick up my girlfriend, Linda, and we'd go on a date. I'd have her home before midnight. Once Linda was dropped off at her mother's house, I'd swing over to Louie's and we would head out to an Elvis party.

It was exhausting.

Almost every party Elvis threw started around midnight and lasted until five o'clock in the morning. I didn't want to miss out on good times and couldn't bring Linda. Her mom wouldn't let me. She was a prudish bitch.

Elvis parties became less and less exciting. Sleep was what interested me. The girls I hooked up with gave me payment for the event. Sex was the price for admission. They didn't care about me. After the novelty wore off and the challenge was gone, the fun left, too. It became empty. The exciting new challenge was to find a stable job that paid more than three bucks an hour. I wanted to buy a nice home and start a family. It was time to settle down.

Linda was the hottest girl I'd ever seen, so she seemed like the best candidate for a wife. Everywhere we went, guys stared at her: flowing brown hair, beautiful teeth, smooth skin, and a bangin' body. Linda kept everything manicured—polished nails, brushed hair, fresh perfume, pristine makeup, and beautiful clothes. She had the looks. The only problem was, Linda was a bitch.

The country was going up in smoke and all my girl could talk about was lipstick and panty hose.

Look pretty, look pretty, look pretty—she changed her look so many damn times every day that it was annoying. Everything was for image: nails repainted twice a day, hair redone at least as often. She powdered her nose every hour. Linda would be "hurt to pieces" if I didn't notice her new pair of shoes or a flashy new barrette. Anything set her off. She would have a bad attitude for days. I tried to notice all of her midday hairstyle alteration and outfit switches, but it was impossible. I couldn't keep up. I started just complimenting her on the gamut whenever I saw her.

"Your hair looks good. I like your outfit. Did you do anything new recently? That color looks great on you; it really brings out your eyes."

It was relationship hell, every second felt like a chore. Sure, life looked great on the outside, but it was torture on the inside. After six months, I was fed up. It didn't matter how hot this woman looked; she was getting dumped. After a while, I intentionally didn't notice things just to piss her off. We were constantly at each other's throats.

Linda and I had two things in common: we both could scream throughout the night and neither of us liked being alone. Beef-tomato stew simmered on the stove. The aroma filled the apartment. French bread was baking. The smell of garlic and melted butter wafted throughout the room. Lifting a lid added the scent of stewed tomatoes. I dipped a wooden ladle into the soup, pulling out a sample. Blowing the concoction to a manageable temperature, I tasted.

It needed a bit of salt and a dash of crushed red pepper. Diana Ross blared from our transistor radio. I stirred in the seasonings and sang along.

> *Set me free*
> *Why don't you babe?*
> *Get out of my life*
> *Why don't you babe?*
> *Whooowhooow whooo*
> *You really don't want me*
> *You just keep me hangin' on*

Linda entered the apartment, more upset than usual.

"Hey, babe, soup's almost ready."

I kissed her on the cheek, pretending not to notice her frazzled hairdo. She collapsed at the kitchen table and slumped over in the chair.

I went back to stirring and singing.

> *You really don't want me*
> *You just keep me hanging on*

I could feel the breakup develop right before my eyes. Experience was on my side; this was it. All the push-pull work was about to pay off. The next few words out of Linda's mouth were going to be "This isn't working out" or at least "I'm not happy."

"James, we need to talk."

"About what?" I asked.

Here it comes.

"I'm pregnant." Linda's forehead came crashing down onto the kitchen table. *THUD.*

"Oh shit."

I wasn't sure if the last statement was a thought or if the words actually left my mouth. Either way, Linda didn't respond. She was too busy crying, smearing her raccoon makeup job across the kitchen table.

Life moved in slow motion.

"What are you going to do, James?"

Tears ran down Linda's face and onto her jacket. This was my time to shine. I could finally be a hero.

"Let's get married."

A week later, my number was pulled in the draft. It was perfect. I was headed back into the army and then off to Vietnam. I had already been through basic training, so they threw me back into combat engineer school. Linda and I got hitched. We lived together for a couple weeks before I had to report for duty at Fort Leonard Wood, Missouri. Our platoon was going to be shipped off to the front line. I would take fire with all of my 101st Airborne buddies. I would finally get a chance to fight for America, kill Charlie, and with any luck, get killed and escape my marriage.

Jimmy's second time in the army—bottom row, far right

On weekends off, I'd drive my '64 Ford Galaxie two hundred and sixty miles to spend a couple days with Linda. The distance kept us safe. We had a beautiful baby on the way and both of us needed to make sacrifices for the sake of the family. I did what I could. The clock was ticking away; in three days, I was getting shipped off to the jungle.

One of the men shouted, "Ten hut." Our Napoleonic officer, Lieutenant Shorte, entered the barracks. He had a pencil mustache and the body frame of a fourteen-year-old. I wondered if he lied about his age to get in, but didn't ask. I jumped off my bunk and snapped to attention. Lieutenant Shorte was a notorious prick who pulled rank and made everyone salute him, even master sergeants. Asshole. Everyone on base hated him.

Shorte walked up to my bunk and said, "Private Beck, come with me."

Inside a cramped cinderblock office, Lieutenant Shorte rifled through a stack of papers on an oversize desk. Steam rose from a piping-hot cup of coffee; he took a sip. I stood at attention, crisp and motionless.

"At ease."

Staring forward, I switched my stance, right foot never leaving the ground.

"Can I get you a cup of coffee?" he asked.

"Sir, no, sir."

Lieutenant Shorte had a power trip unlike any officer I'd ever known. Every move he made was to show other people that they were beneath him. He was so condescending that even his superiors openly mocked his leadership.

Everyone hates this asshole and he is offering me coffee. What gives?

"Is your family okay?" he asked.

"Yes, sir."

What is this guy getting at?

"What about your father?"

"He's good, sir."

What has that fucker done now? How can he ruin my life from two thousand miles away? I'm not picking up his shit anymore.

Shorte asked, "Do you miss him?"

"Very much, sir." This was a complete lie, but everyone expects you to lie about your family. Plus it avoided an awkward conversation. Thoughts ran through my mind: picking up trash out on Black Diamond Road, him choking Momma, sitting in the car as he walked into a tavern, unlocking the fence when I was a little boy. Projecting a perfect-family image was easier than telling the truth. The faster I got out of Lieutenant Shorte's office the better. I wasn't about to traverse my troubled family history with a pathetic officer whom I barely spoke to.

The lieutenant grabbed a letter off his desk and handed it to me. It was confirmation from the Red Cross: Dad had cancer. The doctors gave him six months to live.

My heart sank. I forgot where I was—stunned and wordless. Ignoring protocol, I sat down. Shorte didn't mind.

The next time I see my father will be the last.

Will I make it in time?

Will the army let me see him?

There is so much I want to tell him: being drafted, getting married to Linda, the baby on the way.

Officer Shorte slipped me another piece of paper and said, "I'm shipping you off to Fort Lewis for the remainder of your service obligation. The base is in Tacoma, a few miles from where your dad lives. It's a compassionate reassignment. You'll be able to take care of him and help him through his final days. You are dismissed."

If you asked me ten minutes prior to stepping into Shorte's office, my greatest desire would be to ship off, fight, and die. It was my way out. My family were just lowlifes from my past. I didn't want to connect with them or know them. I didn't even think I cared about them anymore, but I did. My father might be an old drunk, but he's still the only dad I'll ever have.

I might not ever see him again. Now that he has cancer, things might be different this time. There is still time to change our lives around. We could still have a relationship. We could still be friends.

TACOMA, WASHINGTON, 1968
(TWENTY-THREE YEARS OLD)

A bright red cherry traveled up a half-smoked cigarette, leaving only ash behind. Dad exhaled a fresh puff of smoke. It mixed with the smell of stale nicotine and warm beer. His apartment was run-down. There was no formal furniture to speak of, only a couple mismatched chairs and an oversize wire spool that he flipped on its side and used as a makeshift table. Overlapping stains covered the carpet. Dad fiddled with a pack of Marlboro Reds. A bottle of Jack Daniels was secured between his knees. He looked gaunt, empty, and twenty years older than he should.

"Dad, you should take care of yourself."

"What do ya think I'm doing? Cancer ain't gonna beat me. This is my cure." My father raised his cigarette and took a drag.

"I don't think those will help."

"Doctors don't know shit. Cigarette companies did research and they say it's fine."

He took a pull from the whiskey bottle.

I shook my head.

Things were supposed to be different. Everything was the same, except even more depressing. Nothing ever changes.

"What the hell do you expect me ta do? I'm gonna die soon, ain't I? Gotta enjoy the little bit of life I got left, right?"

"Yeah, I guess." There was no point in arguing.

Dad continued, "I'm gonna last a year longer than those smarty-pants said I would and this is how I'm going to do it."

He lifted his hooch, flashed a grin, downed several gulps, and then handed me the bottle. This was the first time he ever shared his booze.

I stared at the black label and then downed a swig.

"Can't believe your momma won't take care of me. Here I am, her loving husband, dyin' of cancer and the bitch just kicks me out on

The biggest man in Jimmy's life—Jimmy Beck Sr.

the fuckin' street. Women—can't trust dem cunts." His last sentence ended in a thirty-second smoker's hack.

I shook my head; he mistook it for agreement.

Dad avoided details: like the ninth restraining order filed against him due to the latest beating he gave Momma or the morphine that was found lacing her coffee. Whenever Dad got caught, he would tell everyone, "If I'm gonna die, I'm taking the bitch with me."

PORT ORCHARD, WASHINGTON (MONTHS LATER)

The Ford Galaxie idled in the driveway; I sat behind the wheel, savoring a few moments of peace. Dad was dying, but not fast enough. He got more and more cantankerous every day. Momma was meaner than ever. I went back and forth from Momma's house to Dad's apartment, out of the frying pan and into the fire.

Momma hollered at me as I entered. "You left me to visit that good-for-nothin' son of a bitch? You're as worthless as he is."

"He needed some money." I didn't feel like getting into it.

"You gave him money? I need money. I gotta buy groceries."

I pulled out a twenty-dollar bill and handed it to her. Her eyes screwed up; it was an insult.

"I need more than twenty bucks. A carton costs nine. How the hell am I supposed to get food? We're out of oranges and I only have one Pepsi. Stingy little shit, yer always keeping money for yourself. You are just like yer dad."

Her words bounced off my ears like hail hitting the ground. I pulled out forty bucks and handed it over to shut her up.

"How much did you give *him?*"

"Ten."

She smiled, triumphant.

I'm up for reenlistment and can get discharged if I want. Life back in Tennessee isn't so bad. I have a good-looking wife, my own apartment, and a baby on the way. I might even be able to get my old job back at Baptist Memorial Hospital.

Momma yelled out from the bedroom, "You leave, abandon me like everybody else, and then make me beg. Good for nothin' bastard."

That's not a bad idea. Why do I stay here and put up with this shit?

She whined, "You know I need the money. Why do ya make me beg for it?"

All of my clothes are still loaded up in my car. There isn't anything left for me in this town. How much gas do I have in the tank? I wonder how far that will get me?

She peeked around the corner and yelled, "What kind of son leaves his mother?"

I grabbed the last Pepsi and headed out the door.

The Galaxie's engine was still warm.

Momma's voice could still be heard over the roar of the V8 as I pulled out of the driveway and peeled off down the road.

Memphis, Tennessee, 1969 (Twenty-four years old)

Three nights later, my family was twenty-five hundred miles behind me and I stood at the front door of my Memphis apartment. A smile stretched ear to ear. I called from Nebraska and told Linda that I was coming home. I stopped by Piggly Wiggly and picked up a couple steaks and some beer.

KNOCK, KNOCK.

Linda greeted me with a big kiss. She was in her third trimester and looked amazing. It was eleven o'clock. We were going to celebrate! Life was great. Dinner sizzled in a cast-iron skillet. Music blared from the radio.

KNOCK, KNOCK.

It was late. I rushed over to the front door. There had to be some sort of emergency. Someone had to be in trouble.

A spit-shined uniformed infantry soldier stood in the doorway. We were both surprised to see each other.

We sized each other up.

The soldier barked, "Who the *hell* are you?"

Linda had a weakness for military men; it was the uniform. This guy was just her speed. Thinking back to my high school teachers, the situation felt like a karmic bite in the ass. I'd never been on the receiving end. I scanned his patches: a couple stripes but no special forces training. This chump was going down.

"I'm Linda's husband. Who the hell are *you?*"

"Oh, I'm sorry. I, uh, didn't know," the visitor stammered and took a couple steps back.

I asked, "You didn't know I was coming home today, did you?"

"No. I thought Linda was getting a divorce."

The soldier seemed sincere. He wrung his ring finger—covering a wedding band of his own.

Both of us squared off.

I waited, expecting anger to consume me.

At any moment my adrenaline would take over.

I waited.

Nothing happened.

I wasn't sad or upset. I didn't *feel* anything. I was at peace and didn't want it to end. After being angry my whole life, something really bad happened and I felt relieved.

I looked down the hallway.

Linda peered out from the bathroom. Our eyes met. She ducked inside and locked the door.

The soldier stood on the walkway like a lawn ornament, dumb as a box of rocks. I flashed him a grin, slapped his shoulder, and said, "You are right. She is getting a divorce. Come back in an hour and she's all yours."

I cracked a beer and ate my steak.

Linda stayed in the bathroom.

It was awesome. She looked like a cowering, sneaky bitch and I was off the hook. There wasn't anything in the apartment that I wanted. My car was still packed. I finished my beer and walked out the door as the music played on.

Set me free
Why don't you babe?
Get out of my life
Why don't you babe?
Whooowhooow whooo
You really don't want me
You just keep me hangin' on

Linda ran out of the apartment. I fired up the V8. She grabbed on to the hood and pleaded, "James, don't go. We can work this out. Please don't leave me with this baby."

I pulled back slow enough to not hurt her, but fast enough that she couldn't hold on. There was no reason to stay. I'd been engaged dozens of times. Nothing ever lasts. I thought marriage was different, but I was wrong. I never cheated. That is one line you don't cross. It's the measure of a man: how you follow through with your commitments. I'm not like my father. Linda was the one who screwed this up. Plus, women always beg when you leave them. No one likes getting dumped.

Pulling into the hospital parking garage felt freeing. The Memphis party train would be easy to jump back into. Louie would be happy about the divorce. We were still good buddies and he hated Linda. He'd already set up a welcome-back party at his house and a job interview with his uncle down at Union Pacific Railroad. This was just another new beginning.

The night breeze rustled a nearby stack of next-day newspapers, still bound up. No one was around. I slipped one out and walked back to my car. The dome light clicked on, illuminating the classified section. I flipped through the want ads—Firefighters Wanted.

Interesting. I never thought of being a firefighter before.

The next morning, I drove across town for a hot breakfast. Slipping inside a restroom, I took a spit bath: brushed my teeth, shaved, washed my armpits, and combed my hair. I threw on the nicest shirt I had. The Union Pacific interview was at three o'clock, which gave me plenty of time to check out the Fire Department gig.

I pulled up to Fire Station 2 and looked across the street: the Lorraine Motel, where Martin Luther King Jr. got shot.

I walked inside.

The fire captain was a good ol' boy, ex-infantry, and a respectable family man. We shared boot camp stories and chewed the fat about our time in the service.

Barrow said, "You should think about coming to work for me. Full time is ten 24-hour shifts per month."

"Wait a second. You only work *ten* days a month?" It was the best sales pitch for a job I'd ever heard.

The captain nodded. "Full benefits, too."

"I have another job interview at three. Can I give you my answer by the end of the day?" I said.

The captain nodded again. "Swing by before six."

I kept the interview with Union Pacific, but the cargo transfer job couldn't compete. In my heart, I was already a fireman.

Memphis was still burning up over Vietnam. Civil rights protests just added fuel to the fire. All the chaos offered plenty of overtime and kept me away from Linda, although I had to drive past our old apartment every day. I caught glimpses of her putting my baby girl in her car seat or playing on the lawn as we passed by in the fire truck. She planned on getting remarried and they wanted to raise the baby as their own. It seemed best because our divorce was almost finalized.

Fire runs happened several times a day. It was common to fight fires twenty-four hours straight. We'd have to dodge all of the riots and civil rights protests around town. At times crowds containing hundreds, sometimes thousands, of people would circle our fire trucks. The times were tense. One occasion, we got bum-rushed by protesters. I guess because we wore badges and uniforms we were part of the establishment, part of the problem. I had to unleash a two-hundred-fifty-gallon-per-minute water cannon on the crowd, just to allow the other firemen to contain the blaze. The stupid mob couldn't tell

Jimmy Beck the fireman

the difference between riot police uniforms and fire department uniforms. You would think that a big red fire truck should have tipped them off, but it didn't. I understood why the people were mad and I agreed with them, but they picked the wrong time and place to voice their opinions. We had a job to do and nothing was going to get in the way of our saving lives. It was a fully involved three-alarm fire; people were getting burned alive and protesters blocked our way. Our job was to save those people and we did it, rioters be damned.

My father lasted years longer than the time doctors gave him. He just kept on living, making life miserable for others. It was God's cruel sense of humor. He moved back to Memphis and started living over at Grandpa's. His father didn't mind his son mooching off him anymore, because he wasn't long for this world. The disease touched every part of his body: thinning arms, yellowing skin, even his mischievous grin had faded. Day by day, things got worse and worse. He called me all the time, drunk, wanting to hang out. On my days off, I would stop by, and we'd share a few beers.

One day, he asked, "Hey, Jimmy, can you take me down to Greenville, Mississippi? I want you to meet my best buddy from junior high, Ronnie Jenkins."

"That's a three-hour drive."

"He's the last living friend I got. Come on, it'll be fun."

On the drive down, Dad was giddy. He seemed like an oversize kid, except for his leathery skin and the beer bottle squeezed between his legs.

"Dad, I don't remember you ever talking about this 'best buddy' before."

"Oh, sure I have. You just weren't paying attention."

Getting out of the city was a nice change of pace. After a few hours of driving, we pulled up to a rambler. Mr. Jenkins was waiting out on his front porch: a barrel-chested old-timer, slow moving, and larger than he should be.

He made his way to the car and looked over my dad, as if to place him. "Hey, Ron, good to see ya! This is my son, little Jimmy. He's friends with Elvis."

Recognition. Ron smiled. "Well, is that right?"

I shrugged my shoulders, fake modesty. I hadn't gone to an Elvis party for a few months, but there was no sense in admitting it.

The three of us moseyed inside. Passing the refrigerator, Ron pulled out a few bottles of Budweiser—one for each of us.

We all relaxed on the back porch and popped the tops. A breeze blew, offering a slight chill. The three of us men leaned back and sipped our suds. Dad asked Ron, "Remember when Frank Erwin said that he was gonna fight you and we took him out behind the Dumpsters and whipped his ass?"

Ron replied, "Yeah, I remember that."

They chuckled.

Silence.

"So whatcha doin' now?" my dad asked.

"Aw, nothing much. What about you?"

"Not much...just drinking, I guess." Dad tipped his beer to Ron.

"Me, too," Ron replied.

The three of us clinked our glasses together and took another sip.

After about forty-five minutes of pregnant pauses, a few random stories, and another beer, we headed back to Memphis.

Grandma Beck invited some family over for a Sunday pot roast. It was exciting to have everyone together. Even Aunt Ann was coming down from Saint Louis. She had traveled quite a bit, seen the world, went to college, and even spoke Italian. Dad thought his younger sister was a "fuckin' snob" because of learning a second language and all. He tried his best to make us kids hate her.

Dad started drinking and was pissed drunk by the time Ann arrived. When she walked through the door, he started yelling all the Italian words he knew: "Testa di merda. Vaffanculo a Lei, la sua moglie, e' la sua madre. Andate tutti a 'fanculo!" ("Shit head. Fuck you, your wife, and mom. All go to fuck!")

Dad went on and on with his rant.

The madder Ann got the louder Dad became.

There was no calming him down.

It was embarrassing. I hated it.

I gave her a hug and whispered, "Sorry about this."

"There's no need to apologize. I know my brother. I'm just sorry he's your father."

"Me, too," I replied.

"You taking off?" she asked.

"Yeah, I gotta get outta here."

"Well, I'm jealous."

It seemed like every person my father hated, I liked: Aunt Ann, my black friend Quincy, and all those Christians. I decided to only spend time with people my parents hated. That way, I was less likely to cross paths with my parents or even people like them.

The next day, Grandpa Beck bought Dad a one-way bus ticket to Port Orchard. Surprisingly enough, Momma wanted him back. I couldn't understand why she would allow my father to move back in with her after all he had put her through. It was odd that she requested it. I guess she missed having someone around to hate.

It turned out that Dad needed to be there, if the Federal Housing Administration (FHA) was going to give Momma one of those Housing and Urban Development (HUD) homes. She snagged it. Within a few weeks of arriving in Port Orchard, Momma braved the December chill and went to every store in a thirty-mile radius. Armed with a denture grin and a holiday smile, she tried establishing credit lines all over town in Dad's name. Every business turned her down. The name James Beck had a bad reputation. However, when she walked into Sears, she struck corporate gold. With thirty dollars down she snagged a new TV, stereo, washer and dryer, refrigerator, stove, couch, dining room set, vacuum, the works. Her new house was outfitted with all the amenities. All the loot was delivered and installed the following day for no extra charge. Momma finally had everything she'd ever wanted: a house with appliances and furniture. She even had a Christmas tree with presents underneath.

The Fire Department was in full Christmas swing, decorated from top to bottom with garlands, lights, and Christmas cards from local elementary schools. Carols blared from a transistor radio. It was my day off, but one of the other firemen gave me fifty bucks to work his shift. Sucker. My refrigerator was empty and I didn't have any other holiday options. I would have worked the day for free, but I'm not gonna turn down free money.

All of us firemen pitched in on cooking the feast: a huge turkey, honey-glazed ham, and all the trimmings.

RING, RING. I was the newest recruit, which meant I had the least seniority. Lowest seniority meant that you are everyone's bitch. The bitch has to answer the telephone.

RING. "Fire Department, Beck."

"Hi, Jimmy." Momma's voice was cold and matter-of-fact.

"Hey, Mom. Merry Christmas!" I was surprised to hear her voice. Momma usually overlooks holidays and birthdays. She'd never called the department before.

"Yer father's dead."

The only noises heard were the firefighters joking around in the background.

Numb.

"Thought you should know," she continued.

Part of me died. It was a cold finality. No more second chances. I felt empty and alone. The battle was over. Cancer won.

"How did you find out?" I asked.

"Dennis and Mary were banging on the bedroom door, wanting to open presents, since we haven't had so many before. I thought the son of a bitch was tryin' ta piss me off because he kept layin' there. I tried to wake him, but he weren't breathing."

"Is everyone okay?"

"They're fine. Had to make sure none of them came into the bedroom and saw him. He looked like shit. Didn't want to spoil Christmas." Momma said.

"What did you do?" I asked.

"I called the paramedics. They came, put him in a bag, and hauled him off. Then we opened presents."

"Oh, okay." I didn't know what to say.

Momma's voice suddenly got chipper. "Did I tell you about all the great things I got?"

"No, you didn't."

She replied, "I got a Frigidaire refrigerator with through-the-door ice and water. I also go an Electrolux vacuum, an electric stove with four burners and a griddle. Then for the living room I got a…"

CHAPTER 7

SURRENDER ALL

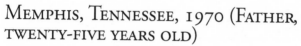

MEMPHIS, TENNESSEE, 1970 (FATHER,
TWENTY-FIVE YEARS OLD)

Two hundred parishioners filled the four hundred-seat auditorium. Church was my slice of heaven, connecting to the Almighty with fellow believers. You wouldn't catch my family in church, so that's where I wanted to be. This place was where I wanted to belong. Bible verses interlaced with statements like "Give it to God" and "Jesus is the cornerstone." Wooden pews groaned under the weight of men in suits, women in sundresses, and young kids in their polished Sunday best. Some parents took copious notes, while others struggled to stay awake. Most children passed messages written on empty tithe envelopes, completely uninterested.

I scoured the city to find God's house and I finally did: at a Baptist church in Memphis. For three months, I'd attended every service available. Even though it was really friendly, I still couldn't break into religious social circles. I relied on a firm handshake and a grin. It was different than the rest of the world and it felt like I lost my touch.

I got smiles and handshakes when I walked through the door from people who wore "Greeter" buttons. There was also a "greet your neighbor" moment at the beginning of the service. After the greeter said "Hi" or "Good morning," we didn't really speak again. I was new at this religious stuff and figured it would just take time to learn the game.

Dressing and speaking the "Christian way" obviously doesn't happen overnight. Becoming a local in a new church was like infiltrating a foreign land. Everything has to be just right before the regulars believe that you meant no harm. Like anything else, time and consistency should take care of it.

Two weeks ago, I got a break. Brother John, the church's song director befriended me. He was a little weird. John stared at people for about three seconds too long—just enough to give everybody the creeps. People gave him slack because a World War II fragmentation grenade left shrapnel in his spine causing his whole right side to go limp, like he had palsy. The guy would joke about his injuries too often, but I didn't think it was Christian-like to bring it up. I'm just fortunate that I didn't look like a stroke victim.

Brother John sure could sing, though. Whenever he belted out a hymn, it felt like his vocal cords connected me directly to God. This church was a holy place of light and truth. It gave hope and inspiration for a new direction in my life. Christian possibilities were endless. The more time I spent sitting in a pew, the more distant my past and my family became. Mingling with religious folk made me feel clean and good. Brother John gave me advice on life and guided me through my divorce. He was generous, would pay for dinner, and even bought me a few shirts. I was proud of my friend when he led the congregation in song. Even though my voice wasn't pleasing to hear, singing along made me feel connected.

All to Jesus I surrender
All to Him I freely give
I will ever love and trust Him
In His presence daily live

While adjusting myself on the hard wooden bench, I often thought about all the people I lied to and hustled. When the preacher spoke of the damaging aspects of sin, I knew the lessons firsthand. Going from memory to memory, remembering the angles: recycling engagement rings, using Elvis to hook up with random women, and sleeping with married teachers. After my dad's death, life went into a tailspin. I didn't belong with good people, but didn't want to hang around bad ones either. Running from problem to problem was exhausting. I was fed up with scams, tired of feeling shame for who

I was. There wasn't a single person in the world who knew me. Even my brothers and sisters were strangers.

Last night, I spent the whole evening curled up in my closet, sitting on work boots. The three-piece suit I was wearing to church hung on a hanger overhead, as a .30-06 Springfield rifle rested under my chin and pressed against my throat.

I cocked it.

No one wants me around.

I hate living.

Why should I even get up tomorrow?

There is nothing to get up for.

The only things I have to account for the past twenty-five years of life are two failed marriages, a young daughter I don't know, an embarrassing family, and a bunch of women who curse my name. My second marriage lasted two weeks and it wasn't much of a story; she didn't run when I put the ring on her finger. Just another embarrassment.

Last week, Brother John told me, "After you accept Jesus into your life, He will speak to God for you. That's how God is able to listen to your prayers. It's why accepting Jesus is so important."

I accepted Jesus Christ into my heart during that conversation, but I expected more to happen. I wanted to feel something. Moments later, I had flushed my pot down the toilet and got rid of my pills. Everything in life that the Bible had a problem with was thrown out. Even my Elvis records got busted up and tossed in the trash. If I was going to give Jesus a shot, I was going to do it right. No more stealing, hustling, or scamming. The family in Alaska who bought me the new coat, the grocery store owners who gave me food, and even Quincy, the Airborne Ranger, were all Christians. I wanted to be like them.

I wanted to be a good man, but I didn't know how. Religion didn't make much sense. How could it? Everything was the opposite from what I had learned my whole life. I moved the barrel away from my chin and called out, "God, if You're up there, help me."

I waited for a voice to reply.

Nothing.

The world remained silent.

I released the safety. It was time.

My thumb reached for the trigger.

Do it! Just do it! Pull the trigger and it will all be over.

An itching sensation erupted in my crotch.

I leaned the gun against the wall and scratched.

More itching.

I investigated.

Little black spots covered my family jewels. Then one moved sideways.

I have crabs?

I can't kill myself with crabs!

The visual of my fellow firefighters finding my body covered with crabs floated into my mind. I already felt like shit. There would be plenty of time to kill myself, once I was crab-free.

The next morning, sitting with fellow believers, I felt God's presence in Brother John's song. I lifted my voice even louder.

> *All to Jesus I surrender*
> *Now I feel the sacred flame*
> *Oh the joy of full salvation*
> *Glory to His name*

While sitting in church, itching my crotch, I half expected someone to ask me to leave.

The large oak double doors swung open. The congregation spilled out of a packed lobby. Parishioners chatted as the mob slowly dispersed. Across the foyer, Brother John talked with some young brunette who I had never seen. I approached and checked her out in an unassuming, Christian way. She was homespun, cute, and wore a handmade dress that was six inches longer than current fashion. She didn't wear makeup or jewelry and looked pretty plain. For some reason, when that girl smiled, she lit up my world.

My three-piece suit was smooth, collared shirt was crisp, and hair looked sharp. Armed with a Bible and a smile, I weaved through the crowd and approached.

"Brother John, are we still meeting today?"

He turned. "Brother Jim, of course. Have you met my friend Susan Lawrence?"

"Not yet."

Susan gave me a polite smile.

She'd be good for me.

I flashed her a grin.

Susan blushed. She was mine.

When Susan and I started dating

Susan Lawrence was God's innocent and simple answer to my prayer. She had round features that neither drew people in nor pushed them away. Everything she did was sweet and kind, opposite of any woman I'd ever dated. The light in her eyes had never been tainted with darkness. She was only nineteen and grew up in Pueblo, Colorado, two hours south of Denver. It was obvious that she had never known a man in the biblical sense. *Pure.* Her parents still lived in the same childhood home she grew up in. *Stable.* Sue was the oldest of four kids and helped raise her siblings. *Responsible.* She was already in her final year of nursing school, because she graduated high school two years early. *Smart.* A Christian woman who was pure, stable, responsible, smart, and kind was just what I needed.

The following Friday evening, Susan was on my arm, walking down a Memphis city street. I was surprised that she had never heard of the band Electric E. It was the rage, best new music around. Tonight was going to impress her beyond her wildest dreams. It was the coolest backyard party in town, invite only. All the people attending were old party friends, but that was my secret. She was about to get a dose of Beck—*gotta play it cool.*

A large wooden gate swung open and the base hit my chest like a wave. *BOOM, BUB-BUB, BOOM.* Large bushes enclosed the gathering, trapping in a purple haze that hovered overhead. A few friends gave groovy handshakes as we strolled by. My buddy Electric Larry led the Electric E on bass guitar. Larry was seven feet tall and was as narrow as a man could be; he looked like a baseball bat with legs. His hair stood straight up like Einstein stuck his finger in a light socket. Charlie, his trumpet player, was as tall as he was wide, which made him look like a beach ball blowing a horn. Mac, a big ol' farm boy, tore up the drums while his little brother Teddy picked away at lead guitar.

The crowd was rocking.

People were dancing.

The party was hot and the band was tight.

I couldn't help but move to the music.

It was amazing.

Everyone was caught up in the funk.

I looked down, eager to check out how impressed my date was.

Her mouth gaped.

I asked, "How is everything? Cool, right?"

Sue pointed to a group of my friends in the corner who were passing around a roach. In a forced yet hushed tone, she said, "Jim, oh my goodness, I think those people are smoking marijuana."

Wow, aren't you a detective.

The ganja haze was so thick that it took only ten steps to get a contact high. That's one of the reasons I wanted to come. I tossed all my pot a couple weeks ago, which got me spiritual. Getting a buzz off other people's sin allowed me to enjoy weed without pissing off God. After all, Jesus hung out with sinners. It was fun to be back in the mix.

"Don't you like the music?" I asked.

"I want to get out of here." She hid her eyes.

"Okay."

Leave the party now? I'm moving to the music and she's trembling. Are we even at the same party? What is this girl's problem?

There were more than a hundred people grooving at the coolest event in town. Everybody loved the music, the feel, except Sue.

Everything is just getting started and my date wants to take off. Great.

Shaking my head, I gave the festivities one final look, taking in what I would soon be missing.

I grabbed Sue's hand and we left.

Halfway down the block, the music still clung to the evening air. Charlie's trumpet took off in a solo, echoing into night sky. I tugged on Sue's arm and asked, "What's wrong?"

She halted in front of me. "What's wrong? You ask me what's wrong? Those guys were smoking *marijuana*! That is what's *wrong*!"

Elephant tears mixed with mascara rolled down her cheeks. She turned away and walked up the street alone, the way we came.

I jogged double-time to keep up. Susan Lawrence was definitely a different breed, wearing loose jeans and a homemade blouse to a Jazz concert. My face turned to the side, hiding a grin. Saying "It was just a little reefer" or anything else to that effect would derail my fast track to success.

Pot isn't that bad, is it? She is a good girl, the marrying type. This party stuff must really be serious to God. Jim, don't screw this up.

I touched her gently on the shoulder. "Are you okay?"

"We just walked right into a group of people doing drugs. *No,* I am not okay." She trembled.

"Sue, that party was probably the safest place in Memphis. Those people didn't even know we were there. They didn't notice us enter and they didn't see us leave. Trust me, you were safe the whole time."

"Well, I was scared to death." Sue threw her arms around my waist and buried her head in my chest. At that moment, I held love for the first time.

SLURP. I vacuumed up the last remnants of a chocolate malt milkshake with a straw. The Three Pigs was the best Memphis barbecue around and the shakes were delicious. If Elvis said it was the best, then it was the best. The rumor was that their smokers had been going for thirty years nonstop. Our plates were empty and the check came. Brother John grabbed it. I voiced my appreciation. My recent divorce kept my wallet thin. I still wasn't technically single, but it was only a matter of time. I was grateful to have a brother in the Lord have my back.

"You know, Brother Jim, I've helped you a lot," Brother John said, staring at me a little too long.

"I know you have. Thank you. I appreciate it. Without you, my life would be very different. These past few months have been the toughest times I've ever faced."

He continued, "I've given you more than I give most people."

"Yeah, I know. You really have impacted my life. I'm not sure what I would have done without you. If I can ever help you in some way, let me know."

Christians do these kind things because they are good people: the airplane tickets to Alaska, groceries as a kid, and even side jobs. I'd love to pay Brother John back and I would do anything for the man: fix his car, paint his house, do some landscaping, anything.

Brother John leaned in and said in a low tone, "I once had a person help me that I couldn't repay and I—"

"What did you do?" I was curious.

Where is this headed?

"I let him..." My Christian friend shook his hand; I thought it was the palsy. I couldn't understand what he was trying to say.

Then Brother John pointed at his crotch.

I took out my wallet and emptied out every bill onto the table. Then I said, "John, thanks for your help, but I'm afraid that I won't be able to pay you back any more than this."

He mumbled, "Well, I was just saying..."

I didn't stick around to hear the rest.

The following Sunday, Sue and I sang hymns across town in a new church. It was independent, premillennial, fundamental, blood-bought,

Bible-believing Bethel Baptist Church. I told my girl that I was led by God and she followed. Fire and brimstone rained down from the pulpit. The new place got me pumped up. This preacher shook his Bible, called out the Devil, blasted sin, and demanded repentance. There was no way that the faggot Brother John would be allowed to attend this place. Longhaired Jesus freaks weren't even allowed in. Pews were filled with silver-haired little old ladies and a few old men. These people knew the Truth.

Three-piece suits were high fashion, leather-bound Bibles were expected, shoes had to be polished, and short haircuts on men were a prerequisite to attending. Women wore dresses, not pants, because that's what Jesus would want. Females in shorts were abominations, cigarettes were of the Devil, and Hollywood movies were just plain wrong.

Can I hear an Amen?

Amen!

For the first time in my life, I had boundaries laid out in front of me. They were easy to follow, rules that secure your salvation. It's was refreshing to finally know the right way to go—doing these things gets you into heaven and this list of activities sends you to hell.

Life became clear. Growing up, there were never any boundaries. Dad slept with anyone who said yes and Mom brought home men whenever Dad was away. My father even sold one of my sisters' virginity to a drinking buddy when she was six years old, for five bucks, to get booze.

The only rule in my childhood: Don't get caught.

Take what you can, when you can. Suckers make survival easy. There was no stability or morality. Lying, cheating, and stealing were a necessary part of life. Anything goes if you don't get caught. Before I found Jesus, I did whatever I had to do to advance my agenda in the moment. These new rules of virtue were a path to God, a road map to a better life, and a better life is what I'd always wanted.

Sue and I had been sitting in church for hours, enjoying the sermon. My stomach grumbled, wanting lunch. The preacher issued his final charge: "Tonight, I am going to deliver a message that will alter the future and transform lives. I want every one of you to invite every person you know. Call up your friends. Invite people you don't know. Ask people from work to come. I don't care if you have to go down to the bars and pull people in. Do it! This will be the best gift you'll ever give them."

I loved it when the preacher called us to action and threw down the Gospel. It revved me up.

That afternoon, I called everyone in my phone book: Elvis friends, Jesus freaks, a couple drinking buddies, my grandparents, and even a few classmates from Memphis Tech. Some firefighters showed up along with several people from the Electric E party. An hour before the evening service, we swung by our favorite bars and got all of our old drinking buddies to join.

Walking into the evening church, I brought at least fifty people with me. We tried to be quiet, but attendance doubled when my gang strolled in. It was impossible to not draw attention. Most of the guests had never been in a church and didn't know protocol. None of them were dressed in three-piece suits and they all smelled like beer and cigarettes, but you can't be held responsible for something nobody ever taught you. I was still on the beginning end of religion's learning curve, so I didn't give much guidance beyond "Just be cool."

The preacher asked us to pull people out of bars. What do they expect? Bars contain smokes and booze; of course they smell like that. Why is everyone staring at us?

Why aren't there more people in the service?

These are the same faces I saw this morning, only fewer. Isn't the preacher delivering a life-changing message? Didn't they hear him this morning? They were supposed to invite all of their friends? Where are all the people?

We were a little late coming in. The head pastor put his Bible on a nearby seat and sat down. If I knew the preacher's life-altering message was so short, I wouldn't have stopped by the last few bars. It was already testimony time.

Damn it, we missed the good stuff.

Mrs. Beverly, a sweet granny, shuffled toward the microphone and froze, stage fright.

"I'm so nervous." She gave a slight laugh.

The crowd listened in encouraging silence.

Mrs. Beverly continued, "I am so blessed."

Everyone waited with bated breath.

"This last week I lost a pair of my favorite shoes. It was a nice pair. They were new. I'd only worn them twice. I prayed and prayed that God would help me find those shoes. Right after I gave up hope, I heard God's voice say, 'Look under the bed.' I went over and looked. Sure enough, those shoes were there."

Mrs. Beverly gave a slight smile and handed the preacher the microphone.

The audience started clapping.

I looked around in amazement.

That's it? This old lady finds a pair of shoes and you guys are impressed? I was dumbfounded.

The preacher asked, "Is there anyone out there that has something to share?"

No one stood.

Everyone scanned the audience to see who would be a courageous Christian and take the stage. I leaned back and whispered to my hippie buddy, "Hey, Frankie, I betcha you can do better than that. Give 'em your testimony."

Frankie jumped up and made a beeline toward the stage. His bandana was down low on his forehead. A flowing paisley shirt camouflaged beads that bounced against his chest with each step. Bell-bottoms flared around soft leather boots. His brown hair was over a foot longer than any Baptist church regulations.

All previous gatherings I had attended with Frankie were held in people's homes with a group of longhaired hippies playing guitar and singing "Kumbaya." When I told Frankie that a really important message would be taught here tonight, he was eager to listen. I figured that because this was his first Sunday at Bethel Baptist that fellow parishioners would cut him slack for his attire and give him a few weeks to pull his Christian look together.

Frankie jumped up on stage, grabbed the microphone, and proclaimed, "I was once a homosexual."

All air in the room was sucked instantly into the congregation's lungs.

Dead silence.

Frozen.

Waiting. Mouths hung open.

It was great; I was on the edge of my seat.

Frankie continued, "I've slept with men. I've whored with women—hundreds. I've had orgies with groups of people. I've been hooked on heroin and smoked reefer."

Frankie went on and on, letting everyone know just how bad his past was. For fifteen minutes, he gave juicy details recounting the darkest moments of his life. The crowd was mesmerized. It was awesome, an amazing testimony. Best of all, it was true. Frankie's story was a million times better than Mrs. Beverly's lost-shoe story. Finally, Frankie said, "And that's when Jesus saved me!"

The senior pastor jumped up, grabbed the microphone from Frankie, and said, "Thank you all for coming to testimony night. We are going to end with a short hymn."

The pipe organ began to play a few notes and the congregation joined in.

All to Jesus I surrender
All to Him I freely give
I will ever love and trust Him
In His presence daily live

CHAPTER 8

THE BEST THING

MEMPHIS, TENNESSEE, 1971 (FATHER, TWENTY-SIX YEARS OLD)

Once a month, on testimony night, my embarrassing past transformed into a gold mine. "The Prodigal Son Returns" or "The Repentant Sinner" were both workable themes. There were many ways I could take the Good News of the Gospel. Street credibility in the secular world combined with a Christian look was the secret recipe for religious success. I kept the short military haircut, had several three-piece suits, and could quote enough scriptures from the Old King James version of my Thompson Chain Reference Bible to make me believable. My Bible even had my name embossed in gold leaf on the cover. The Blood of Jesus Christ washed away my sins. I was redeemed, a new creature. Old things had passed away and all things became new.

The best part of getting the whole "Christian thing" down is when you dress like them long enough, everybody starts believing you are one of them. It just took time, like I figured. After attending multiple services and volunteering around the church, members started listening to what I had to say. The congregation was intoxicated with my heathen background and my words. Cursing was a dead giveaway that you weren't part of the flock, but that was quickly reined in. The first testimony I gave was a game changer. As long as I gave credit to Jesus, it was cool. They wanted as many dirty details about the world as I was willing to give. They seemed like junior high boys who finally get to talk about girls. They craved gritty stories, but not too raunchy. My messages were full of G-rated porn—church porn.

One thing was obvious: religious folks didn't have a clue about the problems kids faced. How could they? They clap for finding a lost shoe. Bible thumpers didn't know what was going on in the world, but I did.

Sue and I started volunteering with the Youth Ministry and they let me preach. It was awesome. I talked about forgiveness, the transformational power of God's love, and how to shut out the Devil. I grew the Children's Ministry so fast—with Jesus's help—that the head pastor invited me to speak on Sundays. Preaching came naturally. Listeners to my messages would storm the Gates of Hell with a squirt gun once I was finished with them. I fought against sin, atheism, and liberalism. The Devil was my enemy. Evil was in trouble when I took the pulpit. The only thing I knew was how to fight.

"Romans 8:31—If God be for us then who can be against us. Can I get an Amen?"

A local theater in Memphis put on a production of *Godspell* and some parishioners wanted to picket. I didn't quite know what sacrilegious meant, so I wanted to check things out for myself before I engaged in battle.

I convinced the group to buy tickets, so we were invited inside. The plan was set. Everyone was ready to follow my lead. God would reveal the perfect moment to attack. We were Christian soldiers.

In the beginning of the second act, the actor who played Jesus placed his hands on Mary Magdalene's boobs and said, "Whatsoever ye shall do, do it with all your might." Then he squeezed her tits like clown horns, moving them all around. I was confident that this was sacrilegious, time to fight for the Lord.

I jumped on stage and yelled, "This is of the Devil. God loves you and has a wonderful plan for your life."

The room froze.

Everyone stared at me.

Crickets.

Nobody stopped me, so I figured God wanted me to continue. "This is not the truth of Jesus Christ. God is a holy and righteous God. This production makes a mockery of His love."

I gave a ten-minute sermon before security realized I wasn't part of the act. They tackled me and dragged me off stage.

People clapped.

The applause was probably for my captors, but I reveled in the glory, nonetheless.

THE THREE-NIGHT Music Hall run of "Godspell" built almost to a sellout for the Wednesday finale, with attendance increasing each night from a Monday low of 1,459. The final performance was spiced early in the second act by an on-stage denunciation by a man, later identified as a Memphis evangelist.

He ran up to denounce the play as not according to the gospel but "according to the devil." The stage manager hustled him off without further friction.

A clipping from the next day's newspaper

It took five minutes before all the other "Warriors for Christ" were cleared out. I felt like a general, with all my lieutenants passing out Gospel tracts and inviting lost souls to Sunday morning service as they were escorted from the theater hall. Eventually, we were all out on the street.

I was so proud.

Sue came by the Fire Department the next day to hear about how last night's mission went. She was speaking with Fire Captain Barrow as I entered.

Captain Barrow asked, "Beck, are you finished polishing brass?"

"Yes, sir."

Captain Barrow looked at Sue with a fatherly smile and said, "Excuse us for a minute. I need to discuss something with my fireman."

He grabbed my shoulder and pulled me into the kitchen. When we were out of earshot, he dug his finger in my chest and shoved his booming voice into a whisper. "Listen to me. I've seen the girls you bring in here, loose women in miniskirts, showing them off in front of the guys. I know what kind of man you are. This girl is different. She is special, a good girl."

"I know, Captain. I'm in love with her."

"If you had any love in your heart, you would stay away from her. You don't deserve a girl like that."

"I'm different now. I'm a Christian."

Captain Barrow eyeballed me. "Are you even officially divorced yet?"

I hung my head. "The paperwork was filed a couple months ago. It should be finalized soon."

The captain leaned in. "I wouldn't let you near any of my daughters. If I can find out how to get a hold of that girl's father and warn him, I will. If I ever find out that you hurt this young girl, it will be my pleasure to make your life a living hell. You got that?"

"Yes, sir. I got it."

Seven months later, Sue and I took our first vacation. The nursing school Sue attended did everything it could to keep the girls focused on their education, but the only way we could live together was if we got married. Her childhood home was eighteen hours away in Pueblo, Colorado. We had just enough time to meet her parents, get hitched, and drive back. Sue was giddy with excitement, gazing at me adoringly as I drove.

PUEBLO, COLORADO

July 24, the small-town Baptist church was packed, over three hundred guests showed up. At the far end of the church, Sue stood next to her father. Warren Lawrence was filled with pride, a barrel-chested steel mill worker with a country smile. The pipe organ played the "Wedding March." Sally, her mother, sat in the front row, admiring the wedding dress she had sewn.

Driving back from Colorado—
on our honeymoon

Sue's father walked her down the aisle. She was my beaming bride—God's answer to my prayer. A sea of faces smiled up at her and she gazed into my eyes.

This town was a clean slate. Sue knew everybody. Looking across the audience, there wasn't a person I recognized. It was perfect.

Sue grabbed my hand. The nerves in my stomach twisted in knots. I had already been married a couple times before, but it always touches your insides. Each one was special. I felt butterflies.

Memphis, Tennessee, 1974 (Twenty-nine years old)

Soapsuds billowed over a kitchen sink. The first Beck family rule: the cook doesn't do dishes. Sue and I alternated preparing meals. I made beans and cornbread, so Sue cleaned the silverware as I sat on the living room floor with our eight-month-old daughter, Rachel. She curled up on my chest and slept.

The moment Rachel was born she owned my heart. That little girl was the most beautiful thing I had ever seen. I spent hours staring at her tiny fingers and nibbling on her toes. She was my baby, Daddy's little girl.

It had been a long couple of days, two back-to-back twenty-four-hour shifts, fighting a three-alarm apartment fire. Right after I got off shift, I spoke in Sunday school with no sleep. Then I spent all afternoon at the revival potluck, preached at the Sunday evening service, and cooked dinner. I felt like the man of the year. Between working at the Fire Department and running our bus ministry for inner-city Memphis kids, there was little time for rest. Moments like this were the only peaceful ones, the times when my infant cooed on my chest.

Reclining on my back, I brought Rachel close to my face and looked into her eyes.

My heart melted.

I didn't think I could ever love this much.

As I lay on my back, I held her like a little airplane.

She spit in my eye and giggled.

I squinted and tried to wipe the gunk off with my shoulder.

In goo-goo talk I said, "Did you spit on Daddy? Huh? Yes, you did. Yes, you did."

I placed her in the crib and walked into the kitchen.

Sue noticed the gunk. "Aw, did she get you?"

"Yeah, she's got good aim. Takes after her dad."

Sue wetted a towel and cleaned off the remaining spit.

I asked, "Hey, Sue, how did you like my sermon?"

She smiled and kept on cleaning. "What do you mean?"

I was expecting her to start singing praise. "Well, do you think I did a good job?"

"I think you were very passionate. People seemed to enjoy it." Sue kept wiping off the puke.

"And?" I prompted, fishing. It wasn't time for subtleties.

"And what?" she replied.

Sue was hiding something.

I was pissed. "You obviously have something to say, so say it."

She looked away, a tad scared.

I felt like a jerk.

"I promise, I won't get mad. Just tell me what you thought about it."

Sue took a long dramatic pause.

I hate these damn dramatic pauses. This is bullshit! She is supposed to support me as a team.

Keep it in, Jim. You gave her your word.

"Well, you were so excited, I didn't want to say anything."

This last statement was followed by another pregnant pause.

It's obvious I want to know your fucking opinion. Why do ya make me beg? Just give me the information!

Oh shit, don't get mad. Calm down. Just be cool.

In a forced calm I asked, "Sue, *please* tell me."

She gathered courage. "You know how you were teaching on Moses and the Ark."

"Yeah," I said.

"Well, that was Noah. Moses was the guy who led the children of Israel out of Egypt, not the Ark."

"Nobody notices things like that," I responded.

"I'm pretty sure they did," she said.

"That's no big deal. I'm sure everyone mixes those names around."

"Uh, not those names. Plus you mixed up the two lives and they are very important biblical figures. The children of Israel didn't march off Moses's Ark, two by two. Animals went two by two. Noah wasn't in the desert...But it sure was exciting."

Thinking back, there were a few moments when I could feel a distinct drop in cabin pressure with the congregation.

I asked, "What about that *Sword of the Lord* mailer. Do you think we should order it?"

"No. Companies should stop mass-producing spiritual work. Spiritual messages shouldn't come from corporations. Spiritual messages should come from God, through a pastor and their own personal walk with Jesus. That mailer encourages pastors to be lazy. Since everyone uses it on the same Sunday, throughout the country, nobody knows that many of the messages are the same. They plagiarize other people's work and pass it off as God's Way. It's awful!"

"Your pastor back home uses it."

"Well, then he isn't a very good pastor."

What is this crazy girl saying? Godly people made that religious publication, so it has to be good. It's a gift and people shouldn't snub gifts from God.

Those letters are exactly what I need to move forward with my Christian ministry so I don't have to study so much. I need to be out there making stuff happen, not sitting in some worthless seminary classroom and reading about it. There is already so much talk and not enough action. I'll wing it. Learn as I go. God honors action; talk is for suckers. I'm sure there is a proverb like that in the Bible somewhere. If not, there should be. The Sword of the Lord is a Baptist publication, sanctioned by the Church. It has their stamp of approval. That is good enough for me. Besides, who's gonna know? There are kids dying out on the street who need my help. Hope doesn't arrive on its own; someone has to bring it. I will be that man.

"I could use that mailer to structure sermons. It can just be a guide. I promise to throw in enough of my own stuff to not plagiarize."

Sue pulled back. "What are you really trying to say?"

I looked my wife square in the eye, mustered up a deep spiritual tone, and said in a commanding voice, "God is calling me into full-time ministry. Sue, I want to start a church and be a pastor."

Sue's mouth fell open. I could tell she was excited.

She stammered, "That is a big responsibility. Do you feel like you are ready? You've only been a Christian for a few years."

"It'll be fine. A couple days ago, I was talking to the manager of a YMCA out in Spanaway, near Tacoma. They have a space available. After a few weeks going door to door, passing out flyers, we can pull in enough people to keep the lights on. Then we'll do some revivals to get the place rolling. It'll be great."

"Jim, we've already moved around Memphis six times in the last three years. I don't want to move again."

"Baby, this time is different. I promise."

She was upset.

Time to pull out the big guns.

"This is what God wants me to do. I need my wife to be by my side on this decision. I need to know right now. Are we a team?"

Sue looked trustingly into my eyes and answered, "Yes, we're a team."

"Good, because my transfer just got approved. We leave in two weeks."

Team Beck—Right before they talked about moving to Washington

SPANAWAY, WASHINGTON, 1975 (THIRTY YEARS OLD)

Sue worked at the Harrison Memorial Hospital Intensive Care Unit (ICU) and I worked for the Pan American Fire Department at the airport. We decided to move near her work and closer to my family. It took some convincing because she was seven months pregnant, but I wanted to get settled before our next baby came. Boxes towered over me, leaning against the walls. A person couldn't tell if we were coming or going. We just landed in our new place and still needed to unpack. Rachel slept on my chest as I laid on the floor, watching her crawl. Sue washed the dishes.

Bethel Baptist Church had been born less than six months ago. The ministry was growing like gangbusters. We had over a hundred in our congregation. Sinners were getting saved. Kids were accepting Jesus. Sue was just about to give birth to our second child. Everyone tells me that I'm getting better with my messages and I could really feel myself grow in Christ.

My newest lesson: Know thy audience.

I spent the better part of last Sunday scaring the "Hell" out of people, getting them to cut their hippie hair and not wear miniskirts. Afterward, I realized that everyone in my audience was over sixty-five years old. Most were happy to have hair. None of them wore miniskirts or hot pants, but everyone shouted at the Devil when I called for it and they said my delivery was great.

Sue called out from the kitchen, "Hey, Jim, can you fix this drain tomorrow? It's still backing up."

"I'll do it later this week. Tomorrow I'm fixing my mom's bathroom floor."

"What about our sink?" she asked.

"I'll finish it after I finish her floor."

"It would really help me if you fixed this first."

"Don't nag me. My mom's bathroom floor is taking longer than I expected. The boards are rotten. She can fall through the floor and break her leg. It has to be fixed."

"I wasn't trying to nag you. It's just that our sink also needs to be fixed."

The next morning, I was over at Momma's home. Her shack was made out of the cheapest material possible and smelled of stale nicotine. Her bathroom floor would have lasted a lot longer if she took better care of it. Momma spilled bathwater and let it settle until it evaporated or soaked into exposed pressure board. The floorboards had been soaked for years and had rotted all the way through.

After a few days' work, the newly installed boards provided a solid footing. I was impressed with my handiwork. I'd never done real construction like this before. Foxfire—do-it-yourself craftsman manuals—answered every question I had. It was easy. I just had to roll up my sleeves and get busy doing the work. There were a few extra materials I had to buy, but they didn't cost much. In the end, the floor turned out a lot better than I expected.

Momma stood in the hallway, watching. She had her false teeth out and looked like a toothless monster. She hovered over me as I worked, as if I was screwing her over on labor costs even though I worked for free and bought all the materials. Her wobbly leg crashed down on the newly installed floorboards. She stomped repeatedly. It didn't budge.

Momma guffawed. The lack of complaints was a good sign. She was satisfied and walked into the living room. "Heard your preachin' is gettin' good."

"Thanks," I followed.

"I didn't say it *was* good. I just said, 'I *heard* it was good.'"

I didn't know who attended my church that knew my momma and didn't ask. It was as good of a compliment as I'd ever received from her.

"What the hell you preachin' about?"

"That."

Blank.

She stared at me. "What?"

"About Hell, Jesus, God's love, and His plan for our lives."

Momma gave out a deep belly laugh, which turned into a smoker's hack. "God doesn't have a plan for our lives. There is no plan."

"Yes, He does."

"Well, it's a shitty plan if you ask me. You preach, but you are still the same." She took a Pepsi out of her refrigerator and popped it open.

"I am different."

"You ain't different. You're crooked, just like your father. You'll leave me again, just like him."

"I'm not like him."

"Yes, you are," she snapped.

A rush of adrenaline coursed through my veins. I caged my rage between clenched teeth. "Would *Dad* have fixed your bathroom? Would *Dad* have moved across the country to make sure you were okay? Did *Dad* give you money every week for years so that you could have food and cigarettes? Did *Dad* put food on the table? No. It was me! It has always been *me*."

She stared at me, then at the bathroom.

Silence.

Momma didn't have to answer. We both knew that Dad never fixed anything in his life.

I sat on the couch. The neighboring armrest contained a thousand cigarette burns in the same place. The fabric was burned down to the wood frame. My elbow avoided the blackened board. Momma gummed her tongue while exhaling fresh smoke from her Winston.

"Do you like your new floor?" I inquired.

"Nope. It's ugly. I like linoleum."

"I wanted you to see how sturdy it was before I laid new linoleum. If you need to go to the bathroom, do it now. Once I lay the glue, you'll have to wait an hour before you walk on it."

"Figures."

I waited for a "Thank you" or "Good job." Instead, she handed me a Pepsi and lit another cigarette.

That was good enough.

Social security assured Momma had smokes, food, and electricity. Dad's final credit line provided every appliance she ever wanted and even afforded a few luxuries that she didn't expect. Best of all, she would never have to move again.

Momma exhaled smoke through a toothless grin and said, "You know what?"

"What, Momma?"

"The best thing your daddy ever did for me...was die."

THE PRESENT...

CHAPTER 9

LOG SITTERS

BREMERTON, WASHINGTON, 1975
(FATHER, THIRTY YEARS OLD)

On April Fool's Day, deafening screams spill from the hospital delivery room and into the hallway, thrusting anticipation into sterile air. Each contraction draws more and more excitement. The bustling staff is ready. We'd been at this for over thirty-six hours. I am the only person out of place.

As a firefighter, I know how to deliver a baby. But when it's your own, things are different. When you are connected to the person in pain, it affects everything. Plus, it is a rarity for me to be a part of the delivery process. Our Fire Department gets a few calls a year to deliver babies. These guys do it every day.

Grabbing Sue's hand from the gurney sidelines, I encourage, "Push, baby, push!"

Sue flexes with all her might. Sweat and pain ooze from every pore of her body. She squeezes my hand so hard that my knuckles pop.

AAAAAAAHHHHH. She lets out another bloodcurdling cry. Her body tenses. The baby's head crowns.

"Come on, Sue! One more push and you've got it." Her back arches and body wrenches with one final contraction.

POP. The baby slides out along with a gush of goop.

The delivery room falls silent.

It is gross to watch your wife's body parts turn inside out.

A nurse washes off the gunk.

The doctor smiles at me. "It's a boy."

"How can you tell?" I ask, chuckling.

The baby wiggles underneath a soft cotton blanket. I poke my pinky inside his mouth.

He gums it.

Anxiety sweeps away. My wife's last three miscarriages are forgotten. Worries surrounding this final pregnancy are over. I should have been content with Rachel. There isn't extra money around for another child, but I wanted a boy more than anything. I wanted someone to take hunting and play baseball with. I would teach him everything I had to learn on my own. My son would never go through life alone like I did.

None of my brothers have boys and there are too many health risks for Sue and I to try again. This was our final opportunity—our last chance at having another kid—and we did it. He is the last in my family line, the only person able to carry on the Beck family name. The name James A. Beck will live on.

Our 1971 baby-blue Toyota Corolla station wagon cruises along Highway 16. It is raining ropes. Mudslides and detour cones are in full effect. Traffic is thick. Instead of a twenty-minute drive, we are stuck in the car for over two hours. Sue feels weak. I focus on traffic, Nixon's recent resignation from the Watergate scandal, and the five-cent increase on the price of candy bars. All irritation slips away as we drive by the Puget Sound Naval Shipyard.

The shipyard is a holy place for a union man, a workingman, a military man, a real man. It provides the lifeblood to our community and I pay respect. The titanic ships that won our freedom in battles across the world are parked in our backyard. Aircraft carriers and battleships look like Wall Street skyscrapers resting horizontal, on the water. The slow traffic is appreciated. My eyes always crave another glance of the floating cities of destruction known as the USS *Missouri*, the USS *Enterprise*, and USS *Mississippi*. I call them all "baby."

"Oh, Sue, look at that baby."

Sue cradles little James in the back of the car. Rachel peaks her head over the white-vinyl front seat to get a better view. My eighteen-month-old baby girl is excited about the living doll her mommy holds.

"Rachel, do you like your new brother? His name is James, just like his daddy. Can you say 'baby brother'?"

Rachel contorts her lips and spits out, "Baaabbbba, Buubuuubba, Bubba."

"Sure, you can call him Bubba."

Port Orchard, Washington, 1979
(Son, four years old)

DING-DONG, DING-DONG, DING-DONG. The doorbell rings over and over at an annoying rate. Mom runs past me to answer it in sweatpants, T-shirt, and bandana—her spring-cleaning outfit. We rarely have visitors now that Dad isn't a pastor anymore. I grip my mom's leg as she opens the door.

"Hi, Ronnie. It's so good to see you."

An odd-looking boy leans against the house. He looks like Dad, but shorter, his ears stick out too far, and his face is smaller. It is like Mom shrank Dad in the wash. The familiar-looking stranger tosses his duffel bag onto the floor and gives my mom an awkward hug. I give him a lengthy stare, the type only little kids get away with.

"Ronnie, Jim said yesterday that you were coming to live with us. We are so happy to have you." Mom grins from ear to ear, happy to help anyone.

Ronnie, Dad's fifteen-year-old delinquent brother, squeaks out, "You must be Bubba. Nice to meetcha little guy." His voice sounds high pitched and nasally, like a record playing too fast.

He rubs my head, messing up my hair as if I were a puppy. I don't like him.

The Beck kids now live beyond their humble beginnings. The penniless children who didn't smile much grew up into young adults of moderate means. They now own homes, cars, cigarettes, and plenty of beer. Gone are the days of funky smells residing in hand-me-down clothes. They now live comfortable lives. Having reasonable success, the Beck siblings made a pact to always look out for the two youngest: Marguerite and Ronnie. Marguerite—known as "Pete"—has Down syndrome and her needs are obvious. Ronnie is a different story, though.

After a few months, it was normal to have a squeaky-toy version of my father living with us. Dad has only four requirements of his brother: stay in school, do chores, stay sober, and keep out of serious trouble. Church attendance was added last week for the good of his soul and as a safeguard against coming home Sunday afternoon to find Ronnie peddling our valuables in the back alley.

Ronnie is the runt of the litter, the forgotten child. He never knew his father and barely knows his mother. He is a survivor, like all of his siblings, in a street rat sort of way. He's the type of shady kid you see lurking around the backsides of shopping malls in a trench coat, selling weed. He bounces from family member to family member, taking up refuge for as long as they allow. Eventually, he moves because of some sort of "frame job."

According to Ronnie, he never breaks into neighbors' homes. Fingerprints are planted, testimonies are doctored, and accusations are falsified. If anyone disagrees with Ronnie/Grandma Beck's version of the story, they are cut out of the will. It is an empty threat because there isn't anything to inherit beyond used household appliances, but it seems to work. As time passes details become murky, the family gets tired of fighting, and everyone eventually accepts Ronnie's side of the story. It is easier that way. The voice that yells the longest and loudest must be telling the truth. It's the Beck family logic and Grandma always wins. The facts about stolen merchandise in Ronnie's possession are brushed aside as hearsay. Ronnie "was framed" and Grandma would not hear otherwise. Any words to the contrary would be sacrilege.

Our family Toyota vibrates in the driveway. Mom still works nightshift in Harrison Memorial's ICU. Dad keeps calling it the graveyard shift, but Mom doesn't think it's funny because it's a hospital. Running down the stairs, my foot slides off the second step, hits the third, and buckles. Head first, I launch down the stairs, toppling end over end.

WHAM. The wall at the bottom of the stairs halts my descent. Head throbbing, stars circle the room, the place keeps moving as I remain still. The door opens. Mom enters. She takes one look and is at my side. "Honey, what happened?"

"I fell." The creases of her nursing uniform press lightly against my cheek. Soon after, a cold washcloth traces my forehead, wiping away the rhythmic throbs pulsing in my head. Mom knows all the tricks. Medication, stitches, shots, and home remedies are her specialty. After taking a couple children's Tylenol, I drift off to sleep. A damp cloth rests on my forehead and a soothing voice whispers, "It's okay, Mommy's here."

Just some good ol' boys
Never meaning no harm...

The Dukes of Hazard theme song blares, ripping me from dreamland. Eyes open, the pulsating throb returns. Bo and Luke Duke slide across the hood of The General. I give an inadvertent grunt. Ronnie cranks the volume and hollers, "Shut up, you stupid brat."

In trouble with law
Since the day they were born...

"Shut da fuck up!"

All of a sudden, hands wrap around my throat. I don't realize I made another sound. Ronnie sits on my chest. All breath leave my lungs. His hands wrap around my throat, flinging my head against the wooden armrest again and again. *WHAM, WHAM, WHAM!*

Making their way
The only way they know how

After a long night in the ICU, Mom doesn't wake up for anything. But for some reason, she comes into the living room to check on the noise. She sees Ronnie sitting on my chest, choking the life out of me.

That's just a little bit more
Than the law would allow

Charging full steam, Mom lunges toward the couch. Her fingers grab Ronnie's greasy locks and pull tight. She throws him across the room. He hits the far wall like a lifeless puppet. Mom storms toward my uncle, as he whimpers in fetal position. She pulls the scrawny boy into the kitchen by his hair. His legs and arms flail to no avail. Mom pushes him into a chair and presses her elbow against his neck, smashing Ronnie's cheek against the kitchen table. With her teeth gritting, she spits out, "I swear, if you ever touch one of my children again, I will kill you."

Ronnie cried.

Mom's quivering grip loosens.

He jerks away and scurries out the back door.

In an instant, my mother runs to my side. I'm still coughing for air. She strokes my brow, whispering, "It's okay. Mommy is here. Mommy is here."

(Father, a little later)

After hearing what happened at home, the fire captain lets me leave the station immediately. The drive can't pass quick enough. I know what needs to be done. My family only learns one way—through pain.

Minutes come slow when you are out for blood. Hours seem like days. The police car finally pulls up with Ronnie in the back. Luckily, our town doesn't offer any long-term hiding spots. After some small talk, the cops leave my little brother in my care. Being a trustworthy fireman comes in handy.

Ronnie cowers for good reason. He should fear me.

"Go to the garage," I demand.

Ronnie follows like a whipped puppy.

The buzz of a sixty-watt bulb transforms pitch-blackness into racks of tools, garden equipment, and a pieced-out carburetor. Everything is a weapon once it is grabbed. I hope my little brother picks one up.

CLICK. The dead bolt twists into place—no escape.

I tell him, "Put up your dukes."

Ronnie slides behind the lawnmower.

"Get your ass over here, you little shit," I command.

He slinks further into the corner.

"If you don't get over here and fight me, I'll make it worse," I challenge. Ronnie whimpers, "I didn't do nothin'."

"Nothin'? You hit my little boy who is more than ten years younger than you. You think that's nothing? 'Do unto others as you would have them do unto you.' I guess you want me to do nothin'."

I throw out a lightning-fast palm strike, smacking Ronnie's face, knocking him from his corner. His arms remain close to his sides, not even trying to block. The kid just stands there, letting me bitch-slap him. My strikes land at will. He sinks to the concrete floor, broken.

It is boring to fight someone who gives up. After spending a few minutes slapping him around, I push him out of the garage. The little shit needs to learn a lesson.

It is just a matter of time before Momma disowns me for beating up her baby boy—what comes around goes around.

Rachel & Bubba visiting Dad's work a few weeks after Ronnie left

BREMERTON, WASHINGTON, 1979
(SON, FOUR YEARS OLD)

Evergreens tower over Anderson's, a little country convenient store, our favorite place to stop by when we drive out to the property. Jerry-rigged fluorescent lights illuminate the candy aisle. Worn wooden floors soak in the light. I'm focused on candy, wondering which one to choose. Only two minutes to decide. My sister is quick. She always picks Toffifay—little caramel cups filled with rich chocolate, a hazelnut, and a little fudge spot on top. Afterward, Dad walks around the store with Rachel.

Toffifays are too small; I'll gobble them up in less than a minute. Sweet Tarts don't melt, but they are boring. Big Hunks are made of tough nougat that makes my jaw tired and makes my teeth feel like they will fall out. Almond Joys are great, but they don't even last as long as Toffifays.

Dad hollers, "You better hurry up, Bubba. We're leaving."

I reach for a familiar candy bar—over a foot long, an inch wide and a half inch high strip of rich strawberry nougat, covered with a thin layer of milk chocolate. The granddaddy of candy bars is also available in vanilla and chocolate, but the name reads the same: Charleston Chew. It is the biggest, therefore it's the best.

A conveyor belt inches a six-pack of O'Doul's and some beef jerky toward the cashier. She rings up Doritos. The Charleston Chew skids up next to the nonalcoholic beer, just in time. Dad leans down and forces a strong whisper, "Bubba, if you keep taking so damn long, next time you won't get anything."

A swift palm hits the back of my head. *WHACK.* It takes a couple steps to catch my balance.

"Sorry," I say.

The cashier says, "That will be $7.23."

Dad smiles and slips him ten bucks.

(FATHER)

I brown-bag the six-pack and push the change deep into my pocket. Beer bottles look bad from a distance. Church people judge appearances from a distance; they don't read actual labels. I can't be too careful and don't have time for nosy questions. It's always nonalcoholic drinks because a man of God has to abstain from all appearances of evil. I'll never be a drunk, but every man is entitled to a cold beer on a hot day.

Gnawing on jerky, I hand the kids their candy.

Bubba bites open his.

Rachel pockets hers for later.

My kids smile up at me as we drive off to the property. I smile back and drive down the road.

Purdy, Washington

Settling down makes me feel like a piece of my spirit is dying. Adventure seems buried, but nothing ever lasts. I have a family now and am a dad. It's time to grow roots. Fathers provide. We have thirteen acres in the heart of the Olympic National Rain Forest, twenty minutes from Tacoma. The surrounding woods are so thick that it takes a machete to cut your way through them. Purdy has one single functional traffic light, a gas station, country restaurant, video rental store, bank, and a public high school. Sue would like to be closer to Tacoma. Thirty minutes away from a major town is close enough for me. I like it out here in the woods where I can raise my family in the way I choose and live in peace.

We are country people and I want a country boy's dream: a log cabin. Foxfire craftsman manuals give all the do-it-yourself information required. There's no need to waste time on blueprints or building plans. I have everything figured out inside my head. We're going to have soft pinewood floors, a kettle stove, log rafters, a wraparound porch, and a river rock fireplace. Tin roofs are cheap; they make rainstorms sound pretty.

The only things I've ever built were a gun rack in the eighth grade and Momma's bathroom floor. A log home can't be much more difficult; it'll just take more time. Do-it-yourself manuals can tell me how to make it happen. They put directions in a list and I can follow a list.

The pioneers who settled this great land had it tough. They pulled off building homes from the raw earth with no support. I have a lumberyard, grocery store, backup chainsaws, and a four-by-four Jeep pickup truck with a two-ton winch. In a couple years, Bubba will be old enough to work by my side. Until then, I'd make do on my own, build as I go, and pay cash. A bulk of the necessities can be taken off the land: log rafters, log walls, log steps, and log furniture. Carpet and drywall can come later.

Stick homes are for suits and city slickers. I don't need French doors or imported tile. I want a man's home, built from the resources of my land, by my own hands, with the sweat of my brow. Plumbing and electrical look a little tricky, but I'll figure it out.

It'll be fun, like Lincoln Logs for a grown man. Chainsaw work is my favorite. Nothing equates with the sound of a chainsaw being fired up. The first three pulls get the engine primed for the real pull: the starter pull. After the starter pull, the machine's dull garble echoes through the trees. Squeezing the trigger brings tension as the grumbling sound transforms into a high-pitched whine, like a motorcycle going full throttle. The machine's shrill voice lowers as the blade sinks into a Douglas fir. Wood-chips spit out in every direction. The air vibrates as the smell of pinesap, the forest floor, and mixed-gasoline fuel swirl together. It's a mountain man's aphrodisiac.

Falling a tree is an art. To an inexperienced logger, the approach is simple: cut a wedge halfway through the evergreen facing the intended drop position, then cut the reverse side. The trick is to leave wood sinew in just the right places so that as you adjust the cutting pattern the tree falls in the desired drop zone and not on your truck.

Evergreens creak as they fall, gathering speed. They snap saplings like toothpicks, landing with a whoosh and a thud. Remaining branches quiver like nerves twitching. Hit the kill switch of the chainsaw and the rumble gives way to the wind sweeping through the woods, carrying the lumberjack fragrance away.

Sap runs during the summertime, so those are the best months for peeling tree bark. It's also the best time to clear my head. With one end of the tree elevated, I'd work a spud (a four-foot-long heavy iron bar with a perpendicular blade, like a gigantic flathead screwdriver with a sharp edge) across the back of the Douglas fir. Fresh sap sprays in all directions, like pinching an orange peel. Peeling logs brings me peace of mind.

Bethel Baptist Church, the place I started from scratch, kicked me out a couple years ago. We were running three hundred people every Sunday and growing fast. Another local pastor got jealous because he never had more than sixty people. He called my home church in Memphis and found out I'd been divorced. After that, it was all over. He spread all sorts of rumors around my congregation. The prick promoted himself as a strong Christian leader who protected my wounded flock through the spiritual crisis he created. I thought everything that happened before you got saved was under the Blood of Christ and forgiven. I thought wrong.

The worst part is my music minister helped the jackass break up my church. It's amazing what religious leaders will do for an increase in salary. At a secretive Denny's lunch, they spun half-truths and convinced all my key leaders to defect. He was good at wielding scripture and even called himself "God's chosen."

In the end I had two choices: split the church I spent years building or bow out gracefully. It was bullshit, but I did what had to be done to protect the people. Six months later, the same music minister ran off with the new church secretary, leaving a wife and three kids, which split the congregation regardless. Live by the sword of the Lord, die by the sword of the Lord.

I know my training as a senior pastor happened on the job, but at least I am a straight-up man. I don't cheat, steal, or lie. I'm not sure where my faith is now. I had faith that God took me down the right path. I also had faith that I was leaving my church in the hands of a good Christian man. That's the last time I trust a minister.

Bethel Baptist Church is now a distant memory. It feels like someone else's life. My time as a senior pastor is over. Sue and I are still on the hunt for a good church with an honorable leader, but we haven't found it yet.

On the good side of things, work at the Pan American Fire Station is going great. They have a confined space entry program and hazardous material training, which should help my career. Work hours are plentiful, income is steady, and I still have plenty of time off to build this home. Sue now works the day shift at Harrison Memorial Hospital, which means I get to keep an eye on Rachel and Bubba as I build our log home. I have the kids straddle the end of logs as I peal the bark off. They think it is an important job, hovering a couple feet in the air.

Babysitting is important. Time to teach my offspring. "Bubba, scoot back a bit further. Sit like your sister."

It's amazing what people can do if they put their mind to it. Common sense, persistence, and determination can accomplish anything. If people just keep on going, they can build a church, a house, or anything. Of course, everyone makes their fair share of mistakes, like when I floored the Jeep in reverse, holding the door open, and a tree stump ripped it off the hinges. The truck doesn't have a door anymore, but I make do and use what I got. A few weeks ago, I cut down a tree and it landed on the truck and I now have matching dents on both sides of the truck bed. So what if they have dents or ripped-off doors. The only thing that matters is if a person finishes what they start.

(Son)

Thick bark scratches against my thighs, through my jeans, as I inch up the tree. Rachel sits where Dad placed her. I have to shimmy back on my own. I go so far

Rachel and Bubba—the professional "log sitters."

that I can't get any closer to my sister without crawling on top of her.

"Dad, is this good?" I ask.

"That's perfect. All right, log sitters, hold on tight."

"Yes, sir." My legs clamp on to the log, bronco style.

Rachel opens her Toffifay; it looks good.

"Can I please have one?" I ask.

"Where's your candy?" she says.

"I already ate it," I reply.

My sister and I are best buddies in everything except when it comes to candy. She always wins. No matter how hard I try, I can't help but finish mine first. I ate the Charleston Chew before Dad parked the truck. Rachel still has two caramel cups left.

"This is mine. You need to learn to save your candy."

The tree quivers between my legs. I grip tight.

Dad pushes the spud down the back of the tree and says excitedly, "You guys are the best log sitters I have ever seen. The balance of this log is perfect because of how you are sitting. Great job! Keep it up."

He goes back to peeling off tree bark. Rachel and I know that our dad tells the truth about our being great log sitters. After all, we know how to sit on a log.

CHAPTER 10

TRUST ME

PURDY, WASHINGTON, 1981 (SON, SIX YEARS OLD)

Storm clouds blanket the evening sky. It's been pouring for days. A fire crackles in a potbelly stove, keeping the house toasty. It's dinnertime. Crocheted hot pads wait on the table for an evening meal. Each family member has the picture-laminated place mat that s/he likes best in front of his/her seat. A herd of elk walking in front of a hunter's cabin is Dad's favorite. Napkins are folded in perfect triangles, point facing out. The silverware is lined up perfectly. Mason jars are filled to the brim with ice water. The table is set just like Dad expects.

Dad says grace from the head of the table. "Dear Lord, thank You for this bounty for which we are about to receive…"

A healthy grin hangs on my cheeks: I did a good job setting the table; he will be proud. The prayer drags on. Legs shift underneath me as I move bruised thighs away from the edge of the chair. Punishments come at least once a week, no matter how hard I try to be good. A steaming casserole tempts taste buds as the smells of cheese and noodles make me salivate. God bless Mom's cooking.

"…and bless the hands that prepared it. Amen." Dad settles into his chair, eyes darting from place mat to place mat, then back at me. Stone cold, he says, "I thought I told you to set the table."

I excitedly reply, "I did."

"Then where is the salt and pepper?"

Salt and pepper?

My gut sinks. I quickly scan the dinner table.

There isn't any salt or pepper. All eyes take turns looking at me and looking for the salt and pepper shakers.

Please, someone pull a saltshaker from behind your back.

Hopeless—the seasoning sits thirty feet away in the kitchen. Everything else was remembered. I even gave Dad his favorite place mat. However, I forgot the salt and pepper.

Leaning back, he asks, "Don't you think we need salt and pepper? We use it every damn meal."

"Yes, sir. I'm sorry, sir."

Red blotches of anger spread across his cheeks and forehead. "Didn't I tell you to put salt and pepper on the table?"

My mind races through the list he gave. *"Put out hot pads, ice water, napkins, place mats, plates, silverware, salt and pepper…"*

He is right. I messed up.

Staring at my plate, I avoid his gaze, hoping he will be lenient. Mom, Rachel, and my foster sister Annette flank my chair. My father is usually nicer when other people are around.

"Either you're stupid or that was direct disobedience. Are you stupid?"

Silence.

"Are you *stupid?*" he repeats his question a little louder, as if I didn't hear him the first time.

If I say, "No, I'm not stupid," then I'll get punished for direct disobedience. If I say, "Yes, I'm stupid," then he'll try to whip the stupidity out of me. Try to look as smart and sorry as you can. Be the victim.

"I'm sorry, Dad."

"Pull your head out of your ass and *answer me!* Are you stupid?"

"No."

"No, *what?*" he yells, demanding an answer.

No more avoiding it. "No, *sir*, I'm not stupid."

"Then go to your room!"

Sitting at the edge of the bed, my feet dangle toward the floor. Whippings like this happen often. The welts on the back of my legs still haven't healed from yesterday when I forgot a book at school.

Why can't I remember things? If I had remembered the salt and pepper before Dad prayed, everything would have been fine. Maybe I am too dumb to realize I'm stupid. Does God allow parents to whip kids for being stupid? Will it get me off the hook if I claim to be stupid? Am I stupid for not embracing stupidity?

The bedroom door flies open, slamming against the wall. My father stands in the doorway. The vein on his forehead pulses rage. The look on his red face warns me to guard my tongue.

"You need to pull the shit out of your ears and listen when I tell you to do something."

How do I pull shit out of my ears?

Dad says that men face problems head-on, so I look into his eyes, as a man. "Okay, fine."

"Fine? You tell me '*fine*'? Boy, I will knock your teeth out and make you pick them up off the floor if you disrespect me like that again. Do you hear me? Don't you tell me 'fine.'"

My chin lowers to my chest. "Yes, sir."

I didn't mean "fine" like that. I meant "I get it." I'm trying to be tough. I don't want another whipping.

Dad's face shifts into a deep purple, a dangerous level.

"I didn't mean to be disrespectful, sir."

Silence. All focus remains on my shoelaces, the only thing safe to look at. One shoelace is untied. I cross my feet, hiding the offense.

My father scrutinizes each movement, the judge, jury, and executioner sizing me up. It was a standoff. The good book says to punish children who disobey and our family follows the Holy Bible. Any flinch or awkward look communicates defiance, doubling the lashes. Only girls are allowed to cry before a whipping is given. Boys who cry early get toughened up with extra whacks.

"What do you get for direct disobedience?"

"Twenty whacks with the belt." Both sets of cheeks clench.

"You better look at me when I talk to you."

The moment of truth: look without expression. I rid myself of all emotion; anything else causes trouble. My gaze lifts, eyes empty and obedient.

Tears show weakness. I am empty. I am not weak.

"Do you understand why you are being punished?"

This is the same question that gets asked every time I get spanked. If I answer with a question, I get the same explanation as before, only louder, followed by more whacks from a belt intended to sink in the message. It is always followed by some lame monkey logic on how his hitting me with a belt or horse bridle will somehow hurt him more than it will hurt me. Lies. All lies. Empty words that make him feel like the victim.

If you hitting me makes you hurt more, then give me the belt. I'll hit you.

Dad and I continue looking at each other, waiting for the other to make a move. I feel like a mouse in a corner, no cover and nowhere to run.

"I asked you a question." Dad's teeth clench.

This is the last chance to escape. Answering this question completes a punishment agreement, ending the dance. There is no way he will budge. The facts are stacked against me. I forgot the salt and pepper, guilty as charged. The choice is simple: Do I choose twenty lashes with the belt or more? "Yes, sir, I understand."

I choose twenty.

"Get ready," he warns.

Time to grab my ankles.

In one fluid motion, Dad pulls his belt out of its loops—snakelike—and folds it in half. Gripping the buckle, he holds the leather firm. Arms spread across the blanket, knees on the floor. My backside is an easy target. Biting into the fabric, I lie waiting.

WHACK, WHACK. My teeth sink into the blanket; the leather strap sinks into my legs. Stinging skin replaces anxiety. I try not to move. Dad likes stationary targets.

WHACK, WHACK. Every so often, the belt smacks non-welted skin, hurting worse, but not as bad as it did yesterday.

Remain still. Keep the lashes in a small grouping.

WHACK, WHACK. Twenty lashes are given, no more, no less.

Dad's leather belt slithers back through the loops on his jeans. The room is peaceful and relaxed. It is over. I sit on the bed, adjusting, finding a comfortable position.

"Did you learn your lesson?"

"Yes, sir, I did."

PURDY, WASHINGTON, 1982

One day, dad says we'll have a big wraparound porch with handrails. For now, the front steps are made from stacked milk crates held together with chicken wire. The top step is three crates high and wobbly. Stepping anywhere but dead center will cause the crates to tip and dump you into mud. The first priority in our log home is finishing all the walls and hanging doors. Right now, double-folded sheets tacked with pushpins into door frames give each room its privacy. Living on a building site means you have to be alert and flexible. The yard is filled with dirt, pealed tree bark, and sharp nails sticking out of loose boards that could puncture your foot while twisting your ankle if you aren't careful. We have our own hayloft, which is awesome. There is a creek out back with plenty of frogs, thick woods all around, and a tree fort. Living here is like camping, but permanent. Dad calls our log cabin "rustic." Mom says it's a "work in progress."

Dad hollers upstairs, "Damn it, Bubba, you better hurry your ass up! We're gonna be late."

When Dad is ready to leave for church, is when everyone else is expected to go. He yells out "five minutes" as a one-minute warning. I used to be the slowest person in the family. However, overnight, I became the fastest and no one knows why. The secret is, I use the next day's clean clothes as pajamas. Right before going to bed, I put on church clothes or my school uniform and sleep in it. Whenever Mom or Dad yells for us kids to get up, I run downstairs ready for the day. Nobody asks me how I do it. Boys' shirts are supposed to be wrinkled, so it's easy.

"Bubba, you better pull the lead out, boy! We are all waiting for you," my father yelled from outside. His initial warning sounded ten minutes ago. It is time to leave for church and the only shoes I can find are my Velcro sneakers that are falling apart.

Out the window, smoke billows from the exhaust pipe of our idling sedan. The heater warms my family as they wait.

The car door slams shut.

Dad walks toward the house.

I panic.

I need to find the other Hush Puppies shoe and fast. They have broad stitching, like someone traced a giant U around the perimeter of my foot. Those shoes are to be worn for Jesus. Today, my Sunday best is one foot wrapped in tan suede leather and the other foot wrapped in a black sock.

Dad stomps up the log staircase and yells, "Don't make me come in there."

My bedroom is the last place I want my father to be. I had been tearing apart my room for the past thirty minutes, looking. Last night, the place was spotless; now, everything is a mess. Blankets are pulled back, boxes are yanked out from underneath the bed; I even turned my closet inside out. Nothing. For the life of me I cannot find my other shoe. So much for my secret plan.

The door to my bedroom swings open, crashing against the sidewall. Dad storms in, furious. "What in the *hell* is taking you so damn long?"

"I can't find my shoe." I keep moving frantically so it seems like I'm working and not being lazy.

He scans the place. "If it wasn't such a pigsty in here, you *would* find it."

Dad shoves me aside. My head knocks against a support beam. "Sorry, Dad. It was clean this morning, I promise."

"Damn it! We just bought those. Do you think money grows on trees?"

He kicks over a box that spills toy cars onto the floor and flings the bed frame into the middle of the room. The mattress dislodges. I stay out of arm's reach.

"Why the hell are you just standing there? Do you have shit for brains? Look for the damn shoe!" my father commands.

"Sorry, Dad."

He slaps the back of my head, sending me stumbling toward the bed. Dad rips apart my closet.

I catch my balance. "I'm sorry," I reply. Then I remember putting my shoes at the end of the bed the night before. I dart toward the footboard, pull back the covers, and my shoe falls from between the sheets.

Dad witnesses the recovery.

"You need to lay your shit out the night before. Pull your head out of your ass and think for once."

"I did."

"Obviously not good enough. You got a week's restriction to think about it."
Dad shoves my shoe on, tweaks my ankle, and yanks the shoelaces too tight.
My foot cramps.

Silence.

There will be plenty of time to retie them once we get to church. The sooner
I get in the car, the sooner I will be around other people. The more witnesses
the better he treats me. I'm happy he gave me only a one-week restriction and no
whipping. One week of not being able to go over to a friend's house or watch TV
isn't bad.

I follow my dad out the door, a few steps behind, out of arm's reach.

Steam covers the car windows. I climb over my foster sister's lap and sit on
the hump, the place reserved for the youngest. Dad slips behind the driver's seat.
Everyone remains quiet.

It's bad to draw attention.

Dad steps on the gas pedal twice as hard as necessary. Gravel sprays twenty
feet behind the car as we fishtail up the driveway. The car skids to a halt. He
palm strikes the steering wheel repeatedly. *WHAM, WHAM, WHAM!*

"What's wrong, honey?" Mom buffers.

Bubba—The ring bearer at
Burley Christian Church

"I forgot my damn Bible and I
have to teach Sunday school this
morning. Damn it! Bubba made us
late again."

"Jim, he's been really good lately."

Dad shoots me a glare in the
rearview mirror. My father's temper
had already been drawn like a ninja
pulling out his katana. It must
experience punishment before it
returns to its sheath.

My eyes stare at my lap,
avoiding his gaze. I ruin everyone's
morning, again. "Sorry, Dad. I didn't
mean to."

Mom draws Dad's gold-embossed Thompson Chain Reference Bible from under her Bible and places it on his lap. She says, "I grabbed your Bible on the way out. We are only five minutes away and still have fifteen minutes to get there."

"Bubba, you got two weeks' restriction to think about it. Maybe that will teach you to pull your head out of your ass and be on time," Dad demands.

Heads hanging low, no one says another word for the rest of the drive. We pull into Burley Christian Church parking lot, ten minutes early.

(Father)

Getting my wife out of the house on time is damn near impossible. Sue is always late. If my schedule were left up to her snail pace, we would miss everything. Bubba is just as bad, maybe worse. If I don't keep riding him, he will never learn. Yelling is just a tool to get people to do what you want. My parents yelled at us kids. Army leadership never stopped yelling and it motivated me.

There is nothing I hate more than being late. Everyone else in the family is hit or miss, sometimes fast and sometimes slow, but Bubba is just like his mom, pokey all the time. If I scream at him, he moves quicker. Nothing else works. If Bubba wasn't so damn slow, I wouldn't have to raise my voice. They are the ones who have the power to change the situation.

Getting mad delivers results. If you yell and someone puts up with it, yell a bit more. If they throw up their guard, you back off. Getting angry is how the world functions—it's a necessary component of life.

Purdy, Washington, 1983

A cup of coffee steams in my hands as I wait on my order, bacon and eggs. Waves crash against a bulkhead, splashing the restaurant windows. Pearls by the Sea is my favorite stop after I work a twenty-four-hour shift. The owner gives a standard 50 percent off to all firemen and police officers in uniform. When he is working, he comps the check entirely. I memorized his schedule to keep this public service benefit flowing. Sue gets the kids ready for church and I get R & R before heading home. It's a win-win.

Sipping coffee, I overhear two city-slicker, wannabe-rustic men chatting. One is frustrated as the other one speaks.

"I know there are a few log homes out here, but they aren't available. Houses have to be on the market. Maybe if we go deeper into the Key Peninsula we can find—"

The other guy cuts him off. "My wife wants to stay on this side of the Purdy Bridge because she works in Tacoma. There has to be something around here. I promised her she would only have a thirty-minute commute to work."

"Are you sure you only want to look at log homes?" the other guy asks.

"Yep. Our minds are made up."

I turn around in my booth. "Excuse me, gentlemen. I couldn't help but overhear your conversation. You are looking for a log home to purchase?" I grin.

"We were, but it doesn't seem like it's in the cards," one of the guys responds.

"Actually, it may be. I recently built a log home right up the street, if you'd like to take a look. We just finished all the major construction work last month."

They light up with excitement. "That would be great!"

The slick guy asks, "Do you have anyone representing your property?"

"Not yet, but if you have someone that you could suggest, I don't mind talking to them," I reply. The air was electric with possibilities.

I dialed Sue from a pay phone. "Sue, go ahead and go to church without me. I have some business to attend to."

After breakfast, the slick real estate agent covers my tab. I didn't tell him it was free. In a few minutes, we were touring my property like old friends. Turns out the slick guy works for Roland and Roland Real Estate Agency. He had a buddy from the agency drive over to represent my side of the transaction. It all comes together perfectly, a gift from God.

"I just finished hanging the drywall, doors, and the trim. The yard still needs some work, but that's just cosmetic."

The buyer and the agents agree.

They love my craftsmanship, especially the river rock fireplace. All four of us are Christians.

Everything is perfect.

I can't wait to push the deal through. The only thing left is Sue's signature.

Later that afternoon, Sue's Toyota cruises up the driveway. I skip toward the car.

She rolls down the window.

"Who are these people? Why are they here?"

"Because I sold the house," I reply, matter-of-factly.

"What?" Sue looks shocked with excitement.

"I sold the house this morning." I am so proud. She can't believe what I had done, all by myself.

She stutters, "We don't even have it on the market."

"I know. Isn't it *great?*" I have a pep in my step and feel like a new man. It's as if we are launching off on a new adventure.

Sue tells the kids, "Take the groceries inside and get ready for supper."

"Sue, this just fell into my lap. It is perfect timing. Aren't you happy?"

"NINE TIMES! You've moved me *nine times* and you ask if I am 'happy'? We've only been married *seven* years. You moved me from Memphis with only two weeks' notice. You sold the house on Conifer, the upstairs–downstairs house in Port Orchard, all me without consulting *me!*"

"Don't worry, I got a good price. You just need to sign the papers." She is pissed, but she always gets pissed when I sell our homes.

"I don't care about the price. I don't want to move. We just finished all of this construction so we have a place to settle down. Now that it is finally looking like a home and not a junkyard, I want to stay. I don't want to start over. Please, don't make me move." Her eyes fill with tears.

The deal is hot right now. If we don't take it, we may never get another shot. I can always build something bigger, something better. Besides, now I know how to do it. I can make custom features that I never would have thought of before.

"After all the work I did to put this deal together and now you don't want to sign? You said you wanted a big family and start a foster home. You said you wanted to build a ministry to help kids. I guess that was just all talk. If you don't want to help kids, that's fine. Just don't get me all excited about something only to smash our dreams when we are at the finish line."

Sue pleads, "I'm not trying to smash our dreams. I just don't want to move. I'm tired of moving. Please don't sell our house."

"We have a Christian buyer, with two Christian real estate agents from the same company. What can go wrong?"

Sue warns, "Any time you rush things too fast, things go wrong. It doesn't hurt to wait."

"Do you trust me?" I reply.

Sue pauses, tears rolling down her cheeks. Each second that passes in silence is one step closer to reaching my goal. Her lips quiver. "Yes, I trust you."

"Look at me."

Sue looks deep into my eyes.

"I promise you that the next house I build will be exactly how you want it. It will be your home. I'll even get you a rainbow."

"To put on my finger?" she says.

"Yes. And after I go out and buy you that rainbow, I'll go out and buy you the moon." It was the first poem I ever wrote Sue, which I lifted off a Russ Hamilton song.

"No tin roof?" she asks.

"No tin roof," I reply. She hates the tin roof.

"A real roof?"

"Yes, a real roof," I confirm.

My wife straightens up, leans in nose to nose, and says, "Will you promise to never make me move again? Will you give me your word?"

"I give you my word. The next house I build will be one hundred percent yours and I will never take it away from you."

Sue gave a dramatic pause, the kind I hate. Nothing good comes from dramatic pauses. "I don't know, Jim. This doesn't feel right."

I can feel her signature slip away.

Time to make a power move. "I can't believe you say you want a foster home and then don't follow through with it. If we want to help kids, then this is what we have to do. I thought we were a team, but maybe not. Maybe I was wrong."

She postures back, "I do want to help kids."

"Then let's sell this place. I promise the new house will be a hundred times better. I've made so many mistakes on this one it will be a relief to start over. We will have a clean slate."

"And you'll never make me move again?" She shrinks back.

"I give you my word."

"Okay, I'll sign."

Reluctant but willing, Sue walks over to the real estate agents and etches her name on the contract.

The deal is done.

The "team comment" worked; it always does. Selling this home "as is" is the financial break we need.

Sue should support me. After all, I built the house. It's mine to sell. It is being sold to Christians, through Christian Realtors. I have been honest, up front, and disclosed everything. It is a sweetheart deal.

What can possibly go wrong? It's not like I'm going to leave my family high and dry like my father. In time, Sue will understand. For now, she will just have to trust me. I'll find us a place to rent. The real estate agent says there is a great mint-green farmhouse out in Key Center that has rolling alfalfa fields split by a quarter-mile gravel driveway. It feels like the perfect place to start over.

CHAPTER 11

AIM HIGH

KEY CENTER, WASHINGTON, 1983
(SON, EIGHT YEARS OLD)

As it turns out, having two Realtors from the same agency representing both sides of a real estate deal wasn't a good idea. As far as Dad was concerned, an "as is" contract *is* cut and dry. But it turns out that this is not the case. Roland and Roland created enough legal loopholes in "as is" to suck out more than just profit. Playing both sides of the fence, they turned the "airtight deal" into a long legal battle that cost my father over sixty-thousand dollars. Dad is still in shock because they claimed to be Christians. He started calling them "the snakes from Roland and Roland"; now, it's just "the snakes."

The *snakes* made out like bandits.

Our family moved into a five-bedroom mint-green farmhouse on thirty acres. A quarter-mile gravel road splits two rolling alfalfa fields, separating our new home from a distant country highway. It is an hour away from Tacoma and the end of the line for public transportation. As far as Dad is concerned, the farther we live out in the woods, the better.

Fluffy clouds sail across treetops. Early morning sunrays peek through the window. It's 7:48 a.m., time for war. Pillow mountains, blanket hideout caves, and foxholes made from shoes cover my bedroom. Transformers, GI Joes, and cheap green army men hide, ready for Armageddon. The battle of the century halts as I switch a Transformer from a racecar to robot. In a flash, the bedroom door flies open and slams against a far wall. The doorknob sinks into plaster leaving a permanent dent in the shape of a crescent moon.

My father stands framed by the doorway, mad as hell. "When I yell for you to come, you *come!*"

"I'm sorry. I didn't hear you." Scrambling to my feet, I stand at attention.

"I called you at least twenty times! There is no way you couldn't hear me," Dad says.

"I didn't hear anything. I promise."

"Then pull the shit outta your ears, you little pecker head. I don't have time to waste. I shouldn't have to look for you all the damn time."

Dad surveys the room. "What is all this?" His foot kicks over the pillow mountains, knocking Transformers across the wood floor. "I thought I *told* you to clean your room."

I try to give a reasonable excuse. "I was just playing."

"When I tell you to do something, you do it!"

"I cleaned up everything else."

"Is your room *clean?*"

Scanning the area, piles of blankets and shoes cover the floor. All of my toys are out in full force. The clothes and boxes that support the pillow mountain range are exposed. The room was clean last night, but because of my playtime it is far from spotless.

"Answer me!" my father demands.

"No, sir, it's not clean."

Dad leans in close, his face inches from mine. He spits his words. "You need to pull your head out of your ass and do what I tell you."

Dad forces his words through clenched teeth. Saliva shoots from his mouth landing on my face. No sudden movements, my breath is soft and short. Control.

"I'm sorry. I thought I did."

"Do what I say, not what you *think* I say!" Spittle hits my eye.

If I wipe the spit from my eye, it could look like I'm crying, then he'll whip me for being a crybaby.

Stay still.

Don't blink.

Ahh, it stings.

"Listen, shit for brains, there is a lot of work to be done around here and I don't have time to hold your stupid little hand and make sure it gets done. If you haven't noticed, there are other people living in this house. The world doesn't revolve around you."

The spit on my face begins to itch. My eye twitches. Dad's gaze bears into me.

"Wipe that look off your face or I'll wipe it off for you!"

What's my look?

I can't see my look.

What's wrong with my look?

How can I change my look if I don't know what I look like?

"I told you to wipe that look off your face and *quit shaking!*"

My body remains motionless. As I glance down, I see my hands trembling. Panic. I place my limbs into a ridged stillness, which forces them to shake even more.

Dad's weathered hands grip my arms. His fingers sink in, bruising flesh. He tosses me to the right, then to the left, back and forth. My head whips around like a rag doll. Louder and louder he yells, "I said quit shaking! Quit shaking!"

His iron grip releases.

My hands and arms tremble worse than ever, traveling up through my shoulders. My whole body convulses violently. This is direct disobedience, the worst sin.

Dad's knuckles sail from his waist, connecting with my jaw. *WHAM!*

The bedroom transforms into a kaleidoscope of colors, spinning in and out of focus. I can't tell the difference between walls, ceiling, or floor.

CRUNCH. A Transformer cracks under my torso, jabbing into my chest. The hardwood floor feels unusually comfortable, something sturdy to hold on to. Objects in the room continue to spin. Peace flows as blood from my busted lip pulses into my mouth, tracing the outlines of my teeth. The red liquid warms my tongue. Dad won't hit me again, not when I'm on the ground. I'm finally obedient, just like he wants.

Gaining balance, I push myself up to my feet. A broken Transformer arm clings to my shirt. Tears and other signs of weakness are swallowed with saliva and blood. He won't see me cry, not today. With my head low, I am careful not to make eye contact. I'm tough, getting tougher.

Void of emotion I say, "I'm sorry, Dad."

My father exits the bedroom. I follow him outside to do what I am told.

Now that we have a big house with several rooms, the foster home is moving into high gear. On any day of the week, a social worker shows up with another kid. Mom is usually taken off guard, but never shocked.

"Hi, Sue, good to see you again." A chubby social worker with a fresh perm stands beside a ragged teenage girl.

Everyone smiles through an awkward silence.

"Hi, Janice, good to see you, too."

Janice eyes the new surroundings. "I am surprised that you moved. What happened to the log house? I loved that place. It was so peaceful."

"Jim and I decided to sell it to make more room for the kids. We had to sacrifice."

"It's really great to see what you are doing for these children. I'm always so happy to bring them over to you." Janice motioned toward the disheveled teen. "This is Kristen. She will be moving in today."

I can't tell if the last sentence is a question or a statement. It doesn't seem like Mom can either.

The social worker notices.

"Is that okay?" she says.

"Of course! Nice to meet you, Kristen. We're so glad to have you," Mom buffers.

"Did Jim tell you I was coming?" the social worker asks.

"I'm sure he did. I just have so much going on that I probably forgot." Mom often tells white lies, protecting Dad. They keep the family safe from prying questions and keeps Dad out of trouble.

"Well, I talked to Jim three times last week. He told me that it was okay to drop Kristen off this afternoon and that he told you." Janice's body language suggests that she knows Dad didn't tell Mom.

"I'm sure he did. Like I said, I've got so much going on these days, I'm not sure which end is up sometimes."

"Are you sure that it's okay?" Janice asks.

"Of course it is. Come inside. I just thought you were coming later this evening. Lost track of time, that's all. You want some fresh cornbread? I just made it."

Mom is flawless at covering things up. All of us kids know that she doesn't know when another foster kid will move in. Most arrivals come as a shock, but she places a higher priority on making newcomers feel welcome than expressing frustration toward Dad's lack of communication.

All of us kids offer welcoming smiles. After introductions and chore assignments, the newest member of our family settles in.

Our house is the random capital of the world. Random kids show up randomly and leave randomly. We own random mismatched dishes, silverware, and furniture bought from random roadside garage sales that we randomly stop by. The Tacoma Rescue Mission gets random grocery donations from distributors and the random excess is passed on to us. Other than bricks of government cheese, our food supply is random. Thrift stores dress us in random hand-me-down clothes. Even our community's rejected animals randomly end up on our doorstep. These creatures are as scarred and unwanted by the world as the foster kids who take care of them: a miniature Shetland pony, a homeless old sheep, feisty goats, a dozen chickens, unwanted pigs, and countless discarded dogs and cats. Feeding random animals is my job.

Mom worked on a dude ranch and taught me everything I know. When family knowledge falls short, Dad says, "Whatever we do for them is better than the 'nothing' they've been getting." That is true, because most come half starved and neglected. Our home operates on a "learn as you go" strategy. It works out most of the time. However, we probably should have learned not to bottle-feed a calf when there are no other cows around before we got the cow.

Right before Dad sold our log house, someone gave us a Jersey cow. We named it Buster. Playing with Buster was a lot of fun when he was the size of a Great Dane. We treated him like our other dogs, but now that he is the size of a Volkswagen, it's a problem. Feeding time is a lot harder when a twelve-hundred-pound cow's main objective is to jump on your back and lick your face.

The winter chill hangs on each exhale. Five flakes of alfalfa are held under my left arm and a blue bucket of grain is on my right. I walk toward the gated field hoping that Buster isn't waiting for me. Rounding the trees, I see him, the faithful opponent. His big cow rump bounces side to side, while his front hooves remain in place. With each approaching step, Buster gets more and more excited, huffing and puffing, sticking his long tongue up one nostril and then the other. The five-acre field is his fenced playpen.

My goal is to reach the feeding trough fifty yards away. Countless mounds of cow patties and horse poop block the my path. Why the animals' feeding trough is so far from the gate is anyone's guess. I put down the blue bucket. It rests by the gate, next to the alfalfa. Reaching inside my pocket, I pull out a secret weapon: a lone apple.

"Hey, Buster, look what I got for ya."

Holding the shiny red apple just out of Buster's reach, I place the fruit on the ground next to an iced-over bathtub, used as a water trough. The cow stares at the apple and then at me.

"You want that apple, don't ya? Well, it's either me or the apple."

A sledgehammer rests against a nearby fence post. Gripping the wood, I plunge it through a thick layer of ice—*CRACK, CRUNCH*—freeing the drinking water. Horses mosey up toward us. Buster keeps his eyes on me, snorting.

"Here, horsey, horsey, horsey. You guys want an apple? I was going to give it to Buster, but he wants to trample me instead."

With apple in one hand and a loose alfalfa flake in the other, I spread some grass just inside the pasture, careful to keep it close to the fence line.

I wave the apple at the oncoming horses. This infuriates Buster. He stomps about, snorting and puffing. There are only fifteen minutes to complete our feeding ritual before I'm late for school. I am cutting it close.

Waiting is key.

The horses walk toward the alfalfa I put out on the ground. One horse finally spots the apple in my hand—game on. I toss the apple into the field. It lands in between Buster and the horse. The battle of wills begins.

The cow remains, staring at me. Every so often, he sneaks a peek, watching the horse walk closer to the apple. He stares back at me, snorting.

As soon as the horse makes a beeline for the fruit, Buster gallops over to the tasty prize and I'm forgotten.

In a flash, I scoop up the remaining alfalfa and bucket of grain, and slip through the fence.

Once inside, I turn and look. The far side of the feeding trough is forty yards away. The horse has the apple in his teeth.

Buster lost.

Hooves dig into frozen earth. A full-grown Jersey cow is aimed directly at me, running full speed. A half-ton of muscle charges in my direction. I take off, running as if the Devil himself is out to get me.

I toss the alfalfa.

It flies into the feeding trough.

I dive in after it.

WHAM. Buster slams into the structure.

The long wooden slats offer protection from our enthusiastic cow. Buster jumps around excitedly, headbutting the boards. My heart beats out of my chest. It takes only seconds to spread out the alfalfa flakes. Our five horses approach, each taking nips off clumps of grass. Shaking the grain bucket, they line up on one side of the feeding trough.

Buster waits on the opposite side, blocking my escape route.

"Come on, you stupid cow. Get over here."

I pull out a handful of oats and offer them to Buster.

He takes some in his mouth. Then he licks his long purple tongue across my hand, sliming my palm. Luckily, eating oats and apples is more important than trampling me. Shaking the blue bucket mesmerizes Buster.

"Buster, if you want some grain, you're going to have to come over here and get it."

I spread some grain out for the horses. They gobble it up. All the animals pack in close, headbutting the boards. I remain safe inside the feeding trough.

Buster rounds the horses and squeezes in to eat his fair share of oats. I pour the remaining grain into the trough, right in front of the cow. The moment he starts eating, I jump out of the feed trough and hit the ground running, dodging mounds of poop. Quick on the mark, Buster stumbles, knocking over the horses as he makes a beeline in my direction.

I run fast.

Buster closes in.

I sprint.

Heavy hooves—the gate is close. I toss the bucket in the air. It lands in the grass on the other side of the fence. Grabbing the fence, I vault over the top and roll to the ground. The frozen grass welcomes my fall. I get up and brush myself off. Buster patiently waits at the fence for a good-bye rub.

He snorts excitedly.

I walk over to the beast.

"Beat ya again, buddy." Buster licks the sleeve of my coat as I scratch his chin. After a few pats, I walk down the fence line, collecting the loose alfalfa I used to lure the horses. Buster trots back over to the feeding trough to eat the leftover grain.

Last week, Dad thought I was being "a lazy piece of shit" because there was fresh alfalfa right outside the fence. I tried to explain why I needed to feed the animals in a strategic fashion, but Dad still thought I was being lazy. No one ever sees this morning feeding ritual; they are still in bed. I don't want another whipping, so it is easier to pick up the evidence and cover my tracks.

Key Center boasts one flashing red light, a gas station, the Huckleberry Inn Restaurant, a grocery store, a volunteer fire station, a health clinic, and a tavern. We are isolated, but have access to all the necessities. Our property line butts up against the imaginary line where the town starts.

Cars barrel down the empty country highway. Buster moos at passersby. He loves humans, machines, and animals, especially our old battered sheep named Clyde. A local farmer dropped Clyde off at our home after wild dogs attacked it. Its wool is useless. The meat is too old to taste good. Because our house is a place for random rejects, Clyde fit right in. Buster and Clyde quickly became tight buddies.

Clyde earned the nickname "Houdini," because he finds small openings in the fence and wiggles his way through. Patches of wool and skin get torn out and cut by barbed wire, but he can't feel it because of the nerve damage from the dog attack. Once on the outside, the sheep bleats for Buster. Cedar poles are no match for the charging head of a Jersey steer. After a few headbutts, the fence lies on the ground and Buster and Clyde stroll into town.

RING, RING. The telephone breaks the silence in our house. We all know better than to allow our friends to call after nine o'clock. Phone calls this late draw unwanted attention. Mom already corralled most of us kids into our rooms for the night. There are only a couple stragglers. Dad is working a twenty-four-hour shift at the fire station.

RING. Mom answers, "Beck residence, Sue speaking. How can I help you?"

The voice on the phone asks, "Is this Jim Beck's wife?"

"Yes, it is. Is there something wrong?"

"This is Chuck Stanton, down at the Key Center Fire Department. I found your phone number on the, uh, cow tag. Can you come pick up your animals? They are down here checking out our breathing apparatus and blocking the trucks."

"I'm so sorry. I'll be right over."

Mom hangs up the phone, humiliated, mumbling G-rated obscenities under her breath. She drags on a bathrobe and heads out. "Bubba, keep an eye on things here. I'll be right back."

"Okay. What happened?"

"Nothing, just stay here." Mom heads out the door with a lead rope, flashlight, and a box of Cheerios—Buster's coaxing agent.

On the front porch, Mom's flashlight bobs up and down, weaving through the alfalfa field, as she heads toward the Fire Department. Her voice carries into the night. "Stupid, gosh-darn, sorry excuse for an animal. I can't believe Jim got a cow. He doesn't even know how to take care of the darn thing. I have to do it. Just like I have to do everything. He says, 'Figure it out. How hard can it be?' I'll tell him how hard it can be. Next time that darn animal runs away in the middle of the night, he's going to have to catch it. Of course it only happens while he's at work. James Beck has to be the luckiest son of a—"

RING, RING. The telephone extension cord snakes across the room. It has been a couple weeks since we received a late-night call interrupting Mom's evening tea. She sets down a book beside her teacup and answers, "Beck residence, Sue speaking. How can I help you?"

"Hi, Sue. This is Walt from Walt's Fine Foods, the grocery store in Key Center. Could you please come get your cow. He's, uh, in my produce aisle."

Within minutes, Mom takes off into the pasture, armed with a flashlight and box of Cheerios. A couple hours later, she returns.

I ask, "What happened?"

She says, "Those motion sensor doors at the grocery store opened up and let Buster and Clyde in. They knocked over everything. Some of the shelves were down. I found Buster in the produce aisle eating all the vegetables. Clyde was running around, knocking things over."

"Did anyone get hurt?"

"No. I told Walt that I would pay for the damages. Everyone was laughing so hard that nobody cared. I brought them home and tied Buster up to the feeding trough. Clyde will keep close by."

Buster and Clyde—With Susan after another escape

I ask, "How did you get him home so fast?"

Mom replies, "Shook Cheerios in front of him. I didn't even need a lead rope. Still, I don't think I'll ever be able to set foot in that grocery store again. I'm so embarrassed. If that cow escapes one more time, I'm gonna...I'm gonna...Well, I don't know what I'm gonna do. But I'm gonna do something."

It is dark outside, late. Dad is at work. Mom reclines in her favorite chair with a book. Most of the foster kids are in their rooms for the night. There is an Eskimo-looking olive-skinned boy who just moved into my room. He smells like stale rice. I don't like him. It sucks to have to share my room with someone that stinky. I hang out in the living room for as long as Mom lets me.

RING, RING. Mom jumps up from her chair and picks up the phone. She gives the alfalfa field the stink-eye and answers in an expectant drone, "Beck residence, Sue speaking. How can I help you?"

"Hey, Sue, Bill here. I'm over at Key Center Tavern. I got your number from the cow tag. Do you have—"

Mom answers through gritted teeth, "Yes, that is my cow. What did he do?"

"Oh, nothing. Your cow is welcome anytime, but you might wanna come get him. It's about twenty shots deep and starting to wobble. The sheep is drunk, too."

Mom hangs up the phone, drags on a robe, and grabs the Cheerios. "I swear to…I'm going to make hamburger out of that stupid cow. That goes for that sorry excuse for a sheep, too. If Jim brings home one more random animal, I'm gonna—"

The door slams shut. Mom walks through the alfalfa field, which renders her invisible except for the beam of light bobbing through the tall grass reeds.

After the bar incident, Buster and Clyde became local celebrities. Roughneck bikers easily blow off barflies, but they couldn't resist buying rounds of drinks for our livestock. Business surged. Booze flowed like honey. Our critters received all the love necessary to make return trips inevitable. Everybody in our small town became curious about the family who owned a crazy cow, cared for by foster girls (the ones who used to be found prostituting on K Street in Tacoma) in that mint-green farmhouse, up on the hill.

It's a school night. I lie on the couch, pretending to read. So far, I've successfully avoided my least favorite addition to the family: the Eskimo boy who smells like stale rice. He is my newest foster brother. The rest of the family is in their rooms. Mom relaxes in her nightgown, snuggling up to an Agatha Christie novel.

Distant gravel crunches beneath unknown tires.

Alert, Mom cranes her neck, looking out the window, toward the distant country highway. Parallel cones of light turn toward our house and make their way down the driveway. The moonlight silhouettes a pickup truck sneaking down our private, quarter-mile gravel road. The wind betrays the hushed voices of drunken men riding in the back of the truck. U-turns can easily be made at the entrance of our gravel road. There is no reasonable excuse for a group of men to come up to our house after ten o'clock at night, unannounced.

Mom drags a trench coat over her fluffy pink robe. She turns to me and says, "Bubba, you stay inside. Don't let anyone out of the house until these people are gone. Do you understand?"

"Yes, Mom."

Both hands on her head, she fluffs up her graying hair like Einstein and dashes over to the gun cabinet. With wiry wild hair spiraling up in all directions and a Smith & Wesson revolver in each hand, she slips out the back door. Peeking out the back window, I watch my mother slide into the shadows of towering evergreens to stalk our unwelcome visitors.

The truck slowly pulls around the backside of the house. Exterior motion lights illuminate the trespassers—a beat-up Ford. A half-dozen scraggly men sit in the back of the pickup, with three in the cab. The truck inches toward the carport.

Mom jumps from the bushes with revolvers raised overhead and bum-rushes the oncoming truck, cowboy style.

BANG!

BANG!

Flame shoots out the barrels and into the night sky. She hollers bloody murder as rounds fly into the darkness. *AAAAAAAhhhhh!*

BANG!

BANG!

Muzzle flashes light up the darkness as bullets pierce the empty sky. Everyone in the truck ducks. The driver spins the vehicle around. Gravel spews from underneath bald tires as the vagrants make a hasty escape.

BANG!

BANG!

With trench coat flapping behind her, my mother chases the fleeing truck down the gravel road. Aiming high above their heads, she empties the guns of their bullets.

Foster kids stampede through the house and rush out to investigate. Illuminated by the motion sensor light on the back porch, Mom is doubled over in a fit of laughter.

The kids shout out, "Mom, what happened? Why are you carrying those guns?"

She told the story and then said, "All right, back to bed. You have school tomorrow."

Heading inside, Kristen asks, "What did the guys look like?"

Mom responds, "I didn't get a good look. I was too busy shooting."

Brenda asks, "Well, were they cute at least?"

Realizing the world of possibilities that live beyond her imagination, my mom squares off to all the foster girls and forces a commanding tone. "If any of you know those boys, then tell them that the next time they drive down our driveway this late at night, I won't aim at the sky."

All of us kids nodded in understanding. After all, Mom meant it.

CHAPTER 12

HOME SWEET HOME

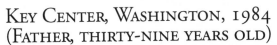

KEY CENTER, WASHINGTON, 1984
(FATHER, THIRTY-NINE YEARS OLD)

The foster home couldn't be better. My entire family enjoys church and receives the love they deserve. Every kid attends Vaughn Christian School and is saved by the Blood of Jesus Christ. Sue and I decided to fill the foster home with mainly girls. Boys are physically bigger and could pose a more significant threat. With my twenty-four-hour shifts at the fire station, Sue is home alone at least two nights a week. We figure that letting several hormone-filled teenage guys sleep under the same roof as a group of street girls who are only sisters on paper isn't a good idea. It is easy to keep one foster boy at a time, but that is the limit. I have to make sure Rachel and the other girls are safe.

Every once in a while we take in women from the shelter along with her brood of kids. They never stay long—three or four months at most. Their abusive husbands are always able to persuade them to move back. It baffles me when they do, but I don't stop them. People are free to come and go. It is funny to listen to all of the men use the same words my dad used with my mom growing up. If I had a dollar for every time I heard "I've changed" or "It will be different this time," I would be a rich man. I guess everybody holds out for the hope that people can change. I doubt anyone has the strength to actually make change happen.

Sue and I take in anyone who needs a safe place to stay. Life out on the street is hard. People need a helping hand and I want to give it to them. We are doing this for God. This is how I am going to make a difference in the world.

Life for kids needs to be regimented, like the military taught me. Sue and I run a tight ship. Chores are done on rotation. Everyone knows what is expected of them and we all come together as a family. Things couldn't be better.

Hallway floorboards creak under each of my steps. The noisy old hardwood in this mint-green farmhouse eliminates the possibility of sneaking around.

Leaning up to the door, I listen.

Silence.

KNOCK, KNOCK. "You guys decent?" I ask.

Three young feminine voices respond, "Yes."

I open the door and peek in. Across the room, a nightstand has three quarters taped to the mirror, one for each of them. They are all in bed.

"Good night, Kristen. Good night, Jenny. Good night, Shannon."

"Good night, Mr. Beck," each of them says from their bed.

Foster kids get two choices: they can call me Mr. Beck or Dad. Most of them remain formal. It's easier to leave someone who isn't family. However, in foster care, runaways are unavoidable. The problem is, collect calls cost $1.75 a minute, which is expensive. We average four runaways a month. Add in static and dropped calls and the phone bill adds up. By taping quarters to everyone's dresser, I can cover the whole group for around two bucks. Plus, each quarter that passes through the hands of my foster kids serves as a reminder that they have a place to come home to.

"I love you girls," I say.

"I love you, too," they each reply.

I softly close the door. The wood floor moans underneath me as I continue down the hallway.

I think I should make the quarter for bus fare. Midnight drives into Tacoma are getting old. Maybe it won't be such a glorious homecoming if they have to take public transportation. Riding the bus could be an embarrassing deterrent.

KNOCK, KNOCK. "Come in," a young girl replies.

I open the door and scan the room. A quarter is missing. Laura lies beneath her covers, trembling.

Angie's bed is empty. This is expected. I hadn't seen her for the last couple of hours. Sitting at the end of Laura's bed, I place my hand on her foot. "How are you?"

Laura replies, "I tried to stop her, but she—"

I respond, "It's fine. I'm not mad. Are you okay?"

Laura calms. "Yeah, I'm all right."

Looking around the room, I ask, "Out of Kristen, Jenny, and Shannon, which one would you like to move into your room?"

"Are you kicking Angie out?" Laura panics.

"No, but there are three girls in the room next door and you are in here alone. We need to make things even. If Angie is still gone by the weekend, I'll move one over. You get to choose, but keep it between us. People might get jealous. I hear you are a great roommate."

Laura smiles. "Can I tell you tomorrow?"

"Of course. Good night," I reply.

"Thanks, Mr. Beck. Good night."

As I walk into the hallway, I pretty much know where Angie is headed. She never gets caught and only comes home when she's ready. Angie is as tough as they come. She's street-smart and already lived a large chunk of her life in back alleys. She hasn't run away for almost a year, so it may be more than a month before we see her again.

I wonder if Angie's mom got out of jail? The last time I saw her, she was under a streetlamp on K Street, whistling at cars. Hope for a good life grows slim when the best of times are decades behind you. She can't bring in the same kind of cash that she once could. However, her daughter can. I hope Angie is okay.

Times were tough. At nine years old, Angie was the "bread and butter" solution to her mom's financial problems. Preteen girls can fetch high prices out on K Street. Big money rolled in for three years until Angie was caught and thrown into foster care at age twelve. She was on my doorstep at thirteen. For years, Angie's mom told the courts that she was innocent and blamed the whole thing on her abusive boyfriend. The social worker told me last week that the court decided Angie's mom was more believable than the facts and they were scheduling her release.

Once Angie's mom is out of prison, there is nothing anyone can do to hold Angie back. Smart kids are the most affected by family trauma, blinded by love. They do crazy things to get attention from their parents. Starved of a normal life, we give them as much love as we can. It's a lot better than the "nothing" they are getting. After a few months of receiving our love, they feel like they are finally fixed, as if their family problems were their fault. They always see their parents as good people and run back into their arms. It's really quite sad.

When foster kids run away, they are just trying to bring their family back together. How can someone be upset at that? Some lessons can't be explained; they have to be felt. The kids are just screaming out, "Look, I'm lovable now." It's sad that they have to learn things the hard way. I just try to be there when they do.

I explained all of this to Sue, but she doesn't understand. My wife is great with religion, but not with basic kid stuff. The whole thing is obvious to me. This is further confirmation that I am doing exactly what God wants. He gave me these skills and it is important that I use them for His glory. After all, I have a knack with kids.

House rules evolve, but two never change: (1) Nobody gets kicked out. (2) You can run away as many times as you wish, but only move out once. Once a kid moves his/her stuff out, there is no coming back.

CLICK. The telephone receiver rests on its cradle. It was the cops; they have Angie. She had been gone only a few days. One week is respectable for most of the girls, but for Angie it is nothing, a drop in the bucket. Plus, it's Wednesday afternoon. Runaways call or get caught at night, when fear settles in. Getting nabbed midday doesn't make sense.

Harsh fluorescence bounces off cinderblock walls as uniformed officers buzz around the police station. The occasional cuffed vagrant sits idle, waiting to be told his/her next move. I approach the front desk and check in with a familiar face. "Hey, Larry."

The officer looks up. "Jim, good to see you. I guess you're here to pick up Angie.

"Yep," I reply.

Larry slides me the usual paperwork and says, "How's the home coming along?"

Surveying the room, I reply, "Not bad. Got six kids, room for a couple more. Other than having to come down here, the foster home is going great. How did you catch her?"

"We didn't. She flagged us down."

Angie flags down the cops? This really doesn't add up.

"Give me the quick version," I say.

The officer continues, "Last night, two guys picked her up, gang-raped her, and dumped her on the side of the road. She stalked them all night and found them this morning at Denny's. She flagged down a patrol car and my boys made the arrest."

"They stiffed her?" I ask.

Larry gives a smile of regret. "You know her history. She's too smart to admit the truth, but it does look like a 'nonpayment of funds for services rendered' issue."

"Did you counsel her?" I ask.

The officer replies, "Yeah, the team has been with her all morning. It's not like there is anything new to say. She's heard it all before. You've got your hands full with that one. She's clever. It's the first time I've ever seen a girl leverage assault and statutory rape to turn my police department into her enforcers."

Things begin to make sense.

"You have the guys here that did it?" I wonder out loud.

"Yeah, they are in custody now. She gave a full description, down to details of their genitalia. They aren't getting out of it."

Officers buzz around in the background. Larry and I give each other an awkward look. There is more to be said, but no words come to mind. Being at a police station makes me feel ill at ease.

I ask, "Do I need to sign something?"

Larry nods and slides over the final form.

I etch my name over a line marked "Guardian."

Larry shakes his head and says, "Jim, we really don't know what else to do."

"Yeah, me neither. I'm sure it'll happen again."

Larry shakes his head, not having anything else to say.

Looking around, I ask, "Where is she?"

"Over there." Larry points to a corner bench, across the room.

Angie sits alone, swinging her legs off the bench, chewing bubble gum. She is relaxed. At first glance, she looks like a normal teenager just waiting for friends. Angie spots me and gives a big smile, waves, like I am picking her up from soccer practice or to go to a movie. I expected a few tears or at least some anxiety.

Nothing.

After a week of hooking on the street, being gang-raped and left in a ditch, and hunting men all night, the only thing different about Angie is her fresh bruises and tattered clothes.

I put my arm around my daughter. "Are you okay?"

Angie's smile brightens. "Yeah, I'm fine."

"Do you want to tell me what happened?"

"Can we do it outside? I want to get out of here. The police give me the creeps." She looks around the building as if it were covered in boogers.

Angie and I walk away from the station. I wait for some sort of emotional response. She climbs into the car like a happy teenager and fiddles with the radio.

"Angie, why did you go back on the street? Do you not like it at home?"

"No, I love you guys." She pauses. "I went to my mom's place. Thought it would be different, but her asshole boyfriend—"

She catches herself. We have a "no cursing" rule. "Sorry, Dad. I didn't mean to cuss."

"It's okay. You have a free pass today," I reply.

"Okay, cool." Angie smiles, examining her fingernails and pushing cuticles back. "Her boyfriend made me have sex with him. He said if I didn't, he'd leave my mom and hurt my little brother. I couldn't let that happen. But then, Momma woke up and caught us fuckin'...er...I mean having sex in the living room. She kicked me out and told me to never come back."

"Why didn't you come home?"

She looks away. "It was the first night. I can't come back on the first night. Besides, I can take care of myself. Everything would have been fine if those guys hadn't raped me. At least I got 'em."

The headrest relieves my exhausted neck.

She's only fifteen years old.

I conjure a fatherly tone. "Angie, you need to start thinking about life and your future."

Angie replies nonchalantly, "I do think about my future. My record will be wiped clean when I turn eighteen. I still got time to figure all this shit... uh...I mean figure all this stuff out. When does this free pass on cussing expire?"

"When we get home. Until then, you are fine. Is there anything you need to talk about? What are you feeling?"

My daughter sits back in her seat. She thinks for a few seconds. Breakthrough moments in parenting are rare. They can't be forced, rushed, prepared for, or predicted. They just happen and you have to be ready when they do.

Angie replies, "Yeah, there is."

I wait, ready for anything.

Angie grins and says, "I totally feel like a Happy Meal. Can we stop by McDonald's?"

"Yeah, sure," I reply.

Turning left out of the parking lot, I head for the nearest McDonald's. After all, it was the least I could do.

(SON, NINE YEARS OLD)

CRASH, SMASH. All the girls hate washing dishes. Angie is breaking them, armed with a Cheshire grin.

CRASH, SMASH. Automatic dishwashers are expensive. Dad says we don't need one because every person has two dishwashers attached to their wrists. He also says, "Dishwashers are the number one cause of divorce." He intentionally doesn't mention that this statement is true because everyone in America has a dishwasher.

CRACK, SMASH. The sounds of glass breaking echoes through the house.

All of us kids are dumbstruck, frozen in time as we watch Angie gleefully throw plates and glasses into the kitchen trash. Waste is not an option; flagrant waste is an abomination, direct disobedience. I back off, keeping a watchful eye. There is no way in hell I'm approaching one of my crazy sisters with broken glass around, that's for damn sure.

SMASH. Another glass breaks. Dad peeks around the corner. He walks up behind her, stalking. We all see him, but dare not warn Angie. He needs to catch her in the act, otherwise Angie will lie her way out of it. Angie grabs another plate and throws it into the garbage. *CRASH.*

Dad grabs her wrist and screams with red-faced furry, "What the *hell* do you think you are doing?"

Angie's pearly white smile disappears. She cowers, falling to her knees.

Gripping his pant leg in the fetal position she begs, "Please don't hurt me. I'm sorry. I'll be a good girl and wash the dishes. I promise. Please don't hurt me."

My father looks around. The Eskimo-looking boy slips around the corner. Kristen, Shannon, Jenny, Laura, Brenda, Rachel, and I stare back at him.

His chest heaves with heavy breaths.

Angie keeps both of his pant legs held tight, as if he was going to start kicking her. The tough street kid is now a scared little girl.

Dad reaches down and says, "Get up. We are going to go talk."

Tears stream down Angie's face. "I'll wash the dishes like a good girl. I promise."

Dad looks deep into her eyes. "I don't want you to ever do that again. Do you understand me?" He scans the living room. "That goes for the rest of you, too."

Everyone nods in affirmation: no breaking dishes on purpose. It seems like an obvious expectation, but we got the message. Dad gazes at all onlookers and barks, "You guys get upstairs. Stay there until I say to come down."

He pulls Angie into a downstairs bedroom. All of us hightailed it into an upstairs bedroom situated right above the action. Everyone puts "shush fingers" up to their mouths as I silently pull out a couple of heating vents. My vent has the best angle: a continuous view of Angie and the occasional glimpse of my dad. We take turns eavesdropping. Four heads rub against each other around my vent. Even though our craniums grind against others', sharing becomes effortless. Not getting along in this moment spells equal disaster for all.

Dad sits down next to Angie, placing his hand on her knee. He pulls a calm, disciplinarian tone. "Angie, do you understand what you did wrong?"

Angie responds syrupy sweet. "Yes, I'm sorry. Do you want to have sex with me?"

All of us pull up, looking at each other wide-eyed, shocked. At the same moment, each of our heads plummet back down toward the vent. We bonk foreheads jockeying for position, trying to gain a firsthand account of Dad's response.

Dad jerks his hand away and stammers, "No, that's not...*No!*"

Angie slides up to him, places her hand on his knee, and says in a sultry voice, "It's okay. I won't tell anyone."

Shannon rams my head out of the way. With my line of sight gone, I can only hear. Without hesitation, my father replies, "I will not have sex with you nor will I ever have sex with you. Never ask me that again. Angie, look at me. I'm your father and fathers don't do that with their daughters."

The moment hangs in the air.

Everyone remains huddling around the heating vents.

Angie responds, "Well, okay. Is there anything else?" There is confusion in her voice.

Dad continues, "You are going to have to do the dishes for two more weeks. I don't want this to ever happen again. Do you understand?"

"Yes, Mr. Beck."

Shannon lets me view the conflict. Dad and Angie stand up, facing each other. He says to her, "Let's just forget all this happened, okay? I won't tell the girls why you have to keep doing the dishes; you just do them. Okay?"

Angie nods in agreement. "Okay."

Dad gives her a big hug and they walk out. Moments later we hear, "Kids, you can come down now."

Strolling down the stairs, Kristen asks everyone, "Why doesn't Dad wanna have sex with Angie?"

Nobody gives her an answer.

After Angie's punishment, things in the house feel different. None of my sisters are spooked when people go into their rooms. They hug my father a lot more often. Most of them stopped calling him "Mr. Beck" and now call him "Dad."

Floorboards creak as my father walks down the hallway, performing the nightly headcount. A door opens. "Good night, girls."

My sisters respond in unison, "Good night, Dad."

A few seconds later, the door shuts. He walks down the hall toward my room. The Eskimo-looking boy turns over, already asleep. The room smells like stale rice. His quarter is still taped to the nightstand, unfortunately. I wish he would use it, run away, and never return.

CLICK. The door opens without a knock.

Dad's silhouette stands in doorway. "Bubba, I don't want to see any more alfalfa by the fence. It's pretty lazy to not walk it over to the feeding trough. You've got a week's restriction to think about it. Do you understand me, young man?"

"Yes, sir," I reply.

"Good night, guys," he says.

"Good night, Dad," I respond, while the smelly Eskimo boy snores.

The door shuts. My asshole father's footsteps get fainter and fainter as they move down the hall.

CHAPTER 13

TAKE IT

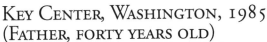

KEY CENTER, WASHINGTON, 1985
(FATHER, FORTY YEARS OLD)

DONG, DONG, DONG. The grandfather clock strikes nine. Family time begins. No calls after 9:15 p.m. or you face trouble. If I don't make every kid enforce this policy with their friends, they would walk all over me. It only takes one week of restriction for each of them to learn. Every person gets one second chance and there is a fifteen-minute grace period, which keeps things fair. If one of the kids' friends breaks our family rule, whomever the call is intended for gets put on restriction. It doesn't happen a second time, the kids make sure of it. Emergencies are the only exception.

The new foster kids are the only ones who test the rules. Veterans know better: one week's restriction is the standard punishment. Everyone has had to serve his/her time. No exceptions or special treatment.

RING. It's 10:22 p.m. Jenny, Shannon, Laura, Rachel, and Bubba freeze from their Monopoly game. I look at the clock. Someone's in trouble.

Kristen peeks up from the couch, taking a pouting break. She doesn't want to play Monopoly. She says, "It's just a stupid game with dice." Then she lobbies for Yahtzee.

Sue peers above her Agatha Christie novel.

RING. I move toward the phone, gripping the receiver.

This call is either from a kid, the police, or the hospital. Angie and Brenda took off the same day. It's been less than a week.

RING. Excitement electrifies the air. I ask the kids, "If you think that it's Brenda on the phone, raise your right hand. If you think that it's Angie, raise your left."

I raise my right. There's no way it's Angie; she's too tough.

Sue raises her left hand, voting for Angie. Kristen agrees with Sue and raises her left.

RING. Shannon yells out, "Kristen, you can't say that you forgot which hand is your right or left this time. You are voting for Angie."

Kristen rolls her eyes. "That only happened one time. I'm voting with Mom."

Sue pipes in, "Since all you guys have already voted and can't switch, Brenda has a secret boyfriend and was planning to run away with him. That's why I don't think it is her."

RING. Everyone playing Monopoly calls out in unison, "It's Brenda; she's the weak one."

Kristen says, "No way, it is Angie. She's weird."

Shannon gives a forced whisper, loud enough for only the game players to hear. "When is Mom going to realize that Brenda lies about everything?"

I hold in a laugh, knowing that Mom never will.

RING. "Hands, I want to see hands. Losers have to dish out ice cream and run around the house three times barefoot screaming, 'Uncle Wiggly wears army boots.'"

Everyone playing Monopoly keeps his or her right hand raised, voting for Brenda. Mom and Kristen hold strong with their left hand, voting for Angie.

RING. I pull the receiver to my ear. "Beck residence, Jim speaking. How can I help you?"

A familiar voice cracks on the other end. "Dad, it's me. Can you pick me up?"

A big grin stretches across my face as I announce the winners. "Brendaaaaa."

The Monopoly players call out, "We win. We win. Go dish us ice cream, Mom. You, too, Kristen."

Fair is fair. Kristen and Sue went into the kitchen to dish out dessert.

I refocus on the call. "Are you okay?"

The young voice mixes with tears. "Dad, I'm at 25th and Pac Ave. Can you please come pick me up?"

"I can, but that drive will cost you two weeks' restriction. That's a long time to be grounded. Why don't you just use the quarter I gave you for the bus?"

"There are no more buses tonight," she pleads.

"There is a bus that can pick you up on McKinley and 38th in thirty minutes. It's about fifteen blocks. You can make it."

I wanted to rescue my daughter, but playing the hero is a slippery slope.

Brenda keeps on. "I lost the quarter. Can you please just pick me up?"

"I can, but rules are rules. It's not fair to make everyone else follow the rules if they don't apply to you, too." I said this loud enough for everyone in the room to hear. A little reinforcement never hurts.

Laura yells out, "Use the quarter, Brenda, like everyone else."

I pull the receiver from my ear and aim it at the room. Everyone chimes in.

Jenny jumps in, "Yeah, rules are rules."

Shannon continues, "Does she think the rules don't apply to her? If I had to be grounded for that, so does she. Dad, don't let her get by with it. She has the quarter in her pocket. Trust me."

Pulling the receiver back to my ear I tell Brenda, "Your choice."

It was time to let my child decide. Sue taught me the benefits of a dramatic pause. After a minute, Brenda says, "I just found a quarter. I'll take the bus."

I reply, "I'll leave the back door unlocked. There are some leftovers in the fridge. See you in the morning."

CLICK. I hung up the phone and unlocked the back door. I'm happy to know that one of the runaways is still alive. I can never tell if the kids are going to come home or if they are just calling to make sure they have a place to come home to. In the end, I guess it doesn't matter.

(Son, ten years old)

It's normal to have several random girls living in my house. The smelly Eskimo boy moved out a couple months ago. Good riddance. Whenever a foster brother moves in, my world turns upside down. They hate me because I represent everything the world stole from them: family, love, and their own bedroom. They are always older, which means they are also bigger and tend to make their own rules that Dad doesn't know about.

Right after they move in, each brother has shoved my stuff aside and replaced it with their stuff. They dare me to challenge. If I complain, they take a sappy sweet tone with my parents and then switch back to their true demon selves when we are alone. It's easier to just let the bastards have the best shelf space from the beginning.

The one good thing about having another guy around is my workload gets cut in half. With the foster brother's help, it is finally possible for my laundry list of chores to actually be completed. Because the guys are bigger, they try to outperform me in order to please my father. I keep the fact—pleasing my father is impossible—a secret. It is something they have to figure out on their own. In the meantime, I get free labor.

Patrick moved in a few weeks ago. He's better than the Eskimo kid, but not by much. Every night, he plays heavy metal—the type that is against the rules—loud enough to keep me awake. My pillow doesn't drown out the noise. Twisted Sister bellows from his boom box.

Oh we're not gonna take it
No, we ain't gonna take it
Oh we're not gonna take it anymore

We've got the right to choose and
There ain't no way we'll lose it
This is our life, this is our song
We'll fight the powers that be just
Don't pick our destiny 'cause
You don't know us, you don't belong

Pat turns to my bed and commands, "Turn off the music."

The stereo is located two feet from his head. There is no way I am getting out of my warm bed to turn off his music when I didn't want to listen in the first place.

"Turn off your own music!" I demand.

Pat sits up in bed. "I told you to turn off the damn stereo!"

"No." I hold my ground, as I lie stiff as a board.

Pat leaps over and lands on my bed. His legs straddle me. The blanket pins my arms beneath his knees. Punch after punch, Pat proves that he is the alpha male in my bedroom. Moments later, I turned off his stereo.

The next morning, as I walk through the kitchen, Jenny pulls dishes from the cabinet, setting the table for breakfast.

Mom notices my bruises and asks, "What happened to your arms?"

Pat shoots me a warning look.

I smile and reply, "A friend and I were wrestling. It's no big deal."

Mom believes me and doesn't dig any deeper. After all, boys will be boys.

Every other week we get a five-dollar allowance. The nights that Dad hands us money are usually the same nights that my siblings run away. They take the quarter taped to their nightstand, slip out the back door, walk through the alfalfa field, and hop on the bus headed to Tacoma. We never know if a kid is going to be stuck in jail or leave forever. It happens at least twice a month, so why worry about it? It's not like there is a shortage of kids that need help. Each of them will be replaced in time. They could be killed and we'd never know about. All we can do is wait and see if they call or show up. Other than being a little bit quieter and chores getting shuffled around, not much changes. The only real change is the number of table settings that get laid out at mealtime.

Plates in hand, rounding the table, Jenny asks, "Hey, Mom, how many should I set the table for?"

Mom yells out from her bedroom, "Angie and Shannon don't have quarters, so they're gone. Set it for eight."

It's 7:30 a.m. A gentle hand rocks my shoulder. My eyes are tired. It takes only a few seconds to realize that I'm at a friend's house, Joe Howard. Joe's mom, hovers over me in a pink bathrobe, holding a telephone. Nobody likes being woken up this early on a weekend, but she hides it well. Mrs. Howard grins ear to ear, accepting some form of flattery from someone on the other line. My father can be charming when he wants to be. After a few chuckles, she hands me the phone.

My stomach twists in knots. I brace myself. "Hello."

Dad's deep voice echoes in the receiver. "Get your ass home, now!" *CLICK.*

I pedal my bike as fast as my legs can move. Morning dew clings to the handlebars. Houses zip by as the wind presses moisture from my eyes. Asphalt hums underneath the tires. Patches of fog hover over neighboring fields, just a few feet in the air.

Most people aren't awake yet, but my father is. The longer I make him wait, the more trouble I am in.

The three-mile ride passes quickly. In a flash, I'm back home and burst through the back door.

Dad is waiting.

"You're trying to get out of doing firewood today, aren't ya? You lazy shit." He is furious.

In a careful tone, I respond, "Mom said I could spend the night at Joe's house if I finished the lawn."

"I don't give a shit what Mom said. You know we are supposed to do firewood today and you are trying to get out of it. You are worthless."

"I was just spending the night," I replied, still unsure of what I did wrong.

"You are grounded. You have two weeks' restriction to think about it. I'm going to teach you not to be lazy. Now, get your ass upstairs and put on some work clothes!"

He punctuated his last statement with a hard slap on the back of my head, lurching me forward. It took a few steps to catch my balance.

Don't hit me, motherfucker! I hate you! Yeah, I wanted to get out of doing firewood. I worked hard all day and asked mom if it was okay. I used the situation to my advantage. I like working; I just hate being around you. Damn cock sucker!

I keep my Christian lips buttoned up tight because that's what good boys are supposed to do. Rachel and I are the only kids who don't have quarters taped to our nightstand. Daddy's little girl doesn't need one, but I do. If I'm home, I get in trouble for breathing. If I'm gone, Dad gets pissed that I'm not around to help him work. I can't win. He screams in my face every day. The only break I have is when he is at the fire station or if I'm gone.

The only sound I hate worse than my father's voice is the fucking high-pitched whine of a chainsaw. When I hear that damn two-stroke engine rev up, my insides twist. I want to punch or be punched; it doesn't matter. Rage pulses through my veins and fuels every breath.

My dad is the stupid fucking moron who can never figure out how much time it takes to finish a job. If he tells me something should take two or three hours, I have to change the word *hours* to *days* in order to have an accurate time estimate. Dad thinks that I should be able to clean the chicken coop in an hour, which takes a day. He also expects me to mow our wraparound three-acre lawn in two hours, even though it is a two-day job under optimal circumstances. He doesn't know why I can't bring together a year's worth of firewood in less than ten days. Forget the fact that thirteen cords would take any mortal the better part of a summer to gather.

I am disappointment wrapped in human flesh.

On the back porch, sifting through a stack of mismatched work gloves, I look for a pair that fits. Dad's angry voice carries from inside the kitchen. "Sue, did you see the woodpile? Bubba didn't do shit yesterday."

Mom calms, "Jim, he worked all day."

"That's all he got done? Damn lazy kid. He needs to pull the lead outta his ass."

"He cleaned the chicken coop and finished the lawn right before it got dark. Bubba worked hard the past three days."

"Bubba is lazy and slow. Quit covering for him."

I find my favorite pair of gloves, shut the back door, and stroll out to the woodpile.

CHAPTER 14

A Hunting We Will Go

KEY CENTER, WASHINGTON, 1985 (SON, TEN YEARS OLD)

The wind rustles pine needles overhead as it flows through the arms of the evergreens. Fresh sawdust covers the surrounding underbrush. Exhaust from the chainsaw is swept away as the scent of pinesap takes over. After Dad slices up a tree, I set the pieces on end. He goes down the row with a maul and splits them into stove-size logs. One by one, I toss them out of the woods and into the truck. Once the truck is full, we drive up to the barn. I dump the load and stack the wood in organized rows while Dad takes a break. I tell him when I'm finished, we go back out, and start the cycle all over again.

Firewood is our only source of heat. It makes sense. We have plenty of free fuel and labor standing around. Day after day, summer after summer, I'd toss, haul, and stack thirteen cords of firewood, which amounts to a couple railroad cars filled to the brim.

About thirty round logs sit upright ready to be split. Dad steps over a recently fallen tree and inspects my work. The wood looks like a trail of big yellow dots breaking up the lush green forest floor.

"Bubba, I want to see if you are 'man enough' to do something."

My father often issues his rite of passage—tasks that need to be accomplished in order to prove manhood: eat a half jar of jalapeño peppers, hold your breath under water for longer than any of my sisters, or do a hundred push-ups. Fulfilling a "man task" is the only way to make my father proud.

"Okay, Dad, what do you want me to do?"

"I want you to swing the ax three times and see if you can split a log with each swing. Do you think you are man enough to do that?"

"Sure, I think I can."

Scouting the ground, I pick the three logs that are big enough to be respectable but without knots so they'd be easy to split.

I grab the splitting maul and set my footing.

Dad got close, as if he was judging an international wood chopping competition. He sets the stage and says, "On your mark. Get set. Go!"

The maul hangs momentarily above my head and plummets into the resting wood. *CRACK*. Two semicircles of wood sail to my right and left.

Another swing. *CRACK*. Another perfect split.

I reposition my feet and swing. *CRACK*. Three for three, a perfect record.

I am the man!

Dad nods his approval. "Good job, son. I think you're ready to start splitting all the firewood."

Great, men must be stupid.

Dad fires up the chainsaw and cuts into a tree. He is the only person who gets to use machinery, the real man's job. I'm just a grunt.

The chainsaw's high-pitched whine pumps tension through my veins—*RAAANAA NAAA NAAA NAAA*—drowning out my mumbling voice. "I'm stupid for swinging so hard. I should have picked a harder piece of wood and got the ax stuck. This sucks. Now I have to split all the damn wood and he gets to take longer breaks. What a fucking asshole, thinking he is so clever."

CRUNCH. The chainsaw engine dies—Dad hit a rock. The blade needs to be resharpened. He tells people all the time that he hasn't hit a rock in over a year, but he's a liar. It happens twice a day.

I keep tossing logs out of the woods. Even from fifty yards away, I can feel my father's rage build. It's better to stay busy than to take the chance of being observed not working.

Keep throwing wood. Don't draw attention. He'll start yelling in three...two... one.

"Damn, fucking, son of a pecker head, shit licker!"

Right on cue and he even strung a new list of curse words together. I've never heard "Damn fucking son of a pecker head shit licker" before. Interesting choices.

Ha, ha, he's mad. Serves the piece of shit right. How about this man test: sharpen the chainsaw with your face.

It is easy to conceal chuckles with work grunts when your back is turned. I keep an eye on him, waiting to see what he'll do next. Sometimes he waves his hands in the air like a crazy man and other times he throws his chainsaw against a tree. This is how he breaks most of his tools.

Dad yells, "Bubba, get over here!"

I run.

"I gotta take this damn saw apart. Go up to the house and get me a Phillips screwdriver. They are on the back porch, in the toolbox."

Even though my father leaves out significant details when he sends me on missions, asking questions reinforces that I'm stupid. Running away too quickly is a sure way to be disrespectful. Waiting too long communicates that I'm lazy.

"Come on, hustle!" he yells.

That's my cue. In a flash, I sprint up the trail toward the house.

I search the back porch, winded.

Will Dad need more than one screwdriver? Where's the toolbox? SHIT!

"Mom, where is the toolbox? I need to get a screwdriver for Dad."

Mom comes running.

Any time my dad needs me to do something, she's quick on the mark to help. She looks around. "I haven't seen the toolbox on the back porch for a long time. I think I have some screwdrivers in the kitchen," she says.

We root through drawers, search cabinets, and gather together all the random screwdrivers we can find, including obnoxiously big ones and ridiculously small ones. Mom sends me off saying, "I'll clean up this mess. You take these to your father."

Running down the trail, I hear her voice echo through the trees. "Don't run with screwdrivers. It's dangerous." She doesn't realize it is even more dangerous not to run.

When I get within eyesight of the truck, I sprint so Dad sees I'm not being lazy. The truck hood is open, blocking his view. A familiar vibrating buzz hangs on the air. I round the back of the pickup. Dad leans over the chainsaw with an electric grinder, sharpening the blade. A screwdriver sticks out of his back pocket.

He looks up, irritated.

Standing in front of him panting, I gather breath. My fingers twist around a dozen odd-shaped screwdrivers.

He shoots me a look of disgust. "What took you so long?"

"I couldn't find the toolbox." I'm dumbfounded.

"I got tired of waiting and did it myself." He grabs the chainsaw blade and begins sharpening.

How in the hell? That is impossible.

I felt stupid until I noticed the toolbox at my father's feet.

Son of a bitch, you had the toolbox the whole time? You gave me the wrong information and made me sprint up to the house for nothing.

Dad glances at my hands. "What are all those for?"

"Screwdrivers, like you asked."

He drops the grinder. "No, I said I needed a Phillips screwdriver—a damn Phillips."

Dad yanks a screwdriver from my hand and pulls out the one from his pocket. The rest fell to the ground.

Pulling my head in close, he sticks the ends of both screwdrivers an inch from my nose. He spits his words through clenched teeth. "Yours is a flathead. That doesn't do me a damn bit of good. That's why I told you to bring me a Phillips. I knew you would screw this up, which is why I have to do everything myself."

Holy crap, he's right. There are two different types of screwdrivers. I didn't know.

"Does this look like a fucking Phillips to you?"

"No, sir."

Dad slaps me upside the head. "Pull the shit out of your ears and learn how to think. I would be stuck here all day if I had to wait for your slow ass. You worthless little pecker head."

(Father)

Being in nature with your son is as good as it gets. Bubba and I work together all summer to fill up the barn with firewood. We even clear land to build a new log home and have a great time doing it. Sue gets on my case for making him work so much. I figure she is right. Boys need to have fun, too.

Then it hits me: Elk season is only a few weeks away!

Hunting with my son is something I've always wanted to do. It's a great way to bond, the perfect father–son adventure. I'll teach him how to track and kill an elk. Guys love learning how to gut an animal. Hunting wild game turns boys into men. Bubba is lucky that he doesn't have to learn on his own. He will never guess in a million years that I'd invite him to go hunting with me.

This is gonna be great!

I palm strike the top of my son's bedroom door. It shakes as it opens. Bubba jumps up from his bed.

Ha, ha, got him again.

Fit to burst with excitement, I say, "Hey, Bub, in two weeks you're coming with me."

"Where?" My boy looks awestruck.

"We are going elk hunting. I'm going to teach you everything you've ever wanted to know."

"What about school?"

School? Ha! What's the point in being a boy's father if you can't get him out of school? I'm his legal guardian and I say that this trip is more important than school. It's healthy for a kid to play hooky.

"I'll write you a note," I say, solving the problem.

"I've got tests and a couple big homework assignments, one is in English," my son replies.

"Don't worry about it. I'll fix it up so you can hand your projects in when you get back."

"Okay." Bubba is speechless.

"Are you excited?" There is no need to ask him. I can tell my boy is ecstatic, grinning ear to ear.

"Yeah, sounds great," he says.

Bubba is so pumped. He never saw this coming. He's probably been waiting for me to ask for years. Ten years old is a good age to start carrying a gun. I'll keep it unloaded on this first trip. Eventually, I'll let him pull the trigger.

"That is really awesome," Bubba replies.

(Son)

Dad keeps standing in the doorway, with a shit-eating grin, thoroughly pleased. "Great! I'll start planning," he says.

Just smile. Nobody gets mad at a grateful kid. I'll sort this out later.

I force a grin.

How can I get out of this? Maybe if I rub a flu-infused tissue on my face I'll get sick and won't have to go? I could jump off the barn, but church camp is coming up and Mom won't let me go with a broken arm. Even if I make myself puke, Dad will say, "Great, now that all that bad bacteria is out of your system, you can come hunting with me."

Why does my father want me to go? I'm the kid who ruins his life and fucks everything up. I hate him. This is the worst punishment imaginable and I didn't even do anything wrong.

God, why do you hate me?

"Real men" go hunting. After splitting three logs in a row, he must regard me as a real man. He also thinks that walking barefoot through the snow, wiping your butt with leaves, and taking baths in glacier streams are fun. If killing with my dad is my path to manhood, then I don't know if I want to be a man. Five minutes ago, hunting season was my favorite time of year because for at least a week I was free of my father. Now, it ranks below going to the dentist. One week of bliss has just been replaced with a tour of hell.

East of Issaquah on I-90, Washington State

Time plays cruel tricks. Weeks before our departure, days raced by. Now that we are en route, minutes move at a snail's pace. Slumped in an oversize sweatshirt, I look out the window of our hunting rig hoping to see something that isn't green. There are green trees, green bushes, and green grass all broken up by gray asphalt, a blue sky, and the occasional lake. I play the shadow game to pass time. The shadow game forces you to hold your breath until your portion of the vehicle drives over a shadow. Big shadows mean big breaths. Long skinny shadows, offered by power lines, allow long shallow breaths. Drives don't seem quite as long when you hold your breath.

Our hunting rig is a converted school bus Dad got from a gun trade. It has most of the amenities of home: a full-size propane stove, refrigerator freezer, bunk beds, card tables, and securable cabinets. The enormous luggage rack welded from scrap metal and red-and-white-checkered curtains scream for attention. People stare. The previous owner stenciled "LUCKY" on the bumper. Our "Lucky Bus" has a Partridge family flavor with a Beverly Hillbillies twist. There are thirty empty seats behind me, but it seems rude to not ride shotgun.

Dad drives in silence.

I sit next to him, holding my breath.

Shifting back and forth, I try to suppress nature's call. A working toilet is the only amenity we don't have. Dad brought a couple pee cans, but they aren't enough. "Dad can we stop? I have to go number two."

"Damn it! You should have taken a dump before we left."

"I didn't have to go back then." Our departure was over two hours ago.

"Just hold it. You'll be fine," he replies.

Dad hands me a clear plastic bag filled with bulk candy: caramel squares and Cinnamon Bears. "Eat this. It'll help."

I unwrap a tiny cellophane package and hold a Cinnamon Bear in my hand. *I am Godzilla. You are helpless in my grasp.*

CHOMP. I bite off the top of the Cinnamon Bear.

Ah, where's my head?

The headless candy runs down my thigh, jumping from leg to leg.

Dad yells at me. "Don't play with it. Just eat it!"

I chew silently.

Each moment spent is one step closer to returning home.

An hour passes. I keep chewing. We pass a brown sign: Welcome to Snoqualmie National Rainforest.

Dad hollers, "Don't eat all the damn candy. You're not going to have any for the rest of the trip, stupid kid."

If I sit perfectly still, maybe I'll disappear.

In the middle of nowhere, Dad turns off the highway onto a dirt road. After a mile into the forest, the road narrows. Branches scrape against both sides of the bus, like fingernails on a chalkboard. Once we reach a small clearing, we stop.

"This is it. This is our spot. Whoohoo! Elk killin' time," Dad proclaims.

My father acts as if this exact spot was predetermined by a celestial design committee to be our base camp. To me, it looks like a random place, on a random road, in a random forest. It looks exactly like our backyard. He eyeballs me, expecting validation.

"It looks great," I comply.

Outside, the brisk mountain air bites my earlobes. Each breath curls into small clouds, hanging just long enough to be replaced by another puffy white exhale. It's damn cold. Butt clench, Mother Nature gives me a friendly reminder that I have to go and quick.

"Hey, Dad, where is the toilet paper?"

Silence.

Instead of handing me a roll, he stares. His jaw tightens. The temperature rises, as his face gets redder by the moment. "You didn't pack it?"

"I didn't know you wanted me to pack it. It wasn't on my list."

I checked, rechecked, and double-rechecked the list he gave me. Mom even went over it. I didn't forget anything.

"What the hell did you think we were going to use? Do you plan on holding it for the whole week?" These words slip through his clenched jaw.

"I packed everything you wrote on my list," I reply.

What the hell? You had your list and I had mine. You said I was responsible for only the things you wrote on my list. If you had put toilet paper on my list, it would be in the bus. It was your job to buy supplies and your job to create my list. Evidently, when you said, "I've got everything else taken care of," it meant that you took care of everything except toilet paper. Don't make forgetting something on your list my problem. I'm about to shit my pants, which is my problem.

"Do I have to spell everything out for you? You are so damn stupid. It was a mistake to bring you," he says.

Yes, on that we agree. It was a mistake. Remember that next year and feel free to take me home at any time.

"Sorry, Dad," I say.

Dad reaches in his duffel bag and pulls out two brand-new handkerchiefs and shoves them into my hand.

"This better be enough because I'm not going to give you my socks," he replies.

"Thanks, Dad."

With wiping materials in hand, I waddle into the woods with a clenched bottom and find the closest fallen tree.

Sitting down, frozen tree sap softens against my backside as little pieces of bark stick to my thigh. All discomfort is welcome as relief is felt. It is going to be a long two weeks. No one likes wiping with leaves, not even "real men," no matter what Dad says.

(Father)

I feel bad for blaming my son. Toilet paper was on my list and I was supposed to buy it when we stopped at the grocery store. I am embarrassed that I forgot. Oops. It is a simple mistake. No big deal. I'll just scrounge a couple rolls from another hunter. Guys up here always forget stuff and have to share. It is all part of the experience. We expect it. Last year, I forgot matches.

At least I gave Bubba a couple handkerchiefs to wipe his butt. He should appreciate that. After all, it's a hell of a lot better than wiping with leaves.

Key Center, Washington, 1986
(Son, eleven years old)

It is another summer, like all the rest. Dad's chainsaw fills the air with a high-pitched whine and sawdust. I hate the sounds and the smells of working in the woods. When I get old enough, I'm moving to a city.

Some things have changed. Flathead and Phillips screwdrivers are now strategically stashed in the truck, lunches are stowed behind the seat to avoid getting squashed or wilted by the sun, and I know exactly where the toolbox is. Every time the splitting maul sinks into a piece of Douglas fir, I imagine it sinking into my father's head. I hate him.

I swing as fast and hard at the beginning of the day as I do at the end. Hatred is powerful energy and I have plenty. It fuels my work.

Son of a bitch, I fucking hate you. You asshole. I wish you would die, motherfucker.

Any words that escape my lips are covered by the hum of the chainsaw ripping through evergreens. Work passes quickly when rage becomes your friend.

(FATHER)

Bubba and I work all day. We get a lot done. It is getting dark, so we should probably head home. I hit the kill switch. The chainsaw goes quiet. The only sound echoing in the forest is wood landing near the truck. *THUD, THUD.*

Bubba is throwing just as fast as he did at the beginning of the day, maybe even faster. That's impressive. He launches heavy logs like they are nothing. He is working harder than I am, not that I'll admit it. My boy is becoming a man, just like me. What is he mumbling under his breath?

"Bring it in, Bub. That's enough."

Bubba pauses with a guilty look. He must have gotten caught up in his work, just like his old man. We both are sweaty and grimy from a hard day of manual labor. I walk over to my boy and give him a pat on the back.

(SON)

Having a gloved hand covered in sawdust scrape against my bare skin makes me want to throw blows. Dad showing me affection usually only happens at church or dinner parties when we are around other people. I hate it when he tries to act like we are buddies.

We aren't friends. We will never be friends.

Pretending to like it, I give him a grin.

This motherfucker doesn't have a clue as to what is going on inside my head. He doesn't want to know.

Our mint green farmhouse is only five miles away. Dad starts up the pickup truck and pulls out onto the highway. He leans over and says, "Good job out there today."

Still panting rage, I reply, "Thanks."

The private country school the Beck kids attended—second row, far right

CHAPTER 15

NEVER AGAIN

PORT ORCHARD, 1986 (FATHER, FORTY-ONE YEARS OLD)

Stale nicotine mixes with the fresh smoke from a Pall Mall cigarette. Momma changed her brand. I'm over at her house and it's a mess. Construction dust, scrap two-by-fours, and drywall cover the living room floor. I haven't step foot in my mother's house or talked to her for years. Last week she called and I answered. I don't remember what our last argument was about, only that it happened. She has been pissed at me ever since I beat up my little brother Ronnie. It feels good to be back in her good graces.

This morning, Sue is taking all the girls to their family members or friends' homes. Bubba should be at home, mowing the lawn. I think there is enough gas. Hopefully he doesn't run out. With the family tied up on personal errands, it seems like the perfect time to help Momma rebuild a dividing wall.

Ronnie has always been Momma's favorite boy, until he persuaded her to pay him union wages to install a partition in the living room. He didn't have a clue what he was doing. There aren't any bracings. The wall is cockeyed and barely held together. It is worse than a built-to-break movie prop. The first time she leaned up against it, the whole thing came crashing down. My little brother pocketed the cash and took off. He evidently never learned not to hustle a hustler. She was his only lifeline left in this world; it was officially severed.

If you screw over Momma, the details will not be altered or forgotten. She yells longer and louder than any of the Becks. There is no forgiveness. After all, Momma taught all us kids how to hate.

Since my little brother was on the outs and I came to her rescue, I am now the favorite son. Being loved by your parents feels like a warm bath when you are frozen to the bone. I'm sure this is what the foster kids feel like in my home. Fixing her wall only costs fifty bucks. It takes me twelve hours, but at least I get to hang out with family.

Momma tells me several times that she is going to put my name back on her last will and testament. It is an empty gesture, but it means a lot. There are at least seven or eight wills floating around. None of us kids keep track anymore. Dying is the only currency she has left. I don't want her to leave things to me. I just want her to leave some love inside of me. I want to connect.

Ronnie's busted wall and my scrap building material lie in a heap in the back of my truck. It takes only two days to be a hero. The wall is built and painted. I even throw an extra coat on the surrounding walls to cover cigarette-stained paint, so the whole room looks fresh and new.

"Momma, it's done. You can test it."

After a solid once-over, she gives the wall a good shoulder shove, as if taking it by surprise.

It doesn't budge.

She is satisfied.

I clean up while Momma pours me a cup of coffee. On the saucer lie two Peppermint Patties. I am officially in her good graces.

We sip coffee in the quiet room as smoke rises from her cigarette.

My cup is empty. It's time to go.

Momma stands in the doorway, watching as I unlock my truck. A lingering question pops in my mind, one that has not been answered in my lifetime. This may be the only time I get. I leave the keys in the pickup and walk over to my mother.

We stand face-to-face, mother and son.

An awkward silence takes over.

Ill-formed words run into my mouth. I ask, "Momma, do you love me?"

She turns her head away and whispers, "Sure."

I wait until our eyes reconnect. I repeat, "Do you love me?"

With a blank look she replies, "Yeah."

"No, Momma. Do you love me?"

"I love all my children," she says.

I stammer, "But do you love *me*? Do you love your Jimmy?"

Silence. Momma shifts from side to side. Her eyes dart back and forth, like an animal trapped. She keeps looking around.

I wait.

Finally, Momma looks into my eyes and mumbles, "Iwuboo."

"Momma, please tell me."

She drops her head and stares at her feet, shifting uncomfortably.

"I never heard it from dad. I need to hear you say those words at least once."

Toeing loose floorboards, face toward the ground, she says, "I love you."

I throw my arms around her. For the first time in my life, I feel like the happiest boy in the world.

I kiss her cheek.

Her jaw clenches. She stiffens and then relaxes.

Two months later, Momma dies.

CHAPTER 16

DEATH OF A SALESMAN

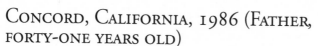

CONCORD, CALIFORNIA, 1986 (FATHER, FORTY-ONE YEARS OLD)

The high life is easy to get used to. For a week, my family has enjoyed the lap of luxury: a heated pool, first-class meals, and star treatment. Sue and I slept on a pillow-top mattress with one-thousand-thread-count sheets. The mansion we are staying at has a high-tech twenty-thousand-dollar alarm system that alerts owners if someone steps on the carpet. It is fancy. This place beats all the KOA campgrounds we stayed at on the drive down. Our Lucky Bus is sturdier than any motor home on the market, but it definitely isn't as swanky as Sue's relatives' place.

Uncle Dick and Aunt Rayetta didn't let me worry about creating an itinerary, figure out sleeping arrangements, cook food, or spend money. They have taken care of everything. I love them.

I'm not use to having family be generous. Our family has two more days of good living before we need to get back on the road. We can't afford to outlive our welcome. That way, we can come back next year. No matter how sweet the deal is, things get messy when you stay too long.

Uncle Dick bought Bubba a new Transformer and each of the girls an outfit. All the kids are upstairs looking at their gifts while we adults kick back in recliners and sip evening tea. It is the perfect night.

Rayetta turns toward me and says, "Everything is going so well. All of your kids listen. Your foster home is a success and your marriage has lasted over thirteen years. James Beck, what is your secret?"

188

The Grahams are full-time marriage counselors, so this is an especially insightful compliment. I pull my wallet and keys out of my blue jeans and place them on the coffee table, next to a tissue box. It's time to get comfortable.

I reply, "Sue and I love each other very much. More importantly, we like each other. If you don't like each other, you can't love each other. However, the secret to the success of our marriage is, we have great communication."

Rayetta claps and says, "You got it. That's it. That is the secret."

The hand clapping is over the top, but my answer is pretty good. Dick quietly sips his tea.

Rayetta looks over at Sue and asks, "Is that how you see it?"

Sue lowers her head and takes in a deep breath—one of her famous dramatic pauses. Then she says, "Well, no…"

Here we go. Sue's gonna try to make a joke.

"…I feel like Jim loves me as much as he can, but I don't think he likes me. He never has. And we have never communicated."

I grin, waiting for a punch line.

I keep waiting.

And waiting.

Sue's antics got old real quick.

I scan the room.

Dick and Rayetta keep looking at Sue as if she is serious.

Instead of laughing, my wife starts crying. After a couple seconds, things begin to sink in. The kids are preoccupied upstairs. Boxes of tissue are strategically placed around the room.

This is a setup!

Sue needs to be put in her damn place. I'm the man of the house. Dick and Rayetta can watch me do it. I don't give a shit. No woman will treat me this way. I'm not a pussy. I won't let her get by with this, not on my watch.

Jumping from my chair, I scream, "How dare you bring me to your family's house and embarrass me like this!"

Rayetta springs to her feet and squares off to me. She says, "Your wife needs your shoulder, not your mouth."

What the hell is going on? She needs my shoulder? Oh really? Then maybe she should have thought about that before she pulled this shit! Sue embarrasses me and expects sympathy. Women are fucking crazy.

Dick is just sitting there, letting his wife do all the work. What a pussy. Now I've got a target on my back because I have a cock hanging between my legs. Sue is crying so everyone sides with her.

Typical.

Fucking typical.

These pricks probably schemed about this all day and now they are having a good laugh. "Look how we pulled one over on stupid James Beck."

I yell, "I don't need this bullshit. Fuck you and fuck this place. I'm outta here!"

I made sure that a curse word was aimed at each of them and stormed out.

WHAM. The front door slams so hard, I look back to check if it came off its hinges.

It didn't. Damn.

There is no way that I am going back to that shithole. I deserve respect. Those assholes need to know who they are dealing with. Damn cocksuckers! I'm not some little pussy boy that can be pushed around. They pissed off the wrong man. I am in control, not them. I can leave anytime I want.

I'm a great dad and a good fucking husband. I provide a roof over everyone's head and food on the table. I've never gone off on a drunken binge, left them stranded. I don't spend all night in taverns and puke on a stranger's lawn. I'm the one who's been helping kids off the street my whole fucking life. Nobody has helped me. I had to do it all on my own. Yeah sure, I have made some mistakes. But who the hell hasn't? At least I've been a better gawdamn father than the one I had.

I jiggle the lever. Our Lucky Bus's back door is locked up tight. Every window and door is secure. MOTHERFUCKER! My keys are on the coffee table, right next to the tissue box. SON OF A BITCH!

I double-check the emergency exit.

It doesn't budge. DAMN IT!

I pat my front pockets for my wallet. My hands plunge into my pockets, searching for cash. They come out empty. COCKSUCKING DICK LICKER!

While pacing up and down the street, I hatch a plan.

All I have to do is grab my wallet and hitchhike home. I'll take a road trip, maybe visit some old friends. I can stay on the road for months. That will teach Sue not to screw with me. She can drive the bus home. See how her lazy ass likes driving a thousand miles. Let her do it since she obviously is the only good parent in our house. She can take care of the damn kids. She won't last five minutes without me. I'll show her.

After two hours, I walk up to the porch. I open the front door half expecting the alarm to go off.

It's still quiet. Sweet. All I need to do is grab a couple things and slip out unnoticed. Freedom is twenty feet away.

"Dad, can I talk to you for a second?" a young, familiar, voice says. I look upstairs. Bubba sits on the landing, waiting. I peer into the living room. My wallet is close.

"What do you need?" I ask.

"Well...I...uh..." Bubba's words come out slower than frozen mayonnaise.

Great. More dramatic pauses, just like Sue. Well, I'm already up for the Shittiest Father of the Year Award. I might as well have one meaningful talk with my son before I leave. It should take only a few minutes.

"Come on, Bub, let's go outside."

We sit down on the cement landing by the front door. Bubba is nervous, staring into his lap. It obviously isn't time to get frustrated, but my patience wears thin. I need to get this show on the road.

"What do you want to talk about?"

"I have to tell you something...something bad."

This grabs my attention. "What is it?" I ask.

"You are going to get really mad at me," he replies.

Bubba's arms start to tremble.

"What did you do?" I ask.

Silence.

Great, he gives me another dramatic pause. Come on, kid, I have to go.

"Son, if you are honest with me and tell me right now, I promise that I will not get mad."

Bubba glances up.

The sooner I get this information, the quicker I can leave. "I give you my word: I will not be angry with you, but only if you tell me now. This is a one-time deal. You know that I will not break my word, right?"

Our eyes meet.

We nod in agreement.

Bubba says, "Do you know the gun that is under your bed? The one in the drawer, underneath the white plastic bag?"

I nod. That revolver is my favorite gun. I keep it next to me when I sleep, for easy access, just in case.

Bubba, you better not have been messing around with it and scratched the handle. This kid is lucky. I can't believe I gave him a free pass on this.

"I put it in my mouth and tried to pull the trigger," Bubba says.

Time stands still.

I heard what my son said, but it can't be right.

Words fail to form. Panic.

"I'm sorry, Dad," Bubba continues.

I stammer. "Why—why did you do that?"

"No one wants me around and I don't want to be around anymore," my son says, staring at his lap.

I need him to look at me. He has to know how much I love him, how much I have always loved him.

"Don't you know I love you?"

"I just get in your way. It seems like you would be happier if I were dead."

Why do you feel like this? You are supposed to be happy. *You are a good boy. You are not supposed to feel...how I feel...how I've always felt. Oh, my God, what have I done?*

Pulling my son in tight, I hug him with all my might. Bubba lets go long before I was ready.

"Dad, thanks for not getting mad at me," he says.

"Of course, son. Can we talk about this in the morning?" I reply.

"Sure," Bubba says with a faint smile.

Climbing the stairs, I wonder what else I am doing wrong. With the covers tucked in around Bubba's shoulders, I kiss him good night.

"I love you, son, remember that. I haven't done a good job showing you, but I really do love you."

"I love you, too," my boy replies, smiling bright, as if he is the happiest boy in the world.

Downstairs, my wallet rests on the coffee table, next to the tissue box. Dick and Rayetta watch me grab it. Sue hides her eyes, crying.

I ask them, "Do any of you know about the conversation I just had with Bubba?"

They exchange glances, clueless.

Maybe it's time to listen.

The last three hours has been a "Jim's an asshole" show. Every time I try to explain myself, Dick or Rayetta says, "Jim, do you see where you are wrong? Do you see how your temper and anger are tearing your family apart?"

At 3:00 a.m. I call an end to the charade and crash on the couch.

I can't sleep.

It is bullshit.

I lie tossing and turning, alone in the dark. I relive the evening's conversations.

My temper isn't a problem. It's an angry world.

Everyone screws up and everyone gets mad. They need to get over it. That snide comment from Rayetta about welfare being able to accomplish what I give my family was out of line. She's a bitch. They ignore all the good that I do. I provide a roof over their head, food, and clothing.

Everyone in my family is a Christian. We all love Jesus. Nobody at church seems to have a problem with me. Those assholes don't take into account the sacrifices I make for them. They act like I'm just like my mom and dad.

Everything I hate about my childhood, they act like I'm doing the same thing to them.

Oh, my God...I am just like my parents.

Fifteen years ago, I had a rifle resting against my head, feeling the way my son feels right now. But he is just little boy and I'm his dad. Raising him is my responsibility. I caused this. The only thing I've ever wanted was to be different than my father.

I failed.

I repeated my dad's cycle.

My son is probably going to repeat it again.

And then his son is going to repeat it again.

Or I can stop it!

Whatever it takes, I will break this cycle.

I'm not sure how, but I can learn. I just need some tools.

Dick and Rayetta have books I can read. They can give me advice.

I'll fix the obvious things and then learn as I go. It will be just like building the log house with my Foxfire manuals.

I'll make a list and look at it every day. I might not know how to be a good father, but I know what lists are.

Nothing is as complicated as it seems. I just have to figure it out. No matter what it takes, I have to change.

A pad of paper lies on the coffee table. I pull off a couple pieces: one for Sue and one for Bubba. After writing a few things down, I tuck them into my wallet and fall asleep.

The next morning, I nudge Sue. "Honey, I want you to know that I am sorry. I realize that the last thirteen years haven't been easy on you, but I am going spend the rest of my life making it up to you. I'll learn how to be a good husband. Things are going to be different this time. I'm going to change. I promise."

We hug and kiss.

It annoys me that I am saying the same bullshit lines my father told to me, but no other words seem to fit. The difference is, I am a man of my word.

I rush over to the office, where Bubba sleeps. He is already up, making his bed.

"Bubba, can I talk to you for a second?"

"Yes, sir. What do you need?"

I take two steps forward.

Bubba takes two steps back. His hands tremble.

Why is he afraid?

I say, "I thought about our conversation last night. It isn't your fault. It is my fault. You deserve a good dad. I don't know how to be a father, but I can learn. I'm going to spend the rest of my life making it up to you. I promise."

Bubba gives a forced smile. "Thanks, Dad."

My son is being cordial. I can tell he isn't convinced. The reply is obligatory. Doubt is still etched on his face.

I take a step forward. Bubba backs up even further. His arms shake.

Even now my son is terrified. Bubba has to know I am serious about this. How can I make him believe?

"Bubba, tell me one thing I can do that will let you know that I'm serious, that I am going to change. Ask anything of me and I'll do it."

"Dad, you never will," Bubba respectfully replies.

"Try me." I look at my son and wait.

Bubba takes a step toward me, but remains out of arm's reach. He says, "Dad, if I never have to work with you for the rest of my life...that would be good."

"Done," I reply.

Bubba takes a few seconds, staring at me as if I were an alien. His hands no longer shake.

All of a sudden, Bubba runs toward me and throws his arms around me. He grips my shoulders tight and doesn't let go. I'm not sure if this means my son believes me, but I hope it does.

(Son)

Yesterday, I watched my dad try to break into the Lucky Bus. He walked up and down the street and cursed the wind for at least a half hour. I'm not sure why I waited so long at the top of that staircase or why I didn't have any anxiety. Usually, his rage ties me in knots.

I wasn't nervous or upset.

I didn't *feel* anything.

It was peaceful.

I was tired of being scared.

I didn't care anymore. If nobody wanted me around, I would go. We put down suffering animals all the time. Using a gun makes the most sense. After all, I am a country boy and I'm comfortable with guns.

Panic was in the past.

After I made the decision to take my life, it was easy to control my emotions. When my father slipped inside the door, I wanted to tell him how he made me feel. I didn't want to hurt anyone, but I didn't want to feel my pain anymore and didn't care how I accomplished it.

The whole thing was simple: Do you love me or not?

I have been hit, screamed at, and told I am stupid my whole life.

I'm not having fun.

I am finished.

I want to be done.

I want to die.

Dad told me that he loved me, but I never felt it.

A man's word is his bond.

I don't understand.

My father seems to want to make things better.

I need answers that make sense. The conversation I had with him last night was not a call for help. It was "last call." If I still wish to end my life, tomorrow is as good as today. Waiting makes sense. It doesn't cost me anything, except time. Maybe he does love me. Time will tell. I will give him one more chance. After all, it's what a good boy is supposed to do.

CHAPTER 17

ROCKY ROAD

TACOMA, WASHINGTON, 1986 (SON, ELEVEN YEARS OLD)

After we get back from California, fixing our relationship becomes priority number one. Dad shows me how he loves me all the time and goes overboard. It's annoying.

I'm not complaining.

It's just weird to be asked, "How do you feel?" several times a day as if I were about to spontaneously combust.

I answer, "Fine."

"Really? Are you really fine?" he questions over and over again.

Let's see, you haven't screamed at me for a month, which is cool. I don't have to work around you, which is awesome. Whenever you start being an asshole, you walk into the woods and yell at the trees. It seems crazy, but I appreciate it. You want to be buddy-buddy all the time, which is uncomfortable. But I'd rather have the new you than the old you. All in all, things are fine.

"Yeah, Dad, things are fine," I reply.

It is awkward talking to the man you are trying to learn not to hate. Until last month I spent my life avoiding my father and walked on eggshells when he was around. Now he walks on eggshells around me.

It is freaky.

His rage still flares up from time to time, but he walks away and deals with it on his own. I notice.

There are few times he starts to ask for my help and then suddenly "forgets what he is saying." A few minutes later, Mom completes the request that Dad "forgot." It is always a reasonable house chore, scheduled when Dad is at the fire station.

It is cool that he tries.

It makes me love him.

Mom told me that Dad has a list in his wallet that has to do with me, but I've never seen it.

Life is good. We'll see how long this lasts.

It's early Saturday morning. Dad and I sit in a smelly gymnasium as silverware scrape against plates. Over a hundred fathers and sons sit around tables, wolfing down sausage links and flapjacks covered in imitation maple syrup. The makeshift buffet line is packed with those getting second helpings of eggs and bacon. Latecomers file in.

When Pastor Buntain announced that the church was having its annual father-son breakfast, my dad was the first to sign up.

The tables in the gym hold social circles. Church leaders and rich businessmen sit closest to the stage. Sports enthusiasts, outdoor adventurers, and small business owners take up the middle section. Blue-collar workers and those of us who live out in the boondocks sit in the back. The gathered crowd joins in song.

All to Jesus, I surrender
Lord, I give myself to Thee
Fill me with Thy love and power
Let Thy blessing fall on me

Hymn time mixes prepubescent screeches from young boys with mature hums from their fathers. Those who never memorized the words can't be bothered to read it off the projector and continue to hum.

Forks shovel last-minute bits into hungry mouths. Volunteers dismantle the buffet line. Plates are put into dish tubs, pulled from the tables. One by one, we stand and sing together.

I surrender all
I surrender all
All to Thee, my blessed Savior
I surrender all

A balding guy hops up on the stage sporting a toothy grin and windbreaker. The way he bellies up to the podium suggests that he is the speaker of the day.

My father likes leaders spit-shined, with trimmed hair, polished shoes, and a silk tie. This guy is not his type of leader. Dad is unimpressed.

The speaker says, "Good morning, everyone. I'm glad you all came out on this Father's Day weekend." He motions to a couple of men in the back. All volunteers file out of the room in an orchestrated fashion.

A projector clicks on. Words fill a fifteen-foot screen.

THE TEST

(Keep answers covered. Five points for each right answer)

1. Favorite ice cream?
2. Favorite type of food?
3. Favorite color?
4. Favorite pet?
5. Favorite family game?
6. Favorite movie?
7. Favorite TV show?
8. Your nickname at school/work?
9. Favorite vacation?
10. Favorite toy?
11. Next place you want to visit?
12. Person you look up to most?
13. Favorite restaurant?
14. Last movie you watched?
15. Who is your best friend?
16. Favorite type of candy?
17. Favorite sport?
18. Three crushes you've had?

The speaker says, "I'd like everyone to grab paper and a pencil. We are going to take a test. It's an easy test. Answer the questions as honestly as you can and don't let anyone see what you write, because you are competing."

Pencils across the room write on slips of paper. Arms guard scribbled words, each test a miniature Fort Knox. Fathers and sons write out their lives, each trying to finish before the other.

Once all the pencils relax, the speaker tells us, "Turn your papers over and keep it hidden. Husbands, if you didn't add your wives as one of your three crushes, now is the time to do it. This is your scorecard. Now I want all the fathers to guess what their sons wrote. Sons in the room, let's see if you know more about your dad than he knows about you. You have ten minutes."

The room falls silent.

Only the sound of pencils etching into parchment can be heard.

I glance up, trying to catch a cheater. My eyes lock with my dad's. He asks, "What you writing?"

"Nothing." We grin at each other.

Favorite ice cream: Rocky Road

Favorite type of food: Mexican

Favorite color: blue

Favorite family game: UNO

Three crushes: Annette Funicello, Patty Murphy, and Mom

The test is over. All answers are final.

(FATHER)

FINISHED!

I slap my pencil onto the table announcing my test's completion. All the other men in the room are still writing.

I finished first! Who's the man? Me!

I'm the man.

James Beck knows kids better than anyone else in the room. This test was a piece of cake. I probably got 85 percent, maybe 90 percent. Bubba doesn't like girls yet; they can't penalize me for that.

My son and I exchange papers while others are still finishing their quizzes.

Losers.

Rocky Road is my favorite ice cream. Correct. Jimbo was my nickname. Correct. Why did Bubba leave "Person you look up to most" blank? Abraham Lincoln is the obvious answer; he built a log cabin. I'll mark that wrong. "Next place you want to visit" and he guessed Hawaii? I made that one up, lucky guess. Correct. Bubba got my three crushes right. Four wrong gives my boy an 80 percent. He gets a B.

We exchange tests.

What? Thirty-five percent? This is bullshit!

There is no way I scored a thirty-five!

I gave him an 80 percent.

That little cheater looked off my paper.

I grab Bubba's answer key and skim the page.

Why did I put GI Joes next to his favorite toy?

"Bubba, I know you love Transformers more than GI Joe. You gotta give me this one."

My son circles it right, bringing me up to 40 percent.

Okay, what else did Bubba mark wrong? Skip-Bo is not his favorite game.

"You like UNO better than Skip-Bo. You beat us at it every night. It's not fair to change answers last minute just because we are taking a test."

My son nods in agreement and I correct his mistake, bringing the score to 45 percent.

Green? Why does he like green?

"Seriously, son, green? Blue is a much better color than green. You wear blue jeans. The sky is blue. Blue goes with everything. It is a much better color."

Bubba marks "blue" correct.

One more right answer, I am up to 50 percent. What else does my son have wrong?

"Bubba, you put mint chocolate chip as your favorite type of ice cream. Your favorite is Rocky Road. Everyone knows that."

(SON)
Oh, hell no!

I don't mind giving Dad a bump in his score for getting Transformers wrong. Hopefully, he will finally get it right at Christmastime.

I like UNO and understand why he would think it is my favorite game. However, I like Skip-Bo more. But nobody ever wants to play Skip-Bo.

Blue and green are a toss-up. I like green more, but not by much.

However, I hate Rocky Road ice cream. Hell will freeze over before I budge on that.

I respond in a firm, yet respectful, tone, "My favorite *is* mint chocolate chip."

Dad screws up his face. "What are you talking about? We never get mint chocolate chip. Every time we go to the grocery store, we pick up a gallon of Rocky Road. You have it all the time because that is your favorite ice cream!"

I whisper back, "No, Dad, *your* favorite ice cream is Rocky Road. We have it all the time because *you* like it. *My* favorite is mint chocolate chip."

(FATHER)
So what if I don't know my son's favorite ice cream. That doesn't mean anything. Screw this windbreaker asshole. Look how fat he is. They let anyone speak in church these days. What are his credentials? He's probably some washed-up, has-been preacher who can't cut it in a real church. Hey, buddy, do these little side events remind you of the glory days? Gluttony is a sin! Write it down and hop on a treadmill.

I lean over.

"Bubba, these questions are stupid. This is a waste of time and the test doesn't prove anything. I've been around kids my whole life and one thing is for sure: I know kids."

My son whispers back, "Yeah, Dad, you know kids, but you don't know me. You don't know Bubba."

Breathable air can't be found.

My test has *50%* written at the top, near a scratched-out *45%*, *40%*, and *35%*. At the bottom of his test are three names: Jami Van Meter, Hayley Cole, and Shannon Murphy. I didn't think my boy even liked girls and yet these are his crushes.

Bubba is right. I have no idea who he is.

Test in hand, I scratch out *50%* and write *35%* at the top.

I pull a significantly smaller piece of paper from my wallet. The note unfolds. I conceal it in my palm. I read over the to-do list I made in California, a month ago. A pencil etches in a fifth entry at the bottom.

> Bubba To-Do List
> 1. Do not yell at Bubba.
> 2. Do not ask my son to work with me.
> 3. Find fun things we can do together.
> 4. Listen to his feelings.
> 5. Learn who Bubba is.

The note slides into my wallet. The guy in the windbreaker doesn't seem to bother me anymore. After the service, I'm going to thank him.

The last few hours of Father's Day slip into the night. Today is 'my day' and I am the biggest fraud I know. I can't get the damn test score out of my head: 35 percent.

Nothing lasts forever and maybe that is a good thing.

With my hands full, I give Bubba's bedroom door a solid kick. It swings open faster than I expect, hitting the wall.

He jumps. A Transformer falls from his grip.

It's funny how skittish Bubba is.

"Dad, what's wrong?" he asks.

Silence.

It's my turn to give him a dramatic pause.

"What did I do?" Bubba asks, squirming.

"What do you mean?" I wonder out loud.

Why does Bubba always think he did something wrong?

The longer I stand, the more nervous my son gets. He evaluates my every move, backing away.

"Seriously, what did I do?" Bubba asks again, shoulders trembling.

"Everything is fine." I try to calm him.

Of course Bubba thinks he did something wrong. Every time I come into his room, I yell at him. Now I'm in his room. He is waiting for me to be the old Jim. But that guy is dead; I plan on keeping it that way.

(Son)

My shoulders are against the wall; there isn't anywhere else to move. My father is ready to explode. I knew it was a matter of time before things went back to normal. I can already hear him scream in the back of my head.

Instead of Dad turning red and yelling, he becomes quiet, nervously shifting from side to side.

I remain still, waiting for his next move.

My father hands me a large bowl filled with mint chocolate chip ice cream. "I wanted to bring you this. It's Breyers, the good stuff. The green ice cream is just food coloring, this is the best."

I take the bowl and eat a bit, wondering if this moment is real. Dad keeps shifting back and forth, looking uncomfortably into his bowl of Rocky Road ice cream, holding his breath.

"Do you like it?" he asks.

I take another bite.

"Dad, it's perfect."

For the next few hours, we talk about all the test questions Dad missed. He tells me he still likes Skippy peanut butter because of Annette Funicello and has been following her since she was on the *Mickey Mouse Club*.

I tell him that I have been trying to work up the nerve to talk to Jami VanMeter, the cutest girl at Key Peninsula Middle School.

"Why don't you get her flowers?" he asks.

"I don't know. Why do girls like flowers?"

Dad chuckles.

"No idea. It's best not to waste your time trying to figure out girls. Just know that you can't go wrong with a box of chocolates and a bouquet of flowers. Do you want me to help you pick some out?"

"Sure," I reply.

My dad suddenly feels like a secret weapon.

"Poetry works too, but—" he looks at his watch "—it's after midnight. We'll save the poetry lesson for another time. I have to work tomorrow and you have to get up early for school."

Dad collects our bowls and heads for the bedroom door.

I didn't want him to leave.

He pauses and asks, "Bubba, how am I doing?"

"What do you mean?" I ask.

"How am I doing as your dad? If I do good, I want to keep doing good. If I screw something up, I want to stop screwing up, fast. I don't want to find out months later. I need to learn and the only way I will learn quickly is if you teach me. So, how am I doing?"

"Do you want me to give you a grade, like in school?" I ask.

"Yeah, why not? It can stay between us. We don't have to tell anyone. It can be our secret. I don't know how to be a good man, but maybe we can learn how to be good men together. Give me whatever grade you think I deserve."

"I don't know what you deserve," I reply.

It feels awkwardly empowering, grading the man I fear.

"Son, you'll never get in or out of trouble for the grade you give me. Just give me a grade for the week and explain why I got that grade. Can you do that?"

He's going to be pissed if I don't give him an A.

"Dad, you got a B this week." I brace for the aftermath.

"Really, I have a B?" he says.

Oh, shit. Here it comes. I should have given him an A.

Instead of a face flushed with purple-red anger, tears rolls down his cheeks.

"Are you mad at me?" I ask.

"No, I'm not mad. B is a pretty good grade for me. The last time I was this happy was the day you were born."

CHAPTER 18

"B" TOGETHER

KEY PENINSULA MIDDLE SCHOOL, WASHINGTON, 1988 (SON, THIRTEEN YEARS OLD)

Turkey feathers dangle from the crown of my head down to the small of my back. Stripes of red clay cross my cheeks, arms, and chest—war paint. In one hand I hold a tomahawk and a door handle in the other, waiting for a cue—the beat of a drum.

I'm ready for battle.

Eighth-grade graduation is quickly approaching. After this summer, I'll be a freshman in high school. The only hurdle in a passing Social Sciences is this oral report. If I get below a C, I will be grounded for a month. However, Dad and I researched the project together. We developed the perfect speech, so I have nothing to fear.

He told me, "It's all about the delivery. Hook them with the entrance, keep up the energy, and when they beg you for more, hit them with a closer."

Book reports and essays are Mom's territory, but public speaking is Dad's domain. After I told Dad that Mrs. Smith let us select the topic for our oral report, he told me to do one on the Yucca Indians. I had no idea what to pick. Because my father volunteered to help, his suggestion was what we went with. After weeks of preparation, we wrote the speech and even perfected the authentic Yucca Indian human sacrifice dance with full costume: headdress, war paint, and weapons.

BUM, BUM, BUM. The drum's rhythmic bass reaches into the hallway. Turning the metal handle, I enter the classroom in full regalia, dancing just like

I had practiced: two clockwise circles with head up, one counterclockwise circle with head down.

BUM, BUM, BUM. The dance leads me center stage and I began my tale:

We Yucca Indians depend on maize, beans, and pumpkins for survival. Every year, we choose a human to sacrifice during the spring, when we sow our crops. Man or woman, it doesn't matter. We dress them in the most costly garments, fatten them on the choicest food, and keep them ignorant of their doom.
    BUM, BUM, BUM.
    Once the sacrifice is fat enough, we bind them to a cross in front of the whole tribe. Then we dance, two circles to the right for the summer solstice and one to the left for the winter solstice.

BUM, BUM, BUM. I dance the circles three times. The drum stops. I let out a bloodcurdling scream and chuck the rubber tomahawk across the room.
    WHACK. It hits the far wall.
    Everyone jumps!

It is I, the chief, who cuts off the victim's head with my tomahawk. My warriors shoot them with arrows. As the blood runs freely, squaws grease the shovels with flesh blood. This makes the great sun god happy. Afterward, the whole tribe dips their farm equipment in the blood and heads out into the field to plant our crops.

Turning away from the classroom, the headdress comes off with the swipe of my hand. Dragging on a flannel, using my sleeves to smear the war paint across my face prepares the next character: a trader.
    I pull out my inner hillbilly and continue.

On April 14, 1837, I remember going up to do some trading with them Yuccas. They had a fourteen-year-old Sioux girl and they treated her real nice up 'til they killed her. Warriors led that poor li'l gal from wigwam to wigwam. At each lodge she got a dab o' paint and some wood. Her body was colored half red and half black. Then those savages strung her up on a gibbet, shot her full of arrows. Poor thing.

The head chief ripped her heart out and ate it in front of the whole tribe. Scared me half to death. Afterward, they cut her up and planted her parts out in the cornfields. The chief dipped grains of corn in her blood and planted 'em. The rest of the tribe did the same, till all the seeds have been covered in blood and rested in the dirt.

The class erupts with applause. A few guys in the back row crack jokes about my feather costume and war paint. All they brought was a stupid mock village made from Popsicle sticks that you have to lean over to see. The tribe they studied didn't even have a real war dance.

At the end of class, Mrs. Smith brings me up to her desk. She says, "Bubba, I really liked your costume and the dance was great. Your speech was very entertaining. Could you spell the name of the tribe you studied?"

"Sure, Yucca. Y-U-C-C-A."

The teacher leans back in her chair and says, "Oh, that explains it. I thought you were doing the Aucas from Ecuador. They have a vicious culture, too."

Hmm, Dad told me that Y-U-C-C-A is the correct spelling. There are so many tribes, it's probably tough to keep track.

Mrs. Smith keeps on, "There is a Yucca Valley near Joshua Tree, but I don't remember ever hearing about any Yucca Indians. Where is this tribe located?"

"The jungle."

Is she trying to trap me? Ha! I've done my research. I might not be able to recall everything Dad told me, but I remember enough.

"I think I remember reading that the Yucca Valley got its name from this tribe. They also had a different type of tomahawk, but this rubber one is safe for school."

I didn't know what I was saying, but everything coming out of my mouth seems to make sense.

I'm surprised Mrs. Smith never heard of the Yucca Indians before. It is such a prominent tribe with a rich and colorful history.

"My costume isn't exactly what they wore. I did my best with what I could find."

The teacher nods her head in understanding. "One of your characters was a 'trader.' What kind of trader was he and where did you source your story?" she asks.

"I read about a trader in a book. He exchanged animal skins with the tribe. My dad said it would be more fun to switch things up and actually speak as the trader," I tell her.

"I agree with your dad. Which books did you use?"

"Library books, I don't know. They are already turned back in."

I don't have any library books at home, so by process of elimination, I must have turned them back in. Who cares which books I used. My dad just talked me through the whole thing…Oh shit!

Mrs. Smith focuses on a clipboard, writing.

Think, Bubba, think. What is that tribe we studied in Sunday school?

"I remember something about a neighboring tribe murdering some missionaries. I think they were the Aucas."

From the looks of it, my comment struck gold.

"Yes, that was the tribe I thought you were doing a report on," Mrs. Smith replies.

"I can ask my mom to check those books out from the library, if it will help."

The teacher nods, scribbling on the evaluation sheet. All of the sudden, I feel stupid in my dirty overalls and smudged face.

Mrs. Smith hands me the clipboard; a large B hangs in the top corner of the paper. "It is very important to reference your sources."

"I understand," I reply.

You can meet my source at the last parent–teacher conference. I'm sure he'll be happy to demonstrate an authentic Yucca Indian war dance for you.

"Bubba, if you would have documented your sources, you would have gotten an A."

I doubt it.

I shoot her a grin.

VAUGHN, WASHINGTON (AFTER SCHOOL)

The high-pitched whine of my father's chainsaw echoes through the trees. Even though it's been a couple years since I've worked around my dad, the sound of his saw still makes my blood boil.

I march toward the noise, pissed.

I'm never asking Dad to help me again. He can keep his "fun version of history." I'll stick with the facts.

Deep in the forest, Dad cuts a tree into stove-size logs. Upon seeing me, he kills the engine.

"Hey, Bub, how did it go today?"

"Is there even a Yucca tribe?"

"Of course there is. Why do you ask?"

"My teacher never heard of it. She heard of the Aucas, but was certain that the Yuccas never existed."

Dad chuckles. "Well, I might have mixed up a few details. If there isn't a Yucca tribe, then there should have been. What grade did you get?"

"I got a B."

"That's great."

No, not great. I danced around like an idiot, talking about a tribe that never existed. You and your stupid "two circles this way and one circle that way."

"The teacher was upset that I didn't cite my sources."

"Aw, what fun would that be?"

"Dad, it wasn't true."

"True? I might have mixed up the details from a few different tribes, but it was all true. Those stories are real. We just took the interesting parts from a few different tribes and put the best stuff together. It's what movies do all the time. If they can do it, you can too."

"But this was for school," I reply.

"People remember things that are fun. I bet you that your speech is the only one those kids remember. It's not going to hurt anyone to add a few juicy details and spiced it up a bit. You got a B. We had a great time putting it together. That's what counts. I'm proud of you."

Dad hangs his head, concealing a grin.

He asks, "So, what grade do I get this week?"

"This week, you get an F," I say.

"Why do I get an F? We got a B together. I helped you pass your class. You have to at least give me the same grade you got."

Maybe he's right. Everything did work out.

I'll always remember it.

The project was fun and we did get a B together.

Maybe that is what's really important.

Posturing up, I tell him, "All right, fine. You get a B this week, but only because that is the grade I got. Otherwise, you would have gotten an F."

Dad laughs. "I told you, 'It's all in the delivery.' Was I right?"

"Yeah, you were right."

CHAPTER 19

THE PLAN

PURDY, WASHINGTON, 1988 (SON, THIRTEEN YEARS OLD)

The halls of Peninsula High School host hundreds of students. They all cross paths before their next class. With more than twelve hundred students, this public school holds the promise of freedom. As a thirteen-year-old, under five feet tall and a hundred pounds, the idea of liberty is limited. Being the smallest and youngest kid in the student body comes with disadvantages. I am unable to blend in.

A couple days ago, riffling through my locker, I looked for an English notebook. The registrar's office assigned me a full-size locker in the seniors' hallway. Most lockers are half size, about three feet tall. Mine is big, really big, six feet tall.

SLAM. A heavy hand pounds against a neighboring locker.

I jump.

A thick, hairy arm leads to a broad shoulder, then to a scruffy face. Marcos Martinez, a senior football player, towers over me. He weighs more than two hundred pounds and is rumored to have a couple tattoos.

His lips move slow and deliberate. "What's your name, boy?"

Stunned, I remain perfectly still.

"I said, 'What's your name?'"

"Bub—Bub—Bubba. Bubba Beck," I reply.

Marcos leans in close. "Bubba Beck, huh? Why does a little runt like you have a locker in my hallway?"

"I d—don't know. They just gave it to me at the registrar's office."

"They did, huh?" he says.

I nod, a victim of circumstance.

Marcos asks, "Do you like your locker?"

I nod again.

Until that moment, I liked it very much.

He presses in close. "Do you want to stay in your locker?"

"Yes, s—s—sir," I reply.

"You called me sir. Good. I want you to stay there, too." Marcos leans back and smiles.

I smile back.

All of a sudden, the star football player picks me up and shoves me in my locker.

The door locks.

It's dark.

Claustrophobic metal walls make it hard to move. Slivers of light illuminate the cramped box. A group of guys laugh as they walk away. I hear Marcos say, "He called me sir. What a little pussy."

I reach toward the lock and feel a thin lever.

I wait for the hallways to clear.

RING. Class starts.

Pushing the lever causes the locker door to pop open. I grab my gear and head off to English, my least favorite class.

The classroom door opens. Mrs. Crommit, my English teacher, a skinny intellectual, is returning our latest writing assignment as I enter.

She continues to hand out papers without looking in my direction. She says, "Hello, James. Glad you could finally make it."

A girl in the back of the class shouts, "His name is Bubba."

Mrs. Crommit eyes me as I sit down and asks, "Is 'Bubba' the name on your birth certificate?"

"No. My sister couldn't say 'baby brother' and said 'Bubba.' So that's what I go by," I reply.

"Well, I call people by their official name. So I will call you James."

Fine, I will call you Vomit. If you won't call me by the name I choose, then I won't call you by the name you choose. Quid pro quo.

I hate Vomit's class more than anything. She tells us "Write down what you feel, organize it later."

How am I supposed to organize what I don't understand? I don't know what I feel. Why do feelings matter?

In Vomit's class, I artistically diagram sentences to make lists of words look like beetles. With essays and book reports, I might as well load commas, colons, and periods into a musket and shoot them onto the page and let physics decide where they land. Punctuation is for decoration.

Mrs. Vomit beckons me to her desk, holding my latest paper.

I approach.

"James, did you even rewrite this assignment? It seems as though you just reprinted what you turned in the first time."

Mustering a sincere tone, I said, "I did my best."

My best for Vomit's class meant waiting until the night before and creating a great first draft. I suck at English, so rewrites are a waste of time. Once a paper lands on a teacher's desk, it might as well be in God's hands.

Please, God, let me get a B. If I get an A, I promise to become a minister. Give me at least a C so my grade doesn't drop any lower. I ask this in Jesus's name. Amen.

Mrs. Vomit hands me my paper. It has a D written on the front.

God, what ever happened to "Ask and ye shall receive"?

I guess you don't want me to be a minister.

Mrs. Vomit says, "You are late. Where were you?"

Embarrassed, I lean in and reply, "In my locker."

"James, you have just as much time as anyone else. Why can't you get to class on time?"

"I was *in* my locker. A senior shoved me *in* my locker and locked me inside. I came to class as soon as I could."

Vomit eyes the classroom; everyone is looking at his/her paper. She points at my D and says, "I am being too magnanimous with you."

"I know." I want to leave.

"No, you don't know. At this rate, you won't pass my class," she says.

"I promise to try harder." I grab my paper and take my seat.

After class, the English paper finds residence in the nearest trash bin.

A ceiling fan rhythmically squeaks overhead, circulating stale air around the congregation. It's Wednesday night and the auditorium is half full. My parents decided that Life Center church in Tacoma is too far to drive.

If Chapel by the Sea is open, my family attends: Sunday morning and evening service, Tuesday night youth group, and Wednesday night church. We are faithful. The only reason our church can brag is in the title: it's by the sea. We have to go somewhere and it is the closest church. That is the only reason we attend. It's definitely not for the people. There are no cute girls, it smells like mothballs, and the pastor is boring.

Nobody knows who the youth pastor is at Chapel by the Sea because we don't have one. Deacons rotate through our Sunday school class and give us lame messages: just say no to drugs, sex is bad, rock music is of the Devil, and Jesus saves. The best days in church are those random Sunday mornings when the adults forget to schedule someone for our Sunday school class. About eight of us kids get to hang out for an hour, which is pretty cool. At night, everyone remains in the sanctuary, which sucks.

The pastor's wife sits at the pipe organ and hits a few notes. The congregation rises. Voices join in song.

Onward, Christian soldiers, marching as to war,
With the cross of Jesus going on before.
Christ, the royal Master, leads against the foe;
Forward into battle see His banners go!

My latest lobby is, switch attendance to Lakebay Community Church. That place is awesome. They have a cool youth pastor and go on missions trips to Mexico. It is packed full of hot girls. I figure that if we are going to heaven, it will be a lot more fun with beautiful chicks. All the popular kids at Peninsula High School go to Lakebay Community Church. Maybe if I get in good with some of the Christian football players, they can tell that meathead Marcos to leave me alone.

When Rachel entered the sixth grade, she and I persuaded Mom and Dad to let us attend public school so we wouldn't become weird homeschooled kids like some of our friends. They seem socially awkward, stuck in their country bumpkin roots. Dad was on board; Mom took convincing. We struck a deal at a family meeting: no more foster kids and Rachel and I get to go to public school. It was a give-and-take for the parents, but a win-win for us kids.

The preacher's wife sways as she pounds on the pipe organ. Latecomers file in as singing parishioners scoot toward the center aisle. Voices from neighboring families blend with the group.

> *Onward, Christian soldiers, marching as to war,*
> *With the cross of Jesus going on before.*
> *Like a mighty army moves the church of God;*
> *Brothers, we are treading where the saints have trod.*

After school, I attempt a preemptive strike on my upcoming progress report. After Mrs. Vomit gave me the heads-up on my upcoming D, I figure that Dad is the best one to turn to because we are finally friends. Being the head of the household gives him the strongest veto power when it comes to punishments.

He sits at his gun reloading station, measuring gunpowder.

"Hey, Dad, I think I have a problem."

"Yeah, what's that?" he says.

"I'm not getting a very good grade in English."

"How bad is it?" Dad meticulously fills a shell with gunpowder and turns toward me.

"I'm getting a D," I reply.

"Ouch. It's probably better to warn us this way than to shock us with a report card," he says.

"Can you help me? You got straight As in high school."

He laughs, hiding a grin. "I think it is better for your mom to help you with this."

"Why can't you tell me how you passed English? I'll do it the same way."

My father laughs again. "The curriculum nowadays is quite a bit different from when I attended school. Trust me, Bub, when it comes to teachers, Mom is a wiser person to follow."

I can't understand why my dad is avoiding my request. He usually jumps at the chance to help me. One by one, he presses primers into shells. I stand by and watch.

"Is there anything else I can do for you?" he asks.

"Yeah, can we try out another church?"

"That is a big request coming from someone who is about to be grounded. Have you asked Mom?"

"No. I was hoping you would."

Dad gives a disgruntled look. "I'm all for it. It would be a great change of pace to try something new, but I am the wrong person to ask. If anyone is able to get Mom to switch churches, it's you. Why don't you like Chapel by the Sea?"

"The youth group sucks. I never learn anything," I say.

"There aren't any cute girls either. If you are going to convince Mom, you'll need to come up with something good. She loves Chapel by the Sea."

"What do I need to say?" I ask.

Dad puts down his bullets and gives me a grin.

A few minutes later, I walk downstairs. Mom is sitting in her recliner, making notes in her Bible, sipping evening tea.

"Mom, can I talk to you?"

She puts down her Bible. "Of course."

"I'm not doing well in English and I need your help. I don't understand it."

"Well, Bub, I'd love to help you."

"I should have come to you earlier. I tried to do it on my own, but it hasn't worked. I'm going to be on restriction when my progress report comes out. I just want to get my grade up before the end of the semester."

Mom gives a gleeful smile, like she just received a new pony. She says, "Why don't you bring me your assignments every night and we'll go through them. It'll be fun."

"Thanks, I appreciate it," I say.

"Any time." Mom picks up her Bible and goes back to reading.

With my back turned, I wait in the doorway, just like Dad instructed.

Eventually, Mom glances up and asks, "Is there anything else?"

I wait for a few moments, giving her a pregnant pause, and then turn.

"Mom, do you learn anything...from church?"

Mom volleys back her own dramatic pause, closing her Bible. Her voice slows in a soothing, concerned way. "What do you mean?"

"I sometimes wish I could just stay home and learn the Bible from you. You are a lot more interesting than Pastor Altig."

By the size of Mom's smile, the compliment sparked her internal happy dance. "It is important that Christians gather together. The Bible says, 'Forsake not the assembly.' We can't stop going to church."

"I know. I just wish I learned more. Some of my friends talk about all the great things they are learning at Lakebay Community Church. At Chapel by the Sea, I can barely stay awake."

"Maybe you just need to get more sleep?" she suggests.

"You're probably right. By the way, what does *magnanimous* mean?"

She lights up and answers, "*Magnanimous* means extra generous, exceptionally kind or forgiving."

"So if someone was too magnanimous?" I ask.

"They would be too generous. Why? Is that going to be on a vocabulary test?"

"Yeah, probably," I reply, irritated at Mrs. Vomit.

The congregation sings on. Mom and Dad belt out the hymn, echoing in my ear.

Onward, Christian soldiers, marching as to war,
With the cross of Jesus going on before.
Crowns and thrones may perish, kingdoms rise and wane,
But the church of Jesus constant will remain.

Noise from the squeaking ceiling fan replaces the organ music. Pastor Altig takes the podium. He says in a meek tone, "Folks, I am not a great speaker. I'm not even a good speaker."

Everyone laughs. This is true.

The pastor continues, "When I was in college, I hated speaking in front of people. To this day, I still get white knuckles."

He lifts his hands and shows the congregation his knuckles; they are bleach white.

The crowd laughs louder.

Mom leans over and whispers into Dad's ear.

He nods and returns a whisper.

A few seconds later, Dad and I lock eyes.

He gives me a wink and a grin.

We are going to Lakebay. Dad's plan was flawless. He gets an A this week.

Pastor Altig continues, "I remember being inside my college dorm, looking into the heavens, and saying 'God, there is one thing I will never do: I will never be a pastor.' Be careful when you tell God that you *won't* do something with your life. The omnipotent Creator has a funny way of turning the universe on its head and getting you to do the one thing you tell Him you won't do."

Squeaks from the ceiling fan get louder.

I'll be grounded soon.

Mrs. Vomit issued another writing assignment. It's due next week. Dread fills my heart, wondering how I will ever get a passing grade in English.

Looking up into the heavens, I defiantly whisper, "God, I will never be a writer."

I grin.

I sense something grin back.

CHAPTER 20

A JEDI'S LIGHTSABER

VAUGHN, WASHINGTON, 1991 (SON, SIXTEEN YEARS OLD)

Four years ago, back when our log home was only half finished, Mom would have me drop off lunch for Dad. She would sit in the car and wave me inside. By the smile on her face, she couldn't hear Dad yelling obscenities inside.

I would stand in the doorway, nervous to approach. Even though I was no longer working around my father, it still felt uncomfortable being around him. With my heart racing, adrenaline pumping, his lunch would tremble in my grasp.

I would round the corner.

Dad wouldn't notice.

One time I caught him screaming at a pile of two-by-sixteen boards, "Stupid pieces of shit!"

He had kicked one of the boards pretty hard.

"Ow, mother son of a bitch. Damn it!" Hobbling around, he noticed me.

Anger shifts to embarrassment.

"Sorry, Bub. I thought I was alone."

"It's okay. Mom and I brought you lunch," I replied.

Dad smiled.

Anxiety dissipated.

(FATHER, FOUR YEARS AGO)

I feel stupid, getting caught yelling at lumber. When it comes to cutting wood, fault lies with the person behind the equipment.

The second log house we built

Sue waves up at us from the car.

I wave back and shoot her a grin, hiding my embarrassment. I ask **Bubba**, "Do you think she heard me?"

"No," he replies.

"Can we keep this between us?" I ask.

"Sure. Why are you so mad?" Bubba says.

"These boards cost twenty bucks apiece and I've already ruined seven." I am at my wit's end.

"What are you trying to do?" my son asks.

"Make a staircase. The boards have to be cut perfectly equal. There are so many cuts, it's impossible to do." Frustrated, I sit on my workbench.

"Why don't you just cut both boards at the same time?" Bubba suggests.

Hot damn, that would work!

"Well, because I didn't think of it. Thanks for the tip," I reply.

"You're welcome." Bubba grins.

My mind wanders to a dark place.

If that little shit had been here five hours ago, I wouldn't have ruined all those fucking boards. He should have been working alongside me. That intuitive little shit paved easy street, "Never work with you again for the rest of my life." He's probably laughing inside right now, mocking me.

"Dad, I hope you like your lunch," my son says.

Knock it off, Jim. He doesn't work with me because of my anger and rage. He wants to be around me and even brought me lunch. If I were a good father, Bubba would want to help and that help would have saved me a hundred forty bucks. Instead, I look like a crazy man who blames his problems on everyone else.

My toe throbs. I forgot I wasn't wearing steel-toed boots when I kicked the twenty-foot two-by-sixteen beam. It didn't give much.

"I sure wish I didn't screw things up with us," I tell my son.
"Yeah, me, too." Bubba hands me my lunch and leaves.

Vaughn, Washington, 1991 (Son, sixteen years old)

It's Saturday, seven o'clock in the morning. I'm awake, lying in bed.

RHHHUUUNNNN. Dad's chainsaw rips through an evergreen. That sound usually pumps rage through my veins. Today is different. The sound of my father's distant chainsaw mixes with a house sparrow's song. The noises of the country are calming. Dad hasn't yelled at me or hit me in years. He never asks anything of me. He built a barn, fixed cars, and cut trees alone.

This morning I feel no anxiety, no rage. Work clothes slide on automatically and I walk downstairs.

Mom gets teary eyed. "Oh, my goodness."

"Mom, stop it. It's no big deal." I grab my favorite set of work gloves.

But it is a big deal. I feel happy and complete, like when I used to be a log sitter. For the first time in over a decade, I wanted to help my dad.

Out in the forest, Dad holds a screwdriver and tightens his chainsaw blade. He is focused.

Each step toward him is awkward.

I want him to see me. He doesn't.

Gravel crunches under my heals.

Dad spins around. Noticing me, he smiles. "Hey, Bub, what do you need?"

"Do you want some help?" I ask.

He looks down at my gloves. Then he scans my appearance; I'm dressed to work.

Silence. We are both ill at ease.

A minute passes.

We look around, uncomfortable.

Dad breaks the tension. "Do you want to use the chainsaw?"

"Sure, but I don't know how," I say.

He screws up his face and says, "What are you talking about? You've been raised around a chainsaw your whole life. You were practically born with one in your hand."

I stand there, feeling stupid.

Dad, I don't know what to tell you. I have never used a chainsaw before. I've seen it used a million times and could probably figure it out. But I still, at this moment, don't know how.

And I stand still, waiting for him to erupt.

My dad looks me in the eye. A dawn of realization sweeps over his face. He asks, "I've never taught you, have I?"

"No." It is as if he read my mind.

"Do you want me to teach you?" he asks.

"Sure," I reply.

The general idea of a chainsaw is easy. Squeeze the handle and the sharp blade goes around. Only touch wood with the sharp blade.

Dad says, "Above all, don't hit a rock."

I yank the cord. The machine garbles. *RUBBUBBUBB.*

Squeezing the trigger flexes the blade. I move the saw around in front of me, getting familiar with the feel. Dad gives me a nod. I lower the blade against the bark of an evergreen. It cuts through the wood like a Jedi's lightsaber. Sawdust bounces off my arms and chest. Cut after cut, the tree transforms into firewood.

Dad stands nearby. He admires my work from a safe distance.

Life is perfect.

CRUNCH. I hit a rock.

Gawdamn motherfucker! Son of a bitch! Why didn't I see that fucking stupid rock?

I cut the engine.

Wind whispers through the pines, sweeping away the scent of the two-stroke engine.

I'm so stupid. I ruin everything. Today was perfect and I fucked it up.

"Are you okay?" Dad asks.

"I'm fine," I lie.

(Father)

Bubba's look tells me he is anything but fine. Rage pulses from him like heat from a red-hot potbelly stove. I know his anger. I've lived with it inside of me for over forty years. It's my anger. I put it inside of him.

Burning with pure hate feels powerful. Hurt or be hurt, it doesn't matter. You want to feel anything else, but can't seem to let go of the rage. Temporary pleasure comes from destroying beauty. Pain is the only welcome distraction.

"You're feeling 'it,' aren't you?" I ask.

Bubba replies, "Dad, I was just—"

"It's okay. You can tell me," I calm.

"I'm sorry. I know you didn't do anything wrong," Bubba says.

"Son, never be sorry with me. I put this demon inside of you. I did this to you. I'm the one that should be sorry. You should hate me."

"I don't hate you," my boy replies.

"If you knew what I stole from you, you would. I hate me. I can't even look at pictures of you as a little boy. Sometimes I wish you would just take a swing at me. Feeling that pain would be easier than facing what I feel inside right now. I'd let you hit me as hard as you want."

"I don't want to hit you," my son says.

"I know. That's what makes this so difficult. I can take a punch, bruises heal, but this ache in my soul doesn't go away."

"I wish there was something I could do to make it go away," Bubba says.

"Keep doing what you are doing. You are perfect just the way you are. I'm proud of you. Please remember that I'm doing the best I can. My father put this rage in me; it's the Beck family curse. It is our demon to conquer. I'll probably carry it for the rest of my life. But no matter what, it stops with me."

I look at my son; he hangs on to my words.

"I feel it inside," Bubba says.

"I know. If you ever change your mind about taking that swing, just say the word."

Bubba frowns. "Hitting the rock set it off. I was trying my best, but it wasn't good enough."

"Son, we all hit rocks. I've been at this for years, have cut thousands of trees, and I still hit rocks. You never stop hitting rocks. Just try your best and when you hit a rock, you sharpen the blade. Ours is dull. Do you want me to teach you how to sharpen a chainsaw?"

"Sure." Bubba smiles.

The chainsaw engine is cold. It rests beneath an evergreen, with a sharpened blade. An empty soda can rests on the forest floor. With perspiration gone and our shirts dry, Bubba and I sit in the shade. The day slips by. I tell him, "You want to go on another double date with me and Mom?"

"No way," Bubba says.

"Why not? The last one was fun," I reply.

"Dad, I can't even look at Angie Martin in the face, much less ask her out again. Those solar-powered flashlight jokes you told are horrible."

"Come on, those are good jokes." I grin.

We both laugh.

My son is right.

They are stupid jokes; nobody ever laughs.

I tell bad jokes on purpose; that's what makes them funny.

Girls come and go, but memories between a father and son last forever. One day, long after I'm gone, Bubba will tell his children about the one double date he went on with his dad. I can almost picture him doing the same, telling the same ridiculous jokes.

"I can't believe you embarrassed me like that," Bubba says in mock frustration.

I grin.

"Son, I am a sensitive guy. I tried really hard. That hurts my feelings," I reply.

"No, it doesn't. You have no soul. You ruined my chances with Angie. I will never double-date with you again."

"Trust me, in college you'll find better," I tell him.

Only now do I regret putting my son through school early. He's only sixteen and next year he will be in college. Our friendship is growing stronger by the day. We both still have rage, just a little less every week. I want more time.

I ask, "Do you plan on going to Liberty University next year?"

"Which school would you pick?" Bubba asks.

"I'd pick Liberty. Jerry Falwell started it," I say, thinking of my days in Memphis when I was a warrior for Christ.

"Who's Jerry Falwell?" Bubba asks.

"Just a man. You'll like him," I say, avoiding the question.

Standing up, gloves in hand, my son gets ready for more work. He asks, "Do you want me to split logs or use the chainsaw?"

There isn't a trace of anxiety. For the moment, the Beck family curse is lifted. But the demon I have caged inside my soul would be back. It always comes back. However, after five years of trying, I finally learned how to beat it. Battling evil happens by listening, not speaking.

I've always tried to be right. As soon as my heart accepted that I was wrong, I'm finally right. The first step was the hardest. The second step was the second hardest. Now, the work is finally getting easier. It took years to get to this point. Our relationship is turning around.

"Son, take the rest of the day off. Joe called you earlier. Why don't you go hang out with him?"

When I think of my dad, this is what I see

"But I want to work with you and we haven't got much done," **Bubba** says.

"I'll finish this tomorrow. There is always more work to do. If you ever want to work with me again, you are always invited."

My son replies, "Thanks, Dad, I will."

Bubba shoves his gloves in his back pocket and gives me a punch on the arm. As he walks back to our log house, I notice all the logs standing on end, waiting to be split in into firewood. My heart burns with joy. More was accomplished in the last hour than the last ten years of my life combined.

The truth is, I want today to end on a positive note. This way, no matter what life brings me, my son will always have at least one good memory of working with his father.

Breakthrough moments are rare. They can't be forced, rushed, prepared for, or predicted. They just happen and you have to be ready for them.

I'll go ahead and mark myself an A this week.

THE FUTURE...

CHAPTER 21

POLISHING ROCKS

TACOMA, WASHINGTON, 1999 (SON, TWENTY-FOUR YEARS OLD)

Lines of church parishioners file into a lobby, like ants leaving an anthill. They march out into civilization with Jesus grins protecting them. The patriarchal head pastor approaches. He has a spit-shine feel and a patent leather sparkle. His shirt is starched and his double-breasted suit doesn't wrinkle. This aged shepherd strolls through the flock with the same haircut as always, a groomed masterpiece.

"James, I want to ask you something," the pastor says.

"Sure, Pastor. What do you need?" I reply.

"Next week is Father's Day and I would like you and your dad to speak at our annual father–son breakfast on Saturday morning."

It's been thirteen years since my father and I attended that event. Thoughts of mint chocolate chip ice cream circle my brain. "Of course. What would you like us to talk about?" I ask.

This could be interesting.

"You guys run a successful business together, are both leaders in our church, and always seem to get along. I'm sure you have a few secrets you can share with the rest of us."

"We may." I grin.

That night, I pull my father aside. "Hey, Dad, we're speaking next week in church, at the annual Father/Son Breakfast."

"Bubba, I'm the last person that should be speaking on that day."

"I disagree. You are the best Dad I know."

What should we talk about?" he asks.

"Our story… and we tell should the truth," I reply.

"Aw, geez." Dad looks from side to side, uncomfortable.

"What's wrong with telling our story?" I ask.

"It's fine for you, you're not the asshole."

"That's true. But all's well that ends well, right? We can design the message together and interweave our talk. We should address the false image that Christian families project."

Dad says, "How come I get the impression that I'm going to regret this?"

"What is there to regret? You've changed."

Dad shakes his head. "Your silver tongue has a habit of talking me into things I later regret."

"Let's create something great, something unique. We don't have to talk. They have three other speakers in the lineup, so they don't need us. I understand if you're not up for it," I goad.

"Who else is speaking?" he asks.

I give him the names.

"I can't stand that guy. He's a stuck-up prick." Dad's jaw clenches.

"Now's your chance to take him out," I reply.

My father turns a mischievous grin. "If we do this, we have to knock it out of the park. I want to crush those men. We can't hold back. We need to be completely open, transparent, and honest. No fluffy religious bullshit."

"It's all in the delivery." I grin.

"Exactly." He grins back.

It's Saturday morning; we crafted our message all week long. My father and I stand on the same stage as the fat man in the windbreaker did, thirteen years ago. It feels good to be on the right side of wrong.

Breakfast hasn't changed.

Forks scrape against plates. Flapjacks dribble imitation maple syrup onto neighboring bacon and eggs. Fathers hum along with prepubescent voices that screech out a song.

All to Jesus I surrender
All to Him I freely give
I will ever love and trust Thee
In His presence daily live

My father and I share the microphone.
We speak of our shame without shame.
It shocks the crowd.
Nobody knew.
How could they?
All of our work was accomplished in secret.
It had to be.
How else could it be trustworthy?

The buzz of our message reaches the higher-ups of the church in a flash. Ironically, no pastors were present to hear our talk. Church deacons relay the message, insisting we speak again for the Sunday, Father's Day, church service. This time it will be in front of many lifelong friends. It feels good to have the church body pull in your direction. Dad tells me not to get used to the feeling because the sword of the Lord cuts both ways.

Sitting on stage, it looks like we have it all together. In truth, we led each other blind and broken. More than a thousand people listen as we share our family's dark secrets. We give our audience the truth, the G-rated church porn version. Friends and family are shocked.

After we finish, more than five hundred familiar faces line up to speak with us. In front, a beautiful middle-aged woman approaches me. She is church royalty and has everything a person should want: the perfect waterfront home, powerful political friends, a good-looking husband and kids, plenty of money, beloved in the community, exotic vacations, beautiful clothes, and expensive accessories. She is the type of person who makes you question the fairness of God. When she walks through the foyer, her strut defines jealousy.

Something is wrong. Mascara streams down her face, staining her ivory-colored Chanel jacket.

She grips my arm and pleads, "My kids hate me, and my husband wants to leave. They say I'm just like my mother and they are right. But I don't know what to do. How did you and your father change everything?"

She believed my lie, like I believed hers.

"I—I don't know how to summarize it. My dad and I worked on our relationship for over a decade. We only recently fixed it. Things that worked for us might not work for you," I reply.

Her tears flow faster and faster. "You have nothing to give me, no advice or specifics?"

I feel impotent.

Finally, I tell her, "Well, there are many things I could say. Some of the stuff we tried worked and some didn't. I could fill books with everything we did. I don't know what you need."

The mascara stain inches down her pristine jacket. She pulls me in close and whispers, "Write it down. Promise me you that you will write it down. Put it in a book. Let me decide what I need."

"Okay, I promise," I reply.

Later that night, my father and I sit in Baskin-Robbins. He has a heaping bowl of Rocky Road in his hand and I have a bowl of mint chocolate chip. This evening's speaking event provides so much closure that new questions rise. "Dad, why me? Why were you so nice to all those other kids and so mean to me?"

"I was hoping you would never ask me that," he replies.

We both take another bite.

I wait.

The first one to speak loses. Dad doesn't have my level of patience. Pregnant pauses bother him. Seconds of discomfort seem like an eternity. On the other hand, I can wait forever. I am the patient one.

"The answer is pretty messed up, but if you want to know, I'll tell you," he says.

"I do," I encourage.

"The man in me wanted to provide a wonderful life for you. But the boy in me was jealous. You had clean clothes and went to school every day to learn.

Santa Claus brought you presents. Your mother loves you. Those are things I never had. The boy in me was jealous and wanted to take them away, so I did."

We keep eating.

Silence.

He asks, "Are you mad at me?"

"No. I forgave you a long time ago," I answer.

"I'm not sure why," he says.

"Because I understand," I explain.

"Is it easier when you understand?" Dad asks.

"Yeah, I think so."

Dad looks deep into his Rocky Road and says, "I wish I could understand."

I wish you could, too. I'd give anything to explain how you taught me how to be a man:

- *Boys take, while men give.*
- *Boys destroy, while men create.*
- *Boys control, while men practice self-control.*
- *Boys force, while men only force themselves.*
- *Boys lie, while men are honest.*
- *Boys manipulate, while men are transparent.*
- *Boys are secretive, while men are discreet.*
- *Boys are stingy, while men are good stewards.*
- *Boys blame, while men take responsibility.*

How can I show my father gratitude for teaching me these lessons through his action, while remaining silent? How can I make him understand?

Then I say, "Dad, can I have your permission to write our story?"

"Why?" he asks.

"I want to write a book," I answer.

"You hate writing," he replies.

This is true. Writing has always been my least favorite activity. I chuckle, remembering the moment I told God that I would never be a writer. "I told someone I would try."

"Did you promise?" Dad asks.

I nod.

Dad raises his brow and says, "Then you have to write it. You have my permission."

A distant part of my soul grins.

We each take a bite of our ice cream.

I keep silent.

Dad breaks the tension. "How will you write this book? You are a C English student and don't know the first thing about getting a book published."

"I'm not sure, but I can figure it out. Learn as I go, make it up as I go along. It has to end up somewhere. I'll just do my best and hope that it is good enough."

He smiles. "If you polish a rock long enough, it's bound to shine eventually."

"Can you imagine our names on the cover of a book?" I ask.

We both laugh.

"Dad, I don't know what it will take or how I'm going to make it happen, but I'm gonna do it. Nothing can stop me."

"Sounds like a plan," he says.

Dad says "sounds like a plan" whenever he doesn't think someone will follow through.

"Let's start now. Tell me about your life, but start from the beginning."

My father relaxes back in his chair and gives a heavy sigh. "The beginning happened back in 1943, a couple years before I was born. The Great Depression was ending. World War II favored the Allies. Your grandfather rode a bus and your grandmother got on that bus. She was heading off to work at an airplane factory."

Dad chuckles.

"Why are you laughing?" I ask.

"Momma always said sitting next to James Beck was the worst mistake of her life."

Dad's tone suddenly shifts to a dark place. "Some people could say the same thing about me."

"Not anymore," I reply.

"You'd be surprised," he says.

"You've changed. You are different now," I tell him.

Dad leans over the table. For the first time in my life, he looks tired. Rocky Road ice cream melts in his bowl. He says, "I doubt people ever change. Even me, I'm the same guy I've always been. My thoughts and instincts have never changed. Every time I go to work, part of me still wants to take off and never look back. At my core, I'm still like my father."

"I don't agree." His words irritate me.

"Bubba, I've tried to kill that bad part of me for years. No matter what I do, the old Jim never dies. I still wonder if anything I've ever done really matters."

"It matters to me. My life is better because of the work you did. Dad, it matters to me!" I reply.

"I know, but—" Dad says.

"Can you call your dad your best friend?" I ask forcefully.

"No," he replies.

"Would you write a book about your father?" I question.

"No, not one that anyone would read," he responds.

I lean in and say, "Then you are not like your dad. You may be connected to your past, but you made sure I wasn't. You rose to the occasion and took responsibility for the problems you created. Since I was eleven, you came to me every week and asked me to grade you until I graduated from high school. Without knowing what to do, we tried. We never stopped trying. You listened to what I said and we figured out how to be good men together. Even though you were broken, for my sake, you picked yourself up. That's how you are different. You taught me how to *rise up*. You taught me that even when you are bruised and broken, a man always carries on. For that, I will always be grateful."

He takes a few bites of Rocky Road and asks, "If you always keep trying, does that mean you've changed?"

"Dad, that's what change means."

CHAPTER 22

THE FOOL'S JOURNEY

NORTH HOLLYWOOD, CALIFORNIA, 2010 (SON, THIRTY-FIVE YEARS OLD)

The Lexus I drive pulls a smooth corner, turning up Laurel Canyon. For the past year, I've worked as the managing partner of an aftercare facility and oversee marketing, nurses, scheduling, and medication. We are located on the ninth floor of the Palomar Hotel and take in post operation patients from top plastic, bariatric, and orthopedic surgeons in Beverly Hills. I oversee the nurses who receive patients sent by the 90210 doctors and even the director of plastics for Cedars-Sinai. Mixing a swanky hotel with twenty-four-hour nursing care seems like a good business model, but what do I know? This is my first try at being a businessman and I've never been busier.

On April Fool's Day 2001, two years after my father and I told our story, I moved down to Los Angeles. I gave myself ten years to write my book, focusing on the moments that transformed our relationship. The ten-year mark is only a few months away. I'm writing the last few chapters now.

The company Lexus is a lot nicer than my 2001 Honda Civic. There is a VIP post operation pickup right after an acting audition. It is the first time I've ever auditioned for the TV show *Glee* or the UDK (Ulrich, Dawson, and Kritzer) casting office. I tell myself that driving the Lexus helps me get into character. UDK casts my favorite shows: *Dexter*, *Criminal Minds*, *Nip/Tuck*, *Battlestar Galactica*, and the list goes on.

I park. Across the street, a guy in a wheelchair rolls by. He's a friend. I holler, "Hey, Toby!"

"Beck, what up?" he replies.

"What are you doing here?" I ask.

"I'm going out for the preacher role in *Glee*."

"Me, too."

I wonder how we will stack up to each other because Toby has less than 10 percent use of his arms; he's a quadriplegic. Even without full use of his limbs, Toby has booked more acting jobs than I have. Head-to-head, it's a toss-up at best. If I don't get it, I hope he does. I'm actually just happy they invited me through the front door. Gone are the days I have to crash auditions. I have an agent, a manager, stellar headshots, and a respectable reel.

Toby says, "Don't think that just because all your body parts work that you can beat me. I can beat you without legs, punk."

"True, but you may need arms," I reply.

"You're right, preachers usually need arms." Toby gives me his best Southern Baptist impersonation. "In the name of Jesus, demon be gone." He then flips his wrists around in a double-dead-fish fashion.

Toby is one of my favorite people in Los Angeles. From the chin up, he is a cool surfer. From the neckline down, he is an unfortunate reminder to cliff divers not to trust hot chicks when they say, "Jump here. It's safe!"

Toby lights ups. "Dude, UDK wins awards for hiring 'crips' like me and I've got to milk this chair when I can. I wish it would pull me chicks."

"You calling yourself a 'crip' these days?" I ask.

"Yep, permanent gang signs, right here," he replies. Toby's hands flop into an almost gang-like position.

I laugh.

"Nobody messes with the guy in a wheelchair. Shit, nobody usually talks to me. If you ever want to go to Disneyland and get great perks, call me. I'll get you in front of the line!"

I grab the back of his chair and push him toward the building. Toby smiles and says, "I can get use to this."

We enter the elevator.

"How's Cityzen, your band, doing?" I ask.

"Great. I wrote a few songs last week. We won Battle of the Bands last month and get to play at the Hard Rock on New Year's Eve in Vegas! Yeah, baby!"

Toby is one more reason why I love Los Angeles.

The waiting room is empty. The casting office staff work behind a long front desk. I expected a full waiting area, but we are the only ones here.

We sign in on a clipboard, assuring our place in a line. I'm last because nobody messes with the guy in a wheelchair.

Ten years ago, I gave up a life in Washington State for a fresh start in Los Angeles. The City of Angels seemed like the best place to learn how to write my book. In the beginning, I lived a Hollywood cliché: sleeping in my car as I carve out the American Dream. Now, I'm grateful for my apartment in Santa Monica; it's a few blocks from the beach. I own a comfy bed with one-thousand-thread-count sheets. Years have passed since I've lived in my car and had to sneak around, pretending to be accepted. Now, professionals invite me through the front door. As long as you dress the part, nobody seems to question you. The time for trespassing is over. I finally belong.

A dark-haired gentleman enters the lobby. He's casually sharp and approaches my friend with confidence. "Hey, Toby, good to see you. Come on in."

Toby wheels down the hallway, calling out behind him, "Later, Beck."

I nod. Ducking around the corner, I whisper, "Red leather, yellow leather, red leather, yellow leather."

This classic mouth warm-up is meant to loosen my lips. It's all part of the game, a ritual to calm the nerves. It creates the illusion of control.

I'm a talisman type of guy and own magic socks. They look like killer whales swallowing my feet. Mom gave them to me for Christmas. I love them because they are magic. As I walk into the room, my childhood innocence follows me inside fabric, metals, and leathers that carry memories of friendship, love, and laughter.

People blow off my ideas. They say magic isn't real, but placebos work 80 percent of the time. I'm banking on the 80 percent; after all, those are pretty good odds.

I have magic underwear from my girlfriend.

My magic shoes were purchased in college.

The magic antique cufflinks I wear are from the 1920s.

Each piece is imbued with a story and is worn for different reasons. It's like socially acceptable battle armor. I believe my cufflinks bring a +10 Dexterity and +15 Destruction versus the Undead. I've got an 80 percent chance of being right. If I don't see any zombies, I win. Even if I'm wrong, I have more fun than anyone else I know. My soul feels a tickle as I put on these articles of magic.

Some think magic is stupid, but that's because they don't have any magic in their life. I feel sorry for them as I wiggle my toes. "Red leather, yellow leather."

The casting guy calls my name, "James Beck."

Toby gives me a silent "you're up" nod for good luck as he rolls out.

I walk over, sporting a grin.

"Thanks for coming in," he says.

"Thanks for having me." I follow him into a casting room, equipped with one cotton killer whale on each foot.

All magic should be kept a secret, shared only through the written word. Otherwise, it loses its magic. When the world sees my shoes, they see black patent leather dress shoes with a capped toe, monk strap, and a gold buckle. I see magic. I bought them in college, when I became student body president of Jerry Falwell's Liberty University. These shoes bring good feelings when I slide them on, so I wear them when I need a twinkle in my smile.

A casting associate fiddles with recording equipment. It feels like a playdate.

My agent and manager stopped calling these meetings "auditions" months ago because I told them judgment kills magic. Playtime creates magic. Once a week, my creative team leaves invitations on my voicemail like, "James, you have a playdate at FOX tomorrow at noon." Auditions don't interest me, but I wouldn't miss a playdate for the world. I'm thirty-five years old and I've never stopped playing.

Gaff tape makes a *T* on the floor.

In acting, this *T* is the universal "stand here" mark. It's the *X* that marks the spot.

I hit my mark.

The associate adjusts the camera, placing me in frame.

Looking down at the paper, the character's lines come into focus. I tell a casting guy, "This is the easiest audition I've ever had."

My host replies, "Why do you say that?"

I respond, "The breakdown reads 'Minister, thirty-five years old' and has me marrying a couple. I am thirty-five, was a minister before I moved to Los Angeles, and performed a wedding ceremony last month using pretty much the same dialogue. I actually wore this suit, so I didn't even have to think about wardrobe."

Conventional wisdom encourages actors to talk about how nervous they are. Nerves don't matter. At this point, it's all in the delivery. With a killer whale on each foot, I'm unstoppable.

"You were a minister?" he asks.

"Yep, got a bachelor's in religion. I worked in a church for three years, and can translate ancient Greek if it will help me book the job."

"Let's lay one down," he says.

A red light flashes as the camera rolls.

The casting room spins out of focus.

It's like I'm back in front of the church congregation, with my father, thirteen years ago.

Words flow like honey.

The posture and movements are effortlessly delivered.

Before I realize it, I'm done.

Attending a right-wing religious university on the buckle of America's Bible Belt offers few Hollywood advantages. I take my breaks when I can get them.

"That was great. Let's try another. Bring up the enthusiasm this time," the host says.

I'll add a little Southern Baptist holy roller and mix in some of Dad's hellfire and brimstone for added flavor.

"That was perfect. I'm Robert, Robert Ulrich."

Ulrich, as in Ulrich, Dawson, and Kritzer? That Ulrich? You're the guy who heads up one of the greatest casting offices in the business, that Ulrich?

"Nice to meet you," I respond.

Be calm.

Be professional.

This is just another day at the office.

Mr. Robert Ulrich views my headshot.

I remain still. The first one to speak loses.

I'm the new kid on the block, standing in a long line of players, and Mr. Ulrich is the captain of the kickball team. He may not be the king of the world, but this definitely is his game.

Words ruin moments like these.

Lips remain tight, savoring the situation.

Robert scans my résumé.

I breathe easy.

His eyes jump up. "You were in *Johnny Flynton*? I almost cast that film."

"Yeah. I was Artie. It was fun." It is a stroke of luck that my only notable Hollywood achievement caught his eye. It was a supporting role in a short film nominated for an Academy Award. I've been able to milk that ten minutes of screen time for enough success to not count myself a Hollywood failure, but not exactly enough to claim success.

Robert continues, "That would have been great to work on. Lexi Alexander is a top-notch director, very talented. She does great work." His mind wanders far from the casting room to a different time and with different people.

"Yeah, she is an amazing fighter, too, undefeated kickboxer," I say.

Robert looks quizzically at my résumé. "It says you trained special forces?"

"Yep. Stu Segal Productions, down in San Diego. I was booked as an actor on a classified Marine Corps training video: *How to Interrogate Insurgents*." It feels cool to have done something "classified."

"How did you train them?" he asks.

"After filming the piece for the marines, they let me suit up as the opposition. I grew out a beard, wore a man dress, and learned some Arabic. They paid me two hundred fifty dollars a day to shoot blanks from an AK-47 at squads of marines. For two months I played war with a support staff."

"Sounds cool." Robert walks over to me.

"It was cool. They had a mock Iraqi village. After a few fake explosions went off, all hell broke loose. The command would give me a signal and I'd open fire. The squad would have to establish 360-cordon security and try to take me out. Sometimes an amputee would jump out a building with a fake bloody stump.

They would do medical drills while others engaged me in a firefight." It felt empowering to be able to talk about something I was proud of, with a man who deserved respect.

"What other kind of training did they do?" Robert asks.

"They had a shoot house. Each of us had two 9mm handguns with 'sim' rounds that are like paintball guns on crack. Sometimes they gave me blue-body [fake] grenades. Marines would stack up at the door, bust in, and we'd start shooting. I would have a High-Value Target or a hostage. The mission would be: Kill us without shooting the target or hostage. Bullets whizzed by inches from my head. It hurts when you get hit. Sim rounds break the skin even through three layers of clothes. You hope the rounds hit body armor. It takes a few firefights before a person can think clearly through the chaos."

Robert folds up my headshot with a smile and says, "Thanks for coming in today. It was nice meeting you."

"Same here." I grin back.

The audition was quicker than expected, plenty of time to reach the Golden Triangle, near Rodeo Drive, for my pickup. When I first arrived in Los Angeles, this area of town held insecurity. It made me feel "less than." However, the backwoods once a "piece-o'-shit" country boy currently rubs elbows with the Who's Who of entertainment and hobnobs with plastic surgeons.

One of my main surgeon clients, the best "eye guy" in the business, made a special request a couple days ago. He asked that I personally handle a VIP. All of his clients are celebrities, richer than third-world countries, or at least have rich boyfriends. They are all a "big deal."

As I enter the elevator to his office, my phone rings. It's my agent. "Elton, what's up?"

"James, I don't know what you did, but you need to do it again. Robert wants you to come in for a general."

"What's a general?" I ask.

"It's a general meeting where the casting director gets to know you. It never happens. At least, they don't request it. This is a first for me. The office just called. I told them yes and even if it's your mother's birthday, your ass will be in their office on Wednesday at 2:00 p.m. So, start canceling whatever it is you thought you had planned."

"I've got a dentist appointment in the morning. After that, I'm free. I don't have to cancel anything," I reply.

"James, you are supposed to tell me how much you have to cancel to make it. It lets me know you are committed," Elton says.

"I will move heaven and earth to make it."

I exit the elevator. The surgeon's smoking-hot patient coordinator approaches.

"Elton, I've got to go. Work stuff."

The coordinator slides up to me. "James, thank you so much for handling this personally. The doctor really appreciates it."

"My pleasure. Why the extra secrecy?"

"The patient runs a major movie studio and doesn't want his name in the tabloids—'Shallow Exec Doing Excessive Plastic Surgery'—that type of stuff. The paparazzi are always around."

"Does he need the procedure?" I ask.

"Definitely. His eyelashes are growing into his eyes. Every time he blinks, it scrapes his eyeball. Imagine having eyelashes in your eye twenty-four hours a day. It's very painful."

I wince.

Having an eyelash in your eye is one of the few things my dad considers an acceptable work excuse. I couldn't imagine having it being a constant problem. Besides, what guy doesn't enjoy doing favors for beautiful women? Luckily, I work with many beautiful women.

Jenni with Dr. Svelack.

Tina with Dr. Lanman.

The whole Motykie office is packed with hotties.

Time off with the nursing staff

Doctors aren't stupid.

Neither am I.

Bringing coffee and pastries to cute chicks is a much better job than shoveling chicken poop and tossing firewood. I have evolved far beyond my country-boy roots.

BEVERLY HILLS, CALIFORNIA, 2010 (NEXT WEEK)

Sitting at my desk, I look out onto Wilshire Boulevard, nine stories below. Traffic moves slowly during rush hour.

Patient pickups are finished.

The VIP rests in his bed. My staff is happy. The head charge nurse, Jerna, will stand guard. If Mother Teresa were a nurse from New Jersey, she would be Jerna. Everything is safe.

I can rest.

The Palomar free-wine hour starts in a couple minutes.

I might as well stay.

I stroll down for a free cabernet and dial my best friend. "Hey Dad, remember me?"

"Bubba! How's the big city?"

"It's good. Just finished work," I reply.

"Is it going well?" he asks.

"Other than feeling out of place every day, things are great."

My dad's voice shifts into that of a Fire Chief. "Son, you always feel out of place at a new job. As time goes on, you work hard, learn the job, and get good at it...then you no longer feel that way."

I reply, "Last year I was Zen boy, only doing massage. Now, I'm asked to make decisions that there are no clear answers to."

"At work, who do you trust most?" Dad asks.

"My head nurse, Jerna."

"She has a nursing license for a reason. Use it. If you don't know something, ask her what she thinks. Do what she says and give her the credit. That is the secret to being a good manager."

"Seems simple," I respond.

"It's universal. By the way, you taught this to me," my father says.

"Well, thanks for teaching it back."

Medical supplies rest neatly in storage bins. Jerna takes a vial of Demerol and fills a syringe with the neural inhibitor. It's happy time for sliced-up clients.

I am sitting at my computer desk staring at a medical shopping website displaying side-by-side comparisons of O_2 condensers. Replacing O_2 bottles with an O_2 condenser tops my nursing staff's medical wish list.

"Jerna?"

"Yeah, Beck?" She keeps working.

"Do you think we should get the five-liter O_2 condenser or the ten liter? The big one costs twice as much, so we'll have to stick with bottles for twice as long."

Jerna cocks back on her heals and balances time and money in her mind. It's the classic matchup of safety and budget.

"Hold out for the ten liter. Our O_2 tanks will keep us afloat till then. Only one patient per year needs that type of output, but it will save our ass when the time comes and it comes about once a year. That's my two cents." Jerna's pen continues scribbling nursing notes.

I respond, "Then, that's what we'll go with."

Jerna stops writing and looks up from her paperwork. "James, I like working for you. You really know what you're doing."

"Thanks, Jerna." I grin.

Her compliments are always earned.

"What's that shit-eating grin you've got on your face?" she asks.

"What are you talking about?" My smile tightens.

"That grin. You always have a grin. You're hiding something from me. I can feel it."

BEEP, BEEP. A patient's intercom interrupts the moment. Jerna talks into a walkie-talkie. "I'll be right there." She turns back. "There is something hiding behind that grin of yours. So help me, God, I'm gonna find out what it is."

"You will, but not today." I laugh.

Jerna points a firm finger. "Your ass better be here when I get back." She exits down the hall, off to give an injection. I slip out of the office.

After all these years, I'm proud to be my father's son.

The dentist is finished; my cavity is filled. Cheeks sag over an exhausted jaw that stayed open two hours too long. I keep poking my face, exploring the boundaries of anesthesia. The smile I rely on is cockeyed.

Mouthwash dribbles down my chin.

A BlackBerry vibrates. It's a text from the casting director's associate. It reads: "Meeting pushed back. Can you come now?"

I text back: "Just finished with dentist. I look like a stroke victim. I don't mind, if you don't."

At Ulrich's office, I carry in a tray with three coffees: soy, decaf, and regular lattes. It looks like I'm kissing up, because I am. It's what I bring to all of my meetings when I feel uncomfortable.

Robert notices the gift. "You didn't have to get us coffee."

"Yeah, I did. This is my first 'general' at a casting office and I don't know what I'm supposed to do. I have coffee with people all the time. If adding coffee makes me comfortable, then it's worth it. Which one would you like?" My words slur from half-numb lips.

Robert and his associate appreciatively pick their beverage.

I take the last one.

"What do you do for a living?" Robert asks.

"On weekends or during the week?"

"Both."

"On the weekends, I'm the massage therapist for NBC's *The Biggest Loser*."

Robert lights up. "I love *The Biggest Loser*. How did you get on the show?"

"I was the massage therapist for *American Gladiators* and they have the same medical staff."

For the next hour we chat. I tell him about my life in aftercare and even growing up in a foster home. Industry labels fade as the five-year-old boy inside each of us become friendly.

North Hollywood, California (One month later)

The UDK casting offices is full of *Glee* hopefuls. Fifty beautiful people pack the waiting area, dripping with "pick me" energy. I hadn't seen Robert since he pulled me in for the general. Bugging a casting director is a career death sentence.

Throngs of actors sit nervously, practicing lines.

"Red leather, yellow leather" whispers are heard.

I approach the front desk.

"Is Robert available?" I ask.

The receptionist looks up with a smile, "No, he's in a meeting. Can I help you with something?"

"Could you let him know that James Beck is here? It will only take a minute."

"Is he expecting you?" the secretary asks softly.

"No, but it will be fine," I reply.

"If he is not expecting you, then—"

"Please, just mention it. If he gets upset, tell him that I insisted. Put the blame on me."

"Okay." She sports a "good luck" grin. If this goes south, I will be the talk of the office and not in a good way.

Five minutes pass.

Robert's door remains shut.

The office is at a standstill.

Gotta go.

Gotta go.

Gotta go.

I've got things to do.

Back at the front desk, I ask, "Can I have a piece of paper? I'll just write him a note."

The receptionist slides paper across the counter. "He should be coming out at any moment."

"I need to get going. Besides, it's better this way."

Nestled into a seat, I write him a note.

It looks a mess.

Spell-checker would've been helpful.

There are too many words squeezed together, like a fifth grader wrote it.

I ask the receptionist, "Can I have another piece of paper? I'm much smarter than my note looks."

The office door opens.

Robert walks out.

He sees me and waves. "James, come over here."

The receptionist invites me beyond the waiting area, where few are allowed to tread.

Robert pulls me in close. "Great to see you. I'm swamped at the moment and don't have much time. What are you doing here?"

I reply, "I've got a couple friends-and-family tickets to *The Biggest Loser* finale. You said you love the show. It's in my buddy Frado's section. I figured you might want to go."

"That's awesome, but I'm going to be on lockdown this week with *Glee*. I won't make it out in time and don't want to take tickets from someone else, especially if I don't think I'll make it."

"No worries. I have a few other friends that will want to go. I'm just offering an invite."

"Thanks. Let me know about the next one, will ya?" he says.

"If I get more tickets, I'll let you know. Looks like you need to get back to the grind." I give him a polite exit. Nobody likes the guy who takes too much attention.

"Yeah, I do," he replies.

There wasn't time to tell Robert the whole truth. Fortunately, the sin of omission is forgivable in a town where time is king. Truth be told, there won't be a next time. After five seasons with *The Biggest Loser* and ten years in Los Angeles, I'm giving it all up: the show, acting, a massage practice, and the medical facility. I don't know if I'll ever be back. After Robert, a key player in the entertainment industry, validated me...well, I didn't feel like staying.

The crazy thing about validation is, once a person has validation, he/she no longer needs it. At this point, Los Angeles no longer holds my interest. Hollywood was always just a game and I was playing. When I arrived in the City of Angels, I was a country boy who was trying to have an adventure and a C English student learning how to write a book. For the last decade, I've had my adventure and written my book. However, there is something else out there in the world that I need to find. It's the adventure hiding in a field, flying in the sky, resting at the bottom of a lake, and buried beneath a burned-out church. *The Biggest Loser* finale tickets are the only things I can give Robert that he can't get himself. It was my way of saying, "Thanks for making me feel worthy."

November 31, 2010, my partner in the medical facility just e-mailed me. We severed ties. She agreed to pay me the sixty-thousand dollars she owes for my year of work. She got off cheap. For the last eight months, I had been on call twenty-four hours a day and worked eighty hours per week, six to seven days a week. The business ran well under my charge. But after working with her for a year and witnessing how she treats "friends," I am confident she isn't going to pay. Time will tell. It always does. I won't risk an additional minute beyond the year I promised to give. Pay or not, either way I'm gone.

It's six o'clock the next morning. I wake up in the same Santa Monica apartment I've lived in for the past eight years. After countless hours of writing, the book is finally caught up in real time as I type these sentences. My decade stint in the City of Angels will be over in exactly four months. Only now do I remember this ten-year commitment to write my father's story. I'm a few months ahead of schedule.

It's early and the city hasn't woken up yet. There is no frame of reference for what I feel, at least not in my world. My entire being vibrates in ecstasy. Life would be annoying if it didn't feel so good. It is like a cosmic giggle courses through my veins. This euphoria has been happening off and on for the past few months, as I walk through Trader Joe's or see children playing with their parents. Emotions are so pure and strong that I have no desire to resist. I am completely sober and yet I find myself high on a sort of spiritual heroin.

Last week, the high-powered studio executive's wife challenged me to ask things of God. It seems like a good idea. After all, we have not because we ask not. Why wouldn't God grant me what I ask? Sliding off my bed, I fall into a half-lotus position. The silence is deafening and I love it. I'm anxious to hear "the Voice."

I call up to heaven. "Hey, God, I'm holding still. Wanna talk?"

The Voice fades in and out as I focus on letting go. It's like my soul turns an old radio dial, trying to tune in. Whenever I hear something, I stop. Even now, I can't tell if I create the Voice or if the Voice creates me. It doesn't really matter as long as it helps me become a better man. The world falls into an infinite black void.

"Let me know Your mind," I said.

The Voice answers in a back-alley whisper, "Give me a year."

"A year? Quid pro quo isn't cheap with You!"

"What would giving You a year look like?"

"Give me a year and I'll show you," the Voice softly responds.

"In the end, will I think it's worth it?" I ask.

"If you give me a year, then I'll show you my heart, too," the Voice says as audible as inaudible can be. It feels like a doubled-up, limited-time offer.

"Deal!" I proclaim. No matter where this voice takes me, instincts say that it's the best adventure in town. A wash of warm emotions flood my chest, reaching to all parts of my body. For years I've questioned if my life was priceless or worthless. Legacy is at risk, all or nothing. If I am priceless, my possessions are of little value. A rush of calm soothes my soul. There is nothing left to decide.

"What am I supposed to do?" I panic.

"Follow your heart without question or resistance. Those that you love will guide your way," the Voice says.

"What happens next?" I ask.

"Give it everything you've got and you'll find out," the Voice says with a chuckle.

There was a pull at my heart. It felt like a test. "What do you mean 'everything'?"

Silence.

"Okay, I'll give everything."

I feel something shift inside my soul, but I can't tell what. I tremble, just like I did when I spoke to my dad as a child.

"Heavenly Father, I'm scared."

"Welcome to Life," says the Voice.

CHAPTER 23

SERFBLISS

SANTA MONICA, CALIFORNIA, 2011

It's April Fool's Day, 2011—my thirty-sixth birthday. Exactly ten years ago today, I arrived in Southern California. Now I'm leaving. My wine cabinet empties into red Solo cups. Friends festively roam around my apartment. Homemade lasagna steams on paper plates. People are happy. The evening's plans fall together as if gravity is on my side.

A friend's cup topples; red wine spills on the couch. She rushes to grab paper towels, dabbing up the liquid. She calls out, "I'm sorry."

I laugh and ask, "Why?"

"I just stained your couch."

"I don't own a couch," I reply.

She asks, "Who owns the couch?"

"I have no idea. Nobody has asked for it yet." The new wine stain is as beautiful as a Picasso. I lean in close, "For the record, I love that couch and I love that you spilled wine on it because you just created the last memory that couch and I will share. Thank you."

"You're welcome," my confused friend replies.

I walk away, smiling. It is a curious feeling to be detached from the possessions I've spent a lifetime collecting and protecting. The less I have, the more the world opens up to possibilities. Before this moment, I never realized that I desire to be a minimalist. It feels as if I'm a fledgling, perched on the edge of the bird nest that has kept me safe my entire life. I'm about to spread my wings and have never felt so free.

When the Voice first said "give everything," I thought it was metaphorical hippie speak. My feeling was, "Sure, I'll give it all I got."

Later that morning, I asked my roommate, "What should I do with all my stuff?"

She said, "You should give it all away."

I felt a pull in my heart. Instinct told me that she was right. Using earthly treasures to express friendship to those I love seems the best path to take, especially because I don't know if I will ever see them again. I am committed to following my heart without question or resistance and believe that those I love will guide my way. This is one of many steps, in that direction.

After my roommate's suggestion, everything that is unnecessary for my journey feels like a burden. Holding on to my past will keep me from flying. So, I decided to give it all away at my birthday party. It is a relief to let it go.

A few friends asked me if I am suicidal. I know what thoughts of suicide feel like and this is definitely not it. My spirit is at the opposite end of the spectrum. I've gone full circle—from worthless to priceless—and now I'm about to reconnect.

There are some friends who are upset with me, thinking that I am running away from life. But they don't see what I'm running toward. The irony is, these same friends scramble for things that I find worthless.

I hold black, construction-grade, trash bags that conceal goodies. The bag in my right hand holds a PlayStation 3 with twenty new games. The bag in my left hand holds seven pairs of designer sunglasses.

"Odd or even?" I ask the next friend that passes by.

Odd is my right and even is my left. Both are awesome choices; you can't lose.

My buddy has a deer-in-the-headlights look. "What do you mean?" he asks.

"Just say 'odd' or 'even'; it doesn't matter which," I reply.

"Even. Why?" the person asks.

I hand over the trash bag filled with expensive sunglasses and say, "Enjoy."

He opens up the bag and pulls out a sleek black pair of Spy Optic sunglasses and asks, "Are these real?"

"Yes, as real as it gets," I reply.

"What am I supposed to do with all of them?" he asks.

"There is a note in the bag. Read it and follow the directions," I say.

This evening was planned over a month ago. It took only a few hours because it's easy to make things happen when you don't wish to control or affect the outcome. Time will give me the answers and we all have plenty of time.

My friend pulls out a slip of paper that reads: "Give the sunglasses to other people at the party. You get to keep the last pair. Happy April Fool's Day!"

He turns to me. "But I won't get to keep the ones I like."

I shrug my shoulders and smile. "Tell people what you want and they will surprise you."

I stroll up the hallway, happy that another bag of stuff has been delivered. There are about fifty more that need to be handed out before the night is over. Either my friend will realize the joy received by making every person feel priceless through giving them the first/best choice or get the sunglasses that they like the best. It's the classic matchup of material possession versus spiritual understanding. Either way, we both win. The only cost is my materialism.

Another friend asks, "James, who is taking your teak table?"

"Nobody," I reply.

"Can I have it?" he shouts as if it were a competition.

The room falls silent.

All eyes look to me.

"If you love it, then you can have it," I reply.

"What about the teak end tables? Can I have them, too?" he asks.

"Yes, you can have those, too."

"Awesome!" he replies.

In moments, he recruits volunteers to hustle the loot out to his car.

I glance around.

Half of my things are gone.

Breath comes easier as each possession leaves the apartment. It's as though all of this stuff has been sitting on my chest. The pressure has been there for so long, I didn't even realize it existed. Freedom is close; I can almost taste it. My soul soars around the room.

Mike Valentino, a longtime friend, whispers in my ear, "I want to knock that guy out."

I laugh. "Why?"

"He is trying to take all the good stuff. This is a cool thing you are doing. He makes it feel cheap."

I understand Mike's frustration. However, teak furniture is heavy. Even though the guy took my best possessions, he made my load lighter and I am grateful. I respond, "Mike, the flat-screen TV is yours. I want you to have it."

"I can't take your stuff. It doesn't feel right," he replies.

"Your ex-girlfriend tossed your TV off the roof of your apartment and you still need one for your business. You are one of my favorite people in Los Angeles. That flat screen is going to someone and it might as well be you."

A knowing smile crosses my cheeks. I've visualized this moment for months, hoping it would come to pass. The time has come and it makes me happy.

Mike chuckles. "Okay, I'll take it. But when you get back into town, I'm returning it."

"I don't plan on coming back," I tell him.

"Where are you going to end up?" he asks.

"I have no idea."

"Why are you doing this? It will take years to get your stuff back," Mike warns.

"I don't want my stuff back," I reply.

"But why? Tell me *why* you are doing this!" he demands.

I had the idea exactly four months ago, decided three months ago to follow through with it, and Mike is the first person to ask "Why?"

My mind begins to wander…

How do I explain something that I'm trying to understand? I've spent the last decade writing about breaking patterns of generational dysfunction and repatterning the mind. Growing up, I hated my father because he made me feel worthless. It was so bad that I tried to take my life. I felt that the world would be better off without me. Many people feel the same dark thoughts that I felt as a child, but they don't have a father willing to be humble and vulnerable who will guide them to a new hope and belief in themselves. Some people don't know how to be good to each other because nobody taught them. We are plagued with the same limiting behavioral patterns that restricted our parents because that is what they taught us. It is also what their parents taught them. We function through our dysfunction because that is what we know and what we are comfortable with.

It doesn't have to stay that way.

There is a higher way of fulfillment and purpose. We can all learn how to be better men and women together. We just need to admit the truth, that we don't have it all together. No individual has all the answers, but collectively we do. We need to embrace the key to transformation: serving each other like my father served me. It repatterned my mind and healed my broken heart. If we, as a society, dedicate ourselves to repattern a generation, then in a decade we could transform our species…and the world. It is the last great adventure, one that we all can take. This is my father's legacy; he was the first to make that change and I have the honor of telling his story.

Ironically, it was my father that tried to hold me back. He said, "Bubba, don't do it. I don't see how it is possible for you to succeed. The road will test you in ways you can't imagine. You will go hungry. You will face pain and discouragement at levels you have never known. You are a dreamer and your ideas live in a honeymoon fantasy. Marrying yourself to an idea and following through is much different. There are no guarantees. The work will be the hardest thing you will ever face. It seems romantic when you hear a story about adventure. I told you the fun side of my travels, but there is a dark side. The truth of the experience is difficult and ugly. Putting yourself in a situation where your only options are success or death is not wise. Do not do this."

I responded, "Dad, there is nothing you can say or do to deviate me from my course. I have made my decision. However, if you have anything new to say, I will listen."

After a pregnant pause, he replied, "Good luck."

"Thanks, Dad."

His tone got somber. "The whole animal kingdom is set up to support the young and once you are old enough, you are kicked out of the family to start one of your own. This is no different. If you are going to do this, then you must do it on your own. I will not support you, nor will I be there to catch you if you should fail. If you want to know what it is like to face the world as a man, then you must do it alone. Because only by succeeding alone can you become the man you wish to be."

"I understand."

This was a concept we had talked about before, yet I have never had to experience the separation.

"Remember that the superior man finishes what he starts. Son, finish what you start."

I smiled and said, "I will."

The work my father and I did transformed me into the happiest person I know. It made me feel priceless. As I look around, it seems like everyone I meet struggles with feelings of being worthless. They still deal with the limiting patterns that their parents passed on to them. What's the point of knowing how to repattern the mind if I don't communicate this understanding with others? I hope by sharing these lessons that they will help people feel as amazing as I have for the past several years. I want to pay it forward.

Mom is usually the conservative one of the family. She says, "Any time you rush things, they tend to go wrong. It doesn't hurt to wait." However, after sharing the idea with her, she said, "Do it and give it all you've got. No matter what happens, you can always pick up the pieces and start over. This risk is worth your life."

As a little kid, I pledged allegiance to the flag of the United States of America. Countless people serve this country with their lives and as a man I have done nothing. But that is about to change. Alexis de Tocqueville said, "America is great because America is good, and if America ever ceases to be good, America will cease to be great." So I believe it is worth my life and my time to encourage people around my country to be good, repatterning minds along the way. I will give myself one year to travel across America, touching all fifty states to show them how.

Benjamin Franklin said, "Visitors and fish smell after three days." So I decided to serve an individual or a family in each state for three days. I won't ask for money for my time, just that they pay it forward. I am going to do the greatest thing I can imagine: show the world what my dad showed me—a way to reprogram the mind through service. There might be other ways, maybe even better ways. However, the best I have is better than the nothing people are getting. Maybe one day, other people will join in on this great adventure of learning how to be better men and women together. Until then, the work is mine and I must do it alone.

If a picture is worth a thousand words, then a video is worth a million. I'll record every step of the journey on a GoPro so people can believe me when I'm finished. It is my experience that the truth gets you made fun of and mocked. By recording and sharing the truth, it is I who will have the last laugh. I will prove that people can thrive in modern-day society by living in a constant state of giving—by DOING it. People forget that we have lived without money for centuries by being a serf and giving more than you take. I will repattern my own mind while exploring the concept and begin by pressing the Reset button on my life. I have to start over. My goal is to attain bliss, so I'll call it SerfBliss.

Not knowing how the process will turn out is the secret ingredient. All I know is, if I am going to survive, I must rely on the dark side of my family in order to make it. My father rejected everything about his parents, but they have something to teach me. My grandfather was a master at starting a new life and my grandmother was a genius at survival; I will need those skills as I travel America. By mixing the goodness of my mother's character with the ability my father, I will repattern my own mind and film the process. It is how I will honor my mother and father.

I'm going to test my theory that if you spend a significant amount of time serving others, then when intense situations occur, instead of your mind being freaked out and withdrawing with fear, your mind relaxes and reconnects to the people you served.

Every week I'll ask the people I serve, "How can I help you?" Then, at the end of the week I'll ask, "How did I do?" Just like my dad did with me. I will post everything on YouTube and Facebook to keep everyone safe, accountable, and comfortable. My massage skills can provide the finances necessary to cross the finish line. People must be good in order for this to work. Society must have progressed enough to sustain a pure-hearted person to live in a constant state of giving. Love must actually be all that I need. My greatest challenge is: I must believe.

I look back at Mike, embarrassed about the rabbit hole my mind just traveled. He is still waiting for a response and says, "Dude, tell me *why* you are doing this!"

I reply, "Because it's cool."

Mike says through a toothy grin, "You're right. It is cool. I'm glad that's your answer. I was afraid you were going to commit suicide."

I laugh and tell him, "No, that was twenty-five years ago."

An awkward silence hangs over the conversation. Talking about my childhood tends to do that.

James's SerfBliss Launch Party

"What are you taking with you?" he asks.

"My car, laptop, camera, toolbox, massage table, and a bag of clothes. I'm calling it 'SerfBliss.'"

The next morning, I sit in my car. I spent ten years writing about the great adventures my father took and I realized that I had never taken a great adventure of my own. I'm at the edge of the nest and I'm about to jump. My dad didn't let anything stop him and neither will I. Finally, I am my father's son.

Ten years ago, I drove to Los Angeles in a Honda Accord with a trunk full of clothes and a toolbox. A decade later, I'm leaving the same way. Reaching down, the Reset button feels a lot like car keys. They say, "Try something so big that it is glorious to fail."

I'm still wondering who "they" are.

I have more questions than answers, but the truth is out there and I aim to find it.

Fingers remain motionless.

A normal life is easy.

Facing the unknown is hard. I can't tell if each passing moment contains more or less courage.

The open road is the only option.

I turn the key.

The engine hums under the hood of my 2001 Honda Civic.

I cruise up the 405.

When Dad comes to visit

Wind pushes moisture from my eyes, forcing salty water to roll across my cheeks.

I holler at the top of my lungs.

I am wide open.

I am free.

I want to be like my dad.

In the end, I am.

The End

EPILOGUE

EVERYONE AROUND ME SAID THE SerfBliss journey was impossible. Fortunately, it only takes one person believing in something to transform the "impossible" into merely "improbable." My yearlong quest was completed without a second to spare. On the road, countless adventures took place. I fell in love, was betrayed by those I trusted most, and had strangers redeem my faith in humanity. I faced death three times: driving through a blizzard in Washington, dodging tornadoes in Oklahoma, and navigating an electrical storm in Ohio. Natural disasters and tragedy seemed to be placed right in front of me: a tornado in Joplin, Missouri; a flood in Wilmington, Vermont; and Hurricane Irene met me as I began working my way down the east coast. A Navajo medicine man sent me on a sacred quest to acquire a ram's horn, which was found on the other side of the world, in Tibet. My service to one woman helped another lady struggling with her weight get on ABC's *Extreme Weight Loss*. I encouraged another woman to become a documentary filmmaker; she now has films showcasing in international film festivals. I helped a high school student get into Cornell. My service to one man helped him become a keynote speaker for his company. I never tried to get attention and yet news outlets picked up my story throughout the country. You may have seen me on national news, *Fox & Friends*, Christmas morning 2011.

Even though I've felt priceless for over a decade, I set out to answer a few question. "Am I worthy? Is society worthy? Is love worthy? Is God worthy?" The only way for me to find my answers was to survive and thrive by living in a constant state of giving. I did. I recently was invited to speak at a TEDx conference in Riverside, California. I'll post that talk along with other videos from my trip on www.serfbliss.com if you want to check it out. Civic leaders and business executives ask to meet with me on a regular basis. I speak at leadership conferences at universities. Even the military invites me to address their men. Accomplishing the "impossible" has become normal after I figured out how to repattern my mind. But the details of how all of this happened on the SerfBliss adventure is another story.

April 1, 2011

Dearest Los Angeles,

I promised to give you ten years. You promised to teach me how to write. It's been ten years and this is what you taught me. Thanks for the lessons. I also wanted to say, thanks for making me feel cool. I spent a lot of time not feeling cool, and feeling "cool" is much better. I'm going to go around the country to try and make someone in every state feel priceless, like my dad made me feel.

When I was a kid, my dad made up games—like SerfBliss—to make me feel better. "SerfBliss to save the world" is the biggest game I can imagine and it's how I plan to honor my father. The journey will be time-stamped on Facebook so you know that I am being honest. I apologize in advance for the amateur nature of my videos. I'm teaching myself how to edit and am creating the journey as I go along.

Someone in LA once told me, "The human spirit will always find a way to break through and overcome." I'm going to test that idea by testing my own spirit in the coolest way I can imagine. Real men do hard things; sharing my dad's work with the world is my hard thing. Thanks again for making me feel cool. I hope you enjoy the SerfBliss adventure!

Much love,

James "Bubba" Beck

June 21, 2015

Hey Dad, Remember Me?

Now do you understand? Because I understand you. I became friends with the boy you were and studied the man you became. I know the road you traveled; Who loves ya? Piff Ridif...doodle doo, doodle doo, doodle doo. Sucker dog. Lucky Bus and lima bean presents. Buck burrs and solar-powered flashlight jokes on double date nights. Let's see where this comment goes..."Dishwashers are still the number one cause of divorce," and it's all in the delivery.

Dad, I understand you. I am you.

Your father gave you a lack of fear. Your mother gave you the ability to adapt. Together they gave you the ultimate gift of survival. You found your heart in me, because I was broken in the same way you were broken. You taught me persistence, determination, and how to do the work within through leading by example. We figured out how to be transparent together. This book holds the milestone moments that we learned our lessons. It is long-winded and filled with pregnant pauses, the type we have grown to love. Hopefully, as you read your voice, you heard your heart speak. That was my goal.

You have always been ashamed to be James A. Beck. I am proud to be James A. Beck. We broke the cycle. I have never known a man to do what you have done. You told me not to take the SerfBliss journey, but I had to. You had your adventure and now I have mine. All I had to do was survive (lessons taken from your parents). Sixteen years ago, I made a commitment that today I get to fulfill. I hope it makes you proud. SerfBliss is my Memphis stage. Thanks for always trying, even when there wasn't any hope. I believe that is the reason we made it. You are worthy. You are priceless. I'm proud to be your son. Starting over, if I were to ask God for a father, I would ask for you.

This is what I believe is true: a real man listens, adapts, and grows—surviving on his own. A good man is open, transparent, and honest—contributing to society. Mom taught me the rest. For the first time in my life I'm going to ask you to give me a grade. Take some time, examine the man you have created, and let me know. Happy Father's Day.

Love,
Bubba

P.S. When grading, just remember that I'll be happy with a B.

To the Reader:

THIS BOOK IS AN INFORMAL letter to my father. I started writing because of a promise. I finished this project because I want my dad to understand me, as I understand him. This 'understanding' is my gift to him for Father's Day, 2015.

This book should remind you of the power you hold in the life of a child. We unintentionally break children in the same manner we are broken, because it is normal for us. However, this cycle can change. The service of my father transformed me from feeling worthless and suicidal to feeling limitless and priceless. I am still the same person, but I feel different. Listening and serving others are the keys to this transformation.

ONE SHOULD NEVER DESTROY SOMETHING without a plan to rebuild. I gave away everything I owned, intentionally destroying my life, in order to fully experience and face the parts of my past that contained my brokenness, fear, and anxiety. It was necessary for me to do this in order to repattern my mind and overcome my generational dysfunction. By purchasing this book, you have helped me rebuild my life. Thank you.

If you have been involved in military service and received this book for free, I would love it if you would review my book on Amazon. Thank you for your service.